Po Jen Yap's new book is a must-read in the growing literature on the role of constitutional courts in democratic stabilization. Its fine-grained analyses demonstrate that the political power and vulnerability of courts in protecting democratic processes as well as their own independence is not fixed or prescribable in the abstract, but varies with the state of democratization and party contestation in which they operate.

Stephen Gardbaum, MacArthur Foundation Professor of International Justice and Human Rights, UCLA

A fascinating tour through the fraught relations between courts and political power. Professor Yap provides a nuanced account of how constitutional courts in Asia balance precariously between semi-authoritarian dominant regimes and the live wire of electoral politics. A magnificent, sophisticated contribution that enriches our understanding of judicial politics in an era of weak democratic institutions.

Samuel Issacharoff, Reiss Professor of Constitutional Law, New York University

Po Jen Yap's analysis of the role of Asian courts in three types of democracies illuminates how the possibilities for effective judicial action in connection with major political issues varies according to the type of democracy in which the courts are located. It is an important contribution to the project of integrating comparative constitutional law with comparative political studies.

Mark Tushnet, William Nelson Cromwell Professor of Law, Harvard University

COURTS AND DEMOCRACIES IN ASIA

What is the relationship between the strength of a country's democracy and the ability of its courts to address deficiencies in the electoral process? Drawing a distinction between democracies that can be characterised as 'dominant-party' (e.g. Singapore, Malaysia, and Hong Kong), 'dynamic' (e.g. India, South Korea, and Taiwan), and 'fragile' (e.g. Thailand, Pakistan, and Bangladesh), this book explores how democracy sustains and is sustained by the exercise of judicial power. In dominant-party systems, courts can only pursue 'dialogic' pathways to constrain the government's authoritarian tendencies. On the other hand, in dynamic democracies, courts can more successfully innovate and make systemic changes to the electoral system. Finally, in fragile democracies, where a country regularly oscillates between martial law and civilian rule, their courts tend to consistently overreach, and this often facilitates or precipitates a hostile takeover by the armed forces, and leads to the demise of the rule of law.

DR PO JEN YAP is an Associate Professor at The University of Hong Kong (HKU), Faculty of Law, where he specialises in comparative constitutional law. He graduated from the National University of Singapore with an LLB degree and he obtained LLM qualifications from both Harvard Law School and University College London. He also has a PhD degree from the University of Cambridge. He is an Advocate and Solicitor of the Supreme Court of Singapore and an Attorney at Law in the State of New York, USA. His publications include *Constitutional Dialogue in Common Law Asia* (2015).

COMPARATIVE CONSTITUTIONAL LAW AND POLICY

Series Editors

Comparative constitutional law is an intellectually vibrant field that encompasses an increasingly broad array of approaches and methodologies. This series collects analytically innovative and empirically grounded work from scholars of comparative constitutionalism across academic disciplines. Books in the series include theoretically informed studies of single constitutional jurisdictions, comparative studies of constitutional law and institutions, and edited collections of original essays that respond to challenging theoretical and empirical questions in the field.

Books in the Series

Proportionality: New Frontiers, New Challenges edited by Vicki Jackson and Mark Tushnet

Constituents Before Assembly: Participation, Deliberation, and Representation in the Crafting of New Constitutions Todd A. Eisenstadt, A. Carl LeVan, and Tofigh Maboudi

Buddhism, Politics and the Limits of Law: The Pyrrhic Constitutionalism of Sri Lanka Benjamin Schonthal

Assessing Constitutional Performance Tom Ginsburg and Aziz Huq

Engaging with Social Rights Brian Ray

Constitutional Courts as Mediators Julio Ríos-Figueroa

Perils of Judicial Self-Government in Transitional Societies David Kosař

Making We the People Chaihark Hahm and Sung Ho Kim

Radical Deprivation on Trial Cesar Rodríguez-Garavito and Diana Rodríguez-Franco

Unstable Constitutionalism edited by Mark Tushnet and Madhav Khosla

Magna Carta and its Modern Legacy edited by Robert Hazell and James Melton

Constitutions and Religious Freedom Frank Cross

International Courts and the Performance of International Agreements: A General Theory with Evidence from the European Union Clifford Carrubba and Matthew Gabel

Reputation and Judicial Tactics: A Theory of National and International Courts Shai Dothan

Social Difference and Constitutionalism in Pan-Asia edited by Susan H. Williams

Constitutionalism in Asia in the Early Twenty-First Century edited by Albert Chen

Constitutions in Authoritarian Regimes edited by Tom Ginsburg and Alberto Simpser

Presidential Legislation in India: The Law and Practice of Ordinances Shubhankar Dam

Social and Political Foundations of Constitutions edited by Denis J. Galligan and Mila Versteeg

Consequential Courts: Judicial Roles in Global Perspective edited by Diana Kapiszewski, Gordon Silverstein and Robert A. Kagan

Comparative Constitutional Design edited by Tom Ginsburg

COURTS AND DEMOCRACIES IN ASIA

PO JEN YAP

The University of Hong Kong

Associate Professor, Faculty of Law

CAMBRIDGE
UNIVERSITY PRESS

CAMBRIDGE
UNIVERSITY PRESS

University Printing House, Cambridge CB2 8BS, United Kingdom

One Liberty Plaza, 20th Floor, New York, NY 10006, USA

477 Williamstown Road, Port Melbourne, VIC 3207, Australia

4843/24, 2nd Floor, Ansari Road, Daryaganj, Delhi – 110002, India

79 Anson Road, #06-04/06, Singapore 079906

Cambridge University Press is part of the University of Cambridge.

It furthers the University's mission by disseminating knowledge in the pursuit of education, learning, and research at the highest international levels of excellence.

www.cambridge.org
Information on this title: www.cambridge.org/9781107192621
DOI: 10.1017/9781108131513

First published 2017

Printed in the United Kingdom by Clays, St Ives plc

A catalogue record for this publication is available from the British Library.

Library of Congress Cataloging-in-Publication Data
Names: Yap, Po Jen, author.
Title: Courts and democracies in Asia / Po Jen Yap.
Description: New York: Cambridge University Press, 2017. |
Series: Comparative constitutional law and policy |
Includes bibliographical references and index.
Identifiers: LCCN 2017034649 | ISBN 9781107192621 (hardback) |
Subjects: LCSH: Courts – Asia. | Democracy – Asia. | BISAC: LAW / Constitutional.
Classification: LCC KNC986 .Y37 2017 | DDC 347.5/01–dc23
LC record available at https://lccn.loc.gov/2017034649

ISBN 978-1-107-19262-1 Hardback

I dedicate this book to my parents

CONTENTS

FOREWORD

Context is everything at the micro level of an individual case before a court. This book demonstrates that the same is also true at a macro level – comparing how judiciaries in Asia address electoral law issues.

Po Jen Yap's contribution to international legal scholarship here is of his usual high quality. It is grounded in penetrating analyses of the detail of judicial approaches to electoral law issues in nine Asian jurisdictions. Most valuably, it goes further to develop a macro thesis. It links the political nature of each democracy (dominant-party, dynamic, or fragile) to the nature of each judiciary's approach (limited, more central, or risky).

This book demonstrates the power of comparative constitutional analysis. It also demonstrates the validity of the book's avowed fundamental point: that all courts operate within political parameters and that the task of scholars is to explain how these parameters can both empower and constrain courts.

The Honourable Justice Matthew Palmer
High Court of New Zealand
17 January 2017

ACKNOWLEDGEMENTS

I owe a tremendous debt of gratitude to all the comparative constitutional law scholars in my field who have shaped my views over the years. In particular, I would really like to express my deep appreciation to Cora Chan, Chintan Chandrachud, Albert Chen, M. Jashim Ali Chowdhury, Stephen Gardbaum, Tom Ginsburg, Ran Hirschl, Eric Ip, Samuel Issacharoff, Swati Jhaveri, Marva Khan, Ming-Sung Kuo, David Law, Alec Stone Sweet, Khemthong Tonsakulrungruang, Mark Tushnet, and Simon Young, who have all zealously commented on various drafts of this book. They have refined my arguments and saved me from much embarrassment!

Special thanks must also go out to Eric Chan, Francis Chung, Hyunjin Chung, Jiang Zixin, Raymond Ko, Vanessa Lo, Eileen Lou, Florence Sit, and Rosana Tse, all of whom have provided invaluable research assistance and technical support. Joe Ng, my editor at Cambridge University Press, has been an absolute joy to work with, and I am very grateful for his assistance at every stage of this project. This book would not have been completed in time without all their unyielding support.

An abridged version of Chapter 1 was published as 'Courts and Elections in Asia' in Po Jen Yap (ed) *Judicial Review of Elections in Asia* (Routledge 2016) 1–8. An abridged version of Chapter 2 was published as 'Judicial Review of the Electoral Process in Singapore after *Vellama*' in Po Jen Yap (ed) *Judicial Review of Elections in Asia* (Routledge 2016) 84–92. An abridged version of Chapter 11 was published as 'The Conundrum of Unconstitutional Constitutional Amendments' (2015) 4 *Global Constitutionalism* 114–136.

This research project has been generously supported by the Hong Kong Research Grant Council's General Research Fund and The University of Hong Kong's Seed Funding Programme for Basic Research. I am also grateful to Dan Puchniak, Chen Wei-tseng, and Margaret Ang at the Centre for Asian Legal Studies (National University of Singapore) for hosting me for a period during the writing of this book.

ABBREVIATIONS

1MDB	1Malaysia Development Berhad
AL	Awami League
BJP	Bharatiya Janata Party
BN	Barisan Nasional
BNP	Bangladesh Nationalist Party
BORO	Bill of Rights Ordinance
CBI	Central Bureau of Investigation
CEEO	Chief Executive Election Ordinance
CFA	Court of Final Appeal
CFI	Court of First Instance
DJP	Democratic Justice Party
DLP	Democratic Liberal Party
DPP	Democratic Progressive Party
EBRC	Electoral Boundaries Review Committee
ECICO	Elections (Corrupt and Illegal Conduct) Ordinance
FC	Functional Constituency
GC	Geographical Constituency
GNP	Grand National Party
GRC	Group Representative Constituency
HKSAR	Hong Kong Special Administrative Region
IRA	Industrial Relations Act
ISA	Internal Security Act
JP	Jatiya Party
LCFO	Law (Continuance in Force) Order
LCO	Legislative Council Ordinance
LegCo	Legislative Council
KMT	Kuomintang
MMA	Muttahida Majlis-e-Amal (United Action Front)
NCG	Non-party Caretaker Government
NPCSC	Standing Committee of the National People's Congress

NRO	National Reconciliation Ordinance
ODO	Oaths and Declarations Ordinance
PAD	People's Alliance for Democracy
PAP	People's Action Party
PAS	Parti Islam Se-Malaysia
PCT	Pattana Chart Thai (Party)
PDRC	People's Democratic Reform Committee
PDT	Paen Din Thai (Party)
PGN	Prachatipatai Gao Na (Party)
PHAOA	President to Hold Another Office Act
PLC	Provisional Legislative Council
PML	Pakistan Muslim League
PNA	Pakistan National Alliance
PPP	People's Power Party *or* Pakistan Peoples Party
PR	Pakatan Rakyat
ROC	Republic of China
RPA	Representation of the People Act
SMC	Single Member Constituency
TP	Temporary Provisions Effective During the Period of Communist Rebellion
TRT	Thai Rak Thai
VR	Village Representative

1

Introduction

In the past century, as the winds of political change swept across the globe, Asian nations too experienced a wave of democratisation as countries in the region gained independence or transitioned from authoritarian military rule toward more participatory politics. In tandem with this democratisation trend, we have also witnessed a concomitant expansion of judicial power in Asia, whereby new courts or empowered old ones emerge as independent constraints on governmental authority.[1] The rise of the courts, and the accompanying 'judicialisation of politics',[2] is as much an Asian phenomenon as it is a prevalent trend in the West.

There is now a rich corpus of literature on how Asian courts have participated in and even reshaped the human rights discourse in their respective jurisdictions.[3] However, little academic literature has examined how Asian judiciaries have responded to deficiencies in the electoral processes and the concomitant problem of partisan self-dealing. Specifically, partisan self-dealing occurs when the political actors devise electoral rules that govern voting, political parties, electoral boundaries, apportionment, the administration of elections, and campaign finance that are designed to entrench themselves in power.[4] The purpose of this book is to redress this gap in the scholarship by focussing on the cases

[1] Tom Ginsburg, 'Courts and New Democracies: Recent Works' (2012) 37 *Law and Social Inquiry* 720; Tom Ginsburg, 'Constitutional Courts in East Asia: Understanding Variation' (2008) 3 *Journal of Comparative Law* 80; Andrew Harding and Penelope Nicholson (eds) *New Courts in Asia* (London: Routledge, 2010).

[2] Ran Hirschl, *Towards Juristocracy* (Cambridge, MA: Harvard University Press, 2004) 211; Björn Dressel (ed) *The Judicialisation of Politics in Asia* (Abingdon, Oxon: Routledge, 2012).

[3] Po Jen Yap, *Constitutional Dialogue in Common Law Asia* (Oxford: Oxford University Press, 2015); Po Jen Yap and Holning Lau (eds), *Public Interest Litigation in Asia* (London: Routledge, 2010); Albert Chen (ed), *Constitutionalism in Asia in the Early Twenty-First Century* (Cambridge: Cambridge University Press, 2014).

[4] Yasmin Dawood, 'Electoral Fairness and the Law of Democracy: A Structural Rights Approach to Judicial Review' (2012) 62 *University of Toronto Law Journal* 499, 500.

in which the courts in Asia have impeded or enhanced the competitiveness of the political system when addressing this central challenge to democratic governance.

This book critically examines the state of play in nine Asian jurisdictions, i.e. Bangladesh, Hong Kong, India, Malaysia, Pakistan, Singapore, South Korea, Taiwan, and Thailand; and it seeks to illuminate an interesting phenomenon.

In jurisdictions such as Hong Kong, Malaysia, and Singapore, where a dominant political party or coalition has remained in power since independence or decolonisation, the courts may formally superintend the electoral process, but in reality they do so at the fringes of the entity's political life. On the other hand, in dynamic democracies where there have been extended periods of competing political parties taking turns in office, the courts play a more central role in democratic consolidation.[5] Such courts as those found in India, Taiwan, and South Korea have not only provided constitutional redress for vulnerable or unpopular groups that have been excluded from the voting process; they have also ameliorated major systemic inequalities in their electoral systems. Finally, we have fragile[6] or unstable[7] democracies in Thailand, Pakistan, and Bangladesh, where the armed forces are *not* under firm control of the civilian government and the country oscillates regularly between military and civilian rule. In these fragile democracies, Asian courts, which become partisan tools that assist one political camp to dislodge its rivals, as the Constitutional Court of Thailand did, or pose existential threats to military interests, as the Supreme Court of Pakistan did under the stewardship of Chief Justice Iftikhar Muhammad Chaudhry, would only accelerate a political crisis that sends the country over the constitutional cliff. In these unstable democracies, prudent judges should have insulated the courts against political attacks (from the civilian government or the military) rather than engaged in confrontational strong-form judicial review over the electoral process that antagonises political incumbents. This appears to be the path taken by the Supreme Court of Bangladesh (Appellate Division).

[5] Samuel Issacharoff, 'Constitutional Courts and Consolidated Power' (2014) 62 *American Journal of Comparative Law* 585.

[6] Samuel Issacharoff, *Fragile Democracies: Contested Power in the Era of Constitutional Courts* (Cambridge: Cambridge University Press, 2015).

[7] For an excellent collection of essays on unstable democracies in South Asia, see Mark Tushnet and Madhav Khosla (eds), *Unstable Constitutionalism: Law and Politics in South Asia* (New York: Cambridge University Press, 2015).

All courts operate within political parameters, and the task of scholars is to explain how these parameters can empower or constrain courts.[8] As Tom Ginsburg has observed, the extent of political diffusion within the legislative and executive structures determines how successfully courts can assert their judicial power.[9] Constitutions are incomplete contracts, and while all judges are delegates tasked with the interpretation of imprecise text,[10] the courts' 'zone of discretion'[11] is greater when government is divided and opposing parties in the legislature have to cooperate to effectuate any disagreement with the judiciary.

In dominant-party democracies, courts can only take a limited range of actions before they outrun the government's 'tolerance interval'[12] as the government can respond to confrontational judicial decisions by deploying constitutional or unconstitutional means to overrule or 'punish' the courts.[13] While their courts are unable to successfully challenge the core interests of their governments, they must pursue 'dialogic'[14] pathways to constrain the 'structural pathologies'[15] of authoritarian politics. Bipartisan legislative agreement to overrule or punish judges would be less likely and frequent in dynamic democracies as the 'fragmentation of authority across separate institutions makes coordinated attacks on judicial independence more difficult'.[16] Where political power regularly rotates between competing political parties – a cardinal feature of dynamic democracies – the courts can not only facilitate micro-systemic electoral changes to their countries' voting process or provide 'dialogic' electoral redress for

[8] Tom Ginsburg, 'Courts and New Democracies: Recent Works' (2012) 37 *Law and Social Inquiry* 720, 738.

[9] Tom Ginsburg, *Judicial Review in New Democracies: Constitutional Courts in Asian Cases* (Cambridge: Cambridge University Press, 2003), 19.

[10] Alec Stone Sweet, *Governing with Judges: Constitutional Politics in Europe* (Oxford: Oxford University Press, 2000), 22–23.

[11] Alec Stone Sweet, 'Constitutions and Judicial Power', in Daniele Caramani (ed.), *Comparative Politics* (Oxford: Oxford University Press, 2014), 157.

[12] Lee Epstein, Olga Shvetsova and Jack Knight, 'The Role of Constitutional Courts in the Establishment and Maintenance of Democratic Systems of Government' (2001) 35 *Law and Society Review* 117, 128; Stone Sweet (n 10), 23–24.

[13] For a comparative perspective on Japan, see David S. Law, 'The Anatomy of a Conservative Court: Judicial Review in Japan' (2009) 87 *Texas Law Review* 1545, 1587–1588.

[14] Dialogic review herein refers to a judicial practice whereby courts enforce constitutional rights in a way that provides sufficient decisional space to the legislature or allows the legislature to respond in disagreement using the ordinary political process. See Po Jen Yap, *Constitutional Dialogue in Common Law Asia* (Oxford: Oxford University Press, 2015).

[15] Guy-Uriel E. Charles, 'Democracy and Distortion' (2007) 92 *Cornell Law Review* 601, 604.

[16] Georg Vanberg, 'Constitutional Courts in Comparative Perspective: A Theoretical Assessment' (2015) 18 *Annual Review of Political Science* 167, 181.

vulnerable groups, they can also make macro-institutional changes to the political system. Finally, for fragile democracies where the military is not under the firm control of the civilian government and the country regularly oscillates between martial law and civilian rule, their courts – unlike those in dominant-party democracies – tend to consistently overreach. Such high-octane judicial review by partisan or imprudent judges can easily facilitate or precipitate a hostile takeover by the armed forces, and lead to the demise of the rule of law. Courts in brittle democracies should therefore avoid strong-form judicial review unless their institutional independence is under threat.[17]

At the outset, I should clarify that I am herein making *both* a descriptive and a normative claim. My prescriptive claim about how Asian courts *should* behave is also consistent with my descriptive claim of how the Asian judiciaries have enhanced or undermined the state of democratisation within their respective political systems. Furthermore, I should also state that I am not attempting to offer a quantitative or empirical proof of my claims. My claims are more modest, as I merely seek to describe, explain, and account for this phenomenon I have identified, and defend my normative prescriptions. But, in doing so, I have examined in this book all the relevant cases decided by the Constitutional Courts or generalist courts of final resort on the electoral processes in the nine jurisdictions.

In essence, this book explores how democracy sustains and is sustained by the exercise of judicial power and how courts impact and are impacted by the state of democratisation in their countries.[18] Naturally, the role of any court is not static; it can and will change as the state of democracy in that country evolves.

Dominant-Party Democracies

In dominant-party democracies, the main obstacle to electoral competition is not violence typically associated with fragile or unstable democracies, but the overwhelming control asserted by one party/coalition that has successfully consolidated its political apparatus in office.[19] The People's Action Party has been the ruling party in Singapore since the

[17] Stephen Gardbaum, 'Are Strong Constitutional Courts Always a Good Thing for New Democracies?' (2015) 53 *Columbia Journal of Transnational Law* 285.

[18] For a discussion on how courts become effective political players, see Alec Stone Sweet, 'Constitutions and Judicial Power', in Daniele Caramani (ed.), *Comparative Politics* (Oxford: Oxford University Press, 2014), 160–165.

[19] Issacharoff (n 5), 588.

country's independence and the party has controlled over 90% of the elected seats in Parliament since 1968. Malaysia has been ruled by the same political coalition since its independence, i.e., the Alliance Party, which was renamed Barisan Nasional in 1974. In turn, their courts have acquiesced to the state of affairs by playing a more limited role in their countries' political life as their judges are unable to rely on the support of other strong institutional actors to counter any backlash from the dominant government if they engage in robust judicial review over electoral disputes.

Furthermore, both countries are arguably still reeling from judicial crises that have cast a pall over the state of constitutional review. With regard to Singapore, when the Court of Appeal ruled against the government on *constitutional* grounds for the first and last time in 1988, the government overruled the decision with a series of constitutional and statutory amendments within a month.[20] In Malaysia, the Lord President (now known as Chief Justice) Tun Salleh and two other judges on the Supreme Court of Malaysia (now Federal Court of Malaysia) were impeached and removed on trumped-up charges of judicial misconduct in 1988.[21] While it is not uncommon for judges in all countries to act prudentially when they seek to avoid legislative or electoral outrage, this concern about political reprisals is particularly pronounced in these jurisdictions as dominant-party governments can display their displeasure more easily by ousting judicial review or even the judges themselves.

Therefore, it is perhaps unsurprising that in the first and only election case ever decided in Singapore, its Court of Appeal conceded that judicial intervention in election disputes would arise in the most 'exceptional cases';[22] and on the facts of the by-election dispute, so long as its Prime Minister did not openly reject the possibility of a by-election when a casual vacancy arose, it would appear that the Court did not impose any

[20] In *Chng Suan Tze* v. *Minister of Home Affairs*, [1988] 2 SLR(R) 525, the Singapore Court of Appeal, after surveying a litany of Commonwealth precedents, quashed a preventive detention order issued under the Internal Security Act (ISA) against various alleged Marxist conspirators and concluded that the ministerial discretion to detain personnel under the ISA would be subject to an 'objective' test of review by the courts. This decision proved to be sufficiently disquieting to the Executive; the government quickly overturned this decision and henceforth restricted judicial review in ISA cases to only procedural grounds.

[21] For a full discussion, see H.P. Lee, *Constitutional Conflicts in Contemporary Malaysia*, 2nd edn. (Oxford: Oxford University Press, 2017).

[22] *Vellama d/o Marie Muthu* v. *Attorney-General* [2013] SGCA 39, [2013] 4 SLR 1 [85] (Singapore Court of Appeal).

additional limits on the Prime Minister's exercise of his discretion to fill that vacancy.[23] In the same vein, the Malaysian courts have accepted that their state-controlled Election Commission has no statutory obligation to arrange for persons in detention to vote at the requisite polling centres,[24] nor is it obliged to allow Malaysian citizens living abroad to be registered as absentee voters.[25] Furthermore, the Malaysian courts have also consistently refused to review any alleged irregularities in the electoral roll *after* it has been published and certified by the Election Commission.[26]

Hong Kong provides yet another fascinating case study. After the resumption of sovereignty over Hong Kong in 1997, China had deliberately retained the Functional Constituencies (FC) electoral method in Hong Kong, a system in which the right to vote depends upon a person's membership or registration in a recognised social, economic, industrial, commercial, political advisory, or professional body represented in the legislature. In many of these FCs, e.g., Insurance, Transport, Tourism, Finance, Labour, it is not individuals working in these professions that are eligible to vote; instead, it is only the recognised corporate bodies operating in these professions that can vote. It is significant that since the establishment of the Hong Kong Special Administrative Region (HKSAR), the pro-Beijing/ pro-establishment camp has relied on these 'corporate' votes to dominate the FC elections, such that the pro-establishment camp is able to command an overall majority of the seats in the Legislative Council, even though it lags behind in the Geographical Constituencies (GC) elections that are constituted via universal suffrage.[27] (One may note that since the Hong Kong executive government is heavily reliant on the support of the pro-establishment camp in the legislature for the passage of its bills, unrestricted elections by universal suffrage for all of the seats in the Legislative

23 *Ibid.* [87].

24 *Yazid bin Sufaat & Ors* v. *Suruhanjaya Pilihanraya* [2009] 6 MLJ 152 (Federal Court of Malaysia).

25 *Teo Hoon Seong & Ors* v. *Suruhanjaya Pilihanraya* [2012] 4 MLJ 245 (High Court of Malaysia).

26 *Muhammad Sanusi Md* v. *Mohd Tajuddin* [2009] 1 CLJ 1 (Federal Court of Malaysia); *Charles Anthony Santiago* v. *Suruhanjaya Pilihan Raya* [2014] 7 MLJ 271 (High Court of Malaysia).

27 Currently, 35 seats in the Legislative Council are constituted via universal suffrage in Geographical Constituencies (GC) elections while another 35 seats are constituted via Functional Constituencies (FC) elections. Ma Ngok, 'Political Parties and Elections', in Wai-man Lam, Percy Luen-tim Lui, Wilson Wong and Ian Holliday (eds), *Contemporary Hong Kong Politics: Governance in the Post-1997 Era* (Hong Kong: Hong Kong University Press, 2007), 131–132. See also Sonny Lo, *Competing Chinese Political Visions* (Santa Barbara: Praeger, 2010), 130–131.

Council would unlikely be allowed until the pro-establishment camp is able to form a clear majority in the Legislative Council, without the use of the FC system as a political crutch.) Furthermore, the Standing Committee of the National People's Congress (NPCSC) is empowered under Hong Kong's Basic Law to overrule the Court of Final Appeal's decision via a Legislative Interpretation. In light of these political realities, it is thus unsurprising that the Hong Kong judiciary has adopted a haphazard approach in electoral challenges: its traditionally active judiciary has been willing to extend voting rights writ small to disenfranchised prisoners[28] and allow those who had been convicted of minor offences to stand for elections;[29] but the courts have been reluctant to make major *systemic* changes that would invalidate 'corporate voting',[30] a cardinal feature of the FC electoral system.

Dynamic Democracies

On the other hand, courts operating within dynamic democracies function differently. Where there have been extended periods of competing political parties taking turns in office, courts have less to fear as bipartisan legislative agreement to overrule or punish judges is less likely and frequent in such contested environments. Parties in power may also acquiesce to the robust exercises of judicial power as constitutional review by an independent branch of government provides a form of insurance against their electoral competitors when political fortunes turn.[31] For India and Taiwan, since they transitioned from dominant-party to dynamic democracies, their courts have had more opportunities to innovate and can play a more central role in democratic consolidation by making larger systemic changes to the electoral systems. Specifically, such courts improve 'the performance of democratic institutions through time'[32] by ensuring that the political incumbents do not insulate themselves from political or legal accountability[33] and/or overcoming the anti-competitive electoral rules that existing

[28] *Chan Kin Sum* v. *Secretary for Justice* [2009] 2 HKLRD 166 (Hong Kong Court of First Instance).

[29] *Wong Hin Wai* v. *Secretary for Justice* [2012] 4 HKLRD 70 (Hong Kong Court of First Instance).

[30] *Chan Yu Nam* v. *Secretary for Justice* [2010] HKEC 1893 (Hong Kong Court of Appeal).

[31] Ginsburg (n 9). See also Matthew C. Stephenson, '"When the Devil Turns…": The Political Foundations of Independent Judicial Review' (2003) 32 *Journal of Legal Studies* 59.

[32] David Landau, 'A Dynamic Theory of Judicial Role' (2014) 55 *Boston College Law Review* 1501, 1536.

[33] Michael Pal, 'Breakdowns in the Democratic Process and the Law of Canadian Democracy' (2011) 57 *McGill Law Journal* 299.

partisan forces erect or manipulate to entrench themselves in power.[34] In short, courts in dynamic democracies can adopt what John Hart Ely terms a 'participation-oriented, representation-reinforcing approach to judicial review'[35] and serve as a crucial safeguard against 'self-interested lock-ups'[36] of the electoral process by political incumbents and their allies.

In India, after the Congress Party lost its hyper-dominance in national politics, the Supreme Court became zealous in rooting out systemic and prevalent corrupt practices amongst politicians by adopting a very robust reading of the Representation of the People Act (RPA). Accordingly, the Court was able to mandate election candidates to disclose the source of their political donations,[37] their criminal antecedents[38] and even unseat convicted criminals from elected office.[39] Furthermore, the Indian Supreme Court has directed the country's Election Commission to provide each voter with a choice to cast a negative vote against all the contesting candidates because a 'provision of negative voting would be in the interest of promoting democracy as it would send clear signals to political parties and their candidates as to what the electorate think about them'.[40]

In Taiwan, after the dominant Kuomintang (KMT) lost the Presidency for the first time in the nation's history, its Constitutional Court in 2000 invalidated two constitutional amendments passed by the National Assembly in 1999, which had attempted to extend the existing term of the National Assembly delegates by over two years and allow lawmakers in the Legislative Yuan (Taiwan's primary legislative chamber) to appoint delegates to the said Assembly.[41]

In the same vein, the Constitutional Court of Korea has also directly rectified many of the country's systemic electoral defects. The National Assembly is composed of (1) members elected directly by voters in individual electoral districts and (2) proportional representatives, ranked on

[34] See Samuel Issacharoff and Richard Pildes, 'Politics as Markets: Partisan Lockups of the Democratic Process' (1998) 50 *Stanford Law Review* 643.
[35] John Hart Ely, *Democracy and Distrust: A Theory of Judicial Review* (Cambridge, MA: Harvard University Press, 1980), 87.
[36] Pal (n 33) 306; Ely (n 35) 103.
[37] *Common Cause* v. *Union of India* [1996] 3 SCR 1208 (Supreme Court of India).
[38] *Union of India v. Association for Democratic Reforms* [2002] 3 SCR 696 (Supreme Court of India).
[39] *BR Kapur* v. *State of Tamil* [2001] 7 SCC 231 (Supreme Court of India); *Lily Thomas* v. *Union of India* [2013] 7 SCC 653 (Supreme Court of India).
[40] *People's Union for Civil Liberties* v. *Union of India* [2013] 10 SCC 1 [56] (Supreme Court of India).
[41] JY Interpretation No. 499, 24 March 2000 (Constitutional Court, Taiwan).

a party list by their own political parties, whom voters elect indirectly when they cast ballots in favour of their preferred political party. Prior to the 2004 National Assembly election, a voter could only vote for the district representative. But in 2001, the Constitutional Court mandated that each voter be allowed to cast two votes in the National Assembly election: one for his/her preferred individual candidate in the electoral district and the other for his/her preferred political party that would field the proportional representative in the national legislature.[42] Furthermore, the Constitutional Court of Korea has over time also reduced the disparity in size between the most populous electoral district and the least populous district.[43] However, the Court's record is far from perfect; oddly enough, it has largely upheld all of the oppressive rules regulating electoral campaigns[44] that date back to the authoritarian military era in South Korea.

While courts in these dynamic democracies have creatively consolidated the democratic process by amplifying the competitiveness of elections and electoral institutions, they have also displayed remarkable restraint by strategically not removing top leaders. This was so not only when their courts operated within a dominant-party democracy, as India was when its Supreme Court strategically avoided the removal of Prime Minister Indira Nehru Gandhi from office for an electoral-campaign violation after she was re-elected with a super-majority in Parliament,[45] but such judicial restraint was equally practised by courts after the nation transitioned to a dynamic democracy.

In Taiwan, after President Chen Shui-bian was re-elected with a razor-thin margin in the 2004 presidential election, the dissatisfied opposition party – KMT – insisted that he had staged an assassination attempt on his life on the eve of the election[46] so as to gain sympathy votes for

[42] 13-2 KCCR 77, 2000 Hun-Ma 91, 2000 Hun-Ma 112 (consolidated) (19 July 2001) (Constitutional Court, Korea).

[43] 7-2 KCCR 760, 95 Hun-Ma 224 (27 December 1995) (Constitutional Court, Korea); 13-2 KCCR 502, 2000 Hun-Ma 92, 2000 Hun-Ma 240 (consolidated) (25 October 2001) (Constitutional Court, Korea); 2013 Hun-Ma 781, 2014 Hun-Ma 53 (consolidated) (30 October 2014) (Constitutional Court, Korea).

[44] 13-2 KCCR 174, 99 Hun-Ba 92, 2000 Hun-Ba 39, 2000 Hun-Ma 167·168·199·205·280 (consolidated) (30 August 2001) (Constitutional Court, Korea); 17-2 KCCR 160, 2004 Hun-Ba 52 (29 September 2005) (Constitutional Court, Korea); 2014 Hun-Ba 253, Gongbo Vol. 237, 1049 (30 June 2016) (Constitutional Court, Korea).

[45] *Indira Nehru Gandhi* v. *Shri Raj Narain* [1976] 2 SCR 347 (Supreme Court of India).

[46] A gunman attempted to assassinate both President Chen Shui-bian and Vice President Annette Lu when they were campaigning on 19 March 2004, the eve of Taiwan's presidential election; but both of them suffered only minor injuries. This event has been termed the '319 Shooting' in Taiwan.

his re-election. As the KMT retained a parliamentary majority in the Legislative Yuan, it statutorily created a special commission to investigate the foiled assassination attempt.[47] One may note that members of the special commission were primarily KMT affiliates and the deeply partisan commission was statutorily authorised to launch criminal prosecutions relating to the assassination attempt and overturn any factual findings in a court of law if they differed from the outcome of the investigation conducted by the commission. The Constitutional Court accepted that the Legislative Yuan was empowered to create a special commission to investigate the assassination attempt but it decisively invalidated the statutory provisions that authorised the commission to launch criminal prosecutions and revoke judicial findings.[48] The Court's decision, rendered on 15 December 2004, in essence prevented the special commission from overturning a High Court's ruling on 4 November 2004, which decided that the assassination attempt was neither staged by President Chen nor did the gunshot incident illegally interfere with the conduct of the election.[49] Likewise, in impeachment proceedings, the Constitutional Court of Korea also strategically avoided removing President Roh Moo-hyun from power after Roh's Uri Party won resoundingly at the 2004 National Assembly election during the deliberations of the impeachment case.[50]

Fragile Democracies

In contrast, courts that have come too close to the 'live wire of electoral politics'[51] may end up doing a disservice to their country's transition to a stable democracy; and the state may, as a consequence, backslide

[47] See Jiunn-rong Yeh, 'Presidential Politics and the Judicial Facilitation of Dialogue between Political Actors in New Asian Democracies: Comparing the South Korean and Taiwanese Experiences' (2010) 8(4) *International Journal of Constitutional Law* 911, 932.

[48] JY Interpretation No. 585, 15 December 2004 (Constitutional Court, Taiwan) < http://www.judicial.gov.tw/constitutionalcourt/en/p03_01.asp?expno=585> accessed 1 February 2017.

[49] The High Court's ruling was also confirmed by the Supreme Court in 2005.

[50] 16-1 KCCR 609, 2004 Hun-Na 1 (14 May 2004) (Constitutional Court, Korea); see Wen-Chen Chang, 'Strategic Judicial Responses in Politically Charged Cases: East Asian Experiences' (2010) 8(4) *International Journal of Constitutional Law* 885. In contrast, the Constitutional Court of Korea in 2017 decisively removed President Park Geun-hye from office. One must note that President Park's approval ratings were in single digits at the time of her impeachment – the lowest for any sitting President in South Korea – and the court was merely reflecting public opinion when it chose to remove a deeply unpopular President for her role in an influence-peddling scandal.

[51] Issacharoff (n 5), 610.

to some variant of autocratic military rule. In Thailand, since 2006, the Constitutional Court has invalidated two general elections, removed three Prime Ministers and disbanded six political parties affiliated with former Prime Minister Thaksin Shinawatra. The ensuing political impasse that followed from the complete invalidation of the 2006 and 2014 general elections only precipitated a military coup each time. The most recent military coup in 2014 saw the rise of General Prayut Chan-o-cha as the country's premier and the abolition of the 2007 Thai Constitution. If courts become mere partisan tools that assist one political camp to remove its enemies from the country's political life, as the Constitutional Court in Thailand did, the country's transition to a stable democracy can easily be derailed.

As for Pakistan, since its independence in 1947, the country has been governed for protracted periods by the military; democratic transitions to civilian rule do not last long as they are often soon aborted by military coups.[52] In fact, martial law has been imposed five times in Pakistan, though martial law was not officially declared on the fourth and fifth occasions as General Pervez Musharraf had instead declared a State of Emergency throughout Pakistan on 14 October 1999 and 3 November 2007. (Even during civilian rule, the elected government has been dissolved on four separate occasions by the President.[53]) It is noteworthy that during Iftikhar Muhammad Chaudhry's tenure as Chief Justice, the Supreme Court engaged in unprecedented high-octane judicial review insofar as it invalidated Musharraf's privatisation of state-owned enterprises[54] and investigated into the disappearances of hundreds of persons secretly detained for alleged terrorism links.[55] It should come as no surprise that Chaudhry was eventually suspended by Musharraf in March 2007. But, after Chaudhry was reinstated by the Supreme Court in July 2007, he remained undeterred and the Court agreed to examine the legality of Musharraf's re-election in October 2007 as President. Fearing an adverse outcome, Musharraf declared a State of Emergency on

[52] See Aqil Shah, *The Army and Democracy: Military Politics in Pakistan* (Cambridge, MA: Harvard University Press, 2014).

[53] See Osama Siddique, 'The Jurisprudence of Dissolutions: Presidential Power to Dissolve Assemblies under the Pakistani Constitution and its Discontents' (2006) 23 *Arizona Journal of International and Comparative Law* 615.

[54] *Watan Party* v. *Federation of Pakistan*, PLD 2006 SC 697 (Supreme Court of Pakistan).

[55] See Taiyyaba Ahmed Qureshi, 'State of Emergency: General Pervez Musharraf's Executive Assault on Judicial Independence in Pakistan' (2010) 35 *North Carolina Journal of International Law and Commercial Regulation* 485.

3 November 2007 and dismissed over 60 judges on the superior courts, including Chief Justice Chaudhry.

With regard to Bangladesh, since its independence in 1971, the country has experienced two martial law regimes and undergone four States of Emergency. Interestingly, its Supreme Court (Appellate Division) only questioned the legitimacy of these extraordinary governmental measures *after* the crises had ceased. In *Anwar Hossain Chowdhury* v. *Bangladesh*,[56] the Appellate Division in 1989 invalidated the 8th Amendment to the Bangladesh Constitution, which had authorised the establishment of six additional Permanent Benches in different regions of the country that would possess the same powers and functions as the original High Court Division. One may note that these additional Permanent Benches were created in 1982, at the beginning of a period of martial law governance in Bangladesh that lasted until 1986; and the impugned constitutional amendment was enacted in 1988 to formalise this extra-legal arrangement after martial law was lifted in 1986. In the same vein, the Supreme Court of Bangladesh (Appellate Division) invalidated the 5th Amendment[57] and the 7th Amendment[58] to the Bangladesh Constitution, which had attempted to oust the Court's jurisdiction to review laws and orders passed when the country was governed during the two periods of martial law (1975–1979 and 1982–1986). But what is particularly noteworthy is that the 5th and 7th Amendments were respectively invalidated in 2010 and 2011, more than a decade after both martial law regimes had ended, and upon the request of the civilian government. On 10 May 2011, the Appellate Division also declared in a Short Order that the 13th Amendment, which authorised for an interim unelected Non-political Caretaker Government (NCG) to govern Bangladesh before

[56] (1989) BLD (Special) (AD) 1 (Supreme Court of Bangladesh).

[57] The 5th Amendment provided that all amendments or repeals made to the Bangladesh Constitution from 15 August 1975 to 9 April 1979 (inclusive) by any proclamation or Proclamation Order of the Martial Law Authorities were deemed to have been validly made, and could not be called into question before any court or tribunal or other authority. See *Khondker Delwar Hossain* v. *Bangladesh Italian Marble Works* (Civil Petition for Leave to Appeal Nos. 1044 & 1045 of 2009) (Supreme Court of Bangladesh).

[58] The 7th Amendment to the Bangladesh Constitution provided that all proclamations, proclamation orders, Chief Martial Law Administrator's Orders, Martial Law Regulations, Martial Law Orders, Martial Law Instructions, ordinances and other laws made from 24 March 1982 to 11 November 1986 (inclusive) had been validly made, and could not be called into question before any court or tribunal or other authority. See *Siddique Ahmed* v. *Government of Bangladesh* (Civil Appeal No 48 of 2011) (15 May 2011) (Supreme Court of Bangladesh).

every national election, was unconstitutional.[59] But the invalidation of the NCG system was again what the ruling Awami League (AL) government wanted and the decision provided the government with the necessary political leverage to pass the 15th Amendment, within two months of the Court's Short Order, to abolish the NCG system once and for all.[60]

In countries where the armed forces are not under the firm control of the civilian government and the country oscillates regularly between military and civilian rule, high-octane judicial review can often precipitate a hostile take-over by the armed forces and lead to the demise of the rule of law, as we have observed in both Thailand and Pakistan. Therefore, the judiciary's primary and basic goal in these fragile democracies should arguably *not* be antagonistic strong-form judicial review, but the maintenance of its institutional independence instead,[61] as the Supreme Court of Bangladesh (Appellate Division) has done.

Conclusion

This book seeks to provide important insights on how Asian courts can strategically engage with the political actors in their jurisdictions and contribute to (or even impede) their countries' democratic development. Judges do not operate in an institutional or ideological vacuum; they shape and are shaped by the social, political, and economical struggles within their given political systems.[62]

Chapters 2, 3, and 4 will focus on the dominant-party democracies of Singapore, Malaysia, and Hong Kong, respectively, where genuine political competition is absent. Even though the possibilities of political reprisals against judges or constitutional reversals of the courts' decisions in these jurisdictions are real, such that their courts are unable to challenge the hegemonic dominant player by ushering in macro *systemic* electoral

[59] *Abdul Mannan Khan* v. *Bangladesh* (Civil Appeal No. 139 of 2005) (Supreme Court of Bangladesh).

[60] See Adeeba Aziz Khan, 'The Politics of Constitutional Amendments in Bangladesh: The Case of the Non-political Caretaker Government' (2015) 9 *International Review of Law* <http://dx.doi.org/10.5339/irl.2015.9> accessed 1 February 2017. One should note that the full judgment was only issued 14 months after the Short Order was issued. By then, the 15th Amendment, which abolished the NCG system, had already been passed.

[61] Gardbaum (n 17).

[62] Ran Hirschl, 'The Judicialisation of Politics', in Keith Whittington, R. Daniel Kelemen and Gregory Caldeira (eds), *The Oxford Handbook of Law and Politics* (Oxford: Oxford University Press, 2010), 119.

reforms, I shall explore how these courts can extend voting rights *writ small* in dialogic ways that minimise backlash against the judges.[63]

Chapters 5, 6, and 7 will respectively examine how Asian courts in the dynamic democracies of India, Taiwan, and South Korea operate where political power is more fragmented[64] and diffused among the competing political parties or branches of government. I shall illustrate how courts in such environments have facilitated their nations' democratic transformation by making both micro and macro *systemic* changes that enhance the competitiveness and fairness of voting procedures and electoral institutions; and I shall explore how they can further consolidate the respective jurisdictions' democratic processes. Moreover, I will also highlight how the highest courts in these jurisdictions have enhanced the legitimacy of their actions by remaining non-partisan institutionally and have refrained from acting as proxies that merely aided one political camp to remove its enemies from the country's political life.

Chapters 8, 9, and 10 will analyse the fragile democracies in Thailand, Pakistan, and Bangladesh, respectively, where the armed forces pose a real and existential constraint on civic life and the countries have been oscillating between martial law and civilian rule. Where the democracy's institutional processes are functioning poorly, and judicial independence is fragile, I argue that the country's top judges should not rule in partisan or imprudent ways that intentionally or inadvertently foment a military coup.

Finally, in Chapter 11, I shall examine the doctrine of unconstitutional constitutional amendments.[65] In all nine Asian jurisdictions under discussion, this doctrine has been judicially conceived or applied as a safeguard against legislative worst-case scenarios where the political incumbents (or the military) abuse the amendment process to introduce constitutional amendments that erode democratic values. In short, many of these impugned constitutional amendments relate directly to governmental restrictions on voting rights or constitute legislative attacks on judicial

[63] See Po Jen Yap, *Constitutional Dialogue in Common Law Asia* (Oxford: Oxford University Press, 2015).

[64] John Ferejohn, 'Judicialising Politics, Politicising Law' (2002) 65 *Law and Contemporary Problems* 41, 55.

[65] See Po Jen Yap, 'The Conundrum of Unconstitutional Constitutional Amendments' (2015) 4 *Global Constitutionalism* 114; David Landau, 'Abusive Constitutionalism' (2013) 47 *UC Davis Law Review* 189; Rosalind Dixon and David Landau, 'Transnational Constitutionalism and a Limited Doctrine of Unconstitutional Constitutional Amendment' (2015) 13 *International Journal of Constitutional Law* 606.

independence. In this chapter, I shall examine the normative arguments for and against the judicial enforcement of this ostensibly ubiquitous basic structure doctrine and explore how this doctrine, in its various permutations, *should* be applied in these dominant-party, dynamic, and fragile democracies in Asia.

In essence, there is a symbiotic relationship between a country's state of democratisation and the long-term sustainability of the political power that its judges can wield. A stable and dynamic democracy can empower its judges to shape their political environment and further contribute to democratic politics. On the other hand, judges in dominant-party, or even fragile, democracies may not act with impunity. Therefore, prudent and wise judges must always design constitutional rules and doctrines that keep 'democratic transitions on course rather than contributing to pushing them off the rails'.[66]

[66] Gardbaum (n 17), 320.

PART I

Dominant-Party Democracies

2

The Supreme Court of Singapore and the Promise of Enforceable Constitutional Conventions

Since gaining independence in 1965, Singapore has been governed by the same ruling party, the People's Action Party (PAP). The country practices a variant of 'authoritarian constitutionalism',[1] where a semi-permanent party consolidates both legislative and executive power, makes all relevant public policy decisions, and does not take well to aggressive judicial review; and the courts have generally acquiesced by engaging only in 'retail rule of law, insuring that government obeys its own laws until it changes them'.[2] In constitutional systems where a dominant party/coalition is in control, a robust judicial reading of the Constitution may precipitate a constitutional crisis when the government responds by deploying constitutional or unconstitutional means to 'punish' the courts.[3]

Specifically, in Singapore, when the government lost in a constitutional decision before the Court of Appeal in 1988 for the first and last time, the Government swiftly overturned that decision via a series of constitutional and statutory amendments within a month of the judgment. In that seminal decision of *Chng Suan Tze* v. *Minister of Home Affairs* (1988),[4] the Court of Appeal, after surveying a litany of Commonwealth precedents, quashed the preventive detention orders issued under the Internal Security Act (ISA) against alleged Marxist conspirators and also concluded in *obiter* that the Ministerial discretion to detain personnel under the ISA would be subject to an 'objective' test of review by the courts as constitutionally required under Articles 9[5] and 12[6] of the Singapore

[1] Mark Tushnet, 'Authoritarian Constitutionalism' (2015) 100 *Cornell Law Review* 391.

[2] Martin Shapiro and Alec Stone Sweet, *On Law, Politics, and Judicialisation* (New York: Oxford University Press, 2002), 166.

[3] Po Jen Yap, *Constitutional Dialogue in Common Law Asia* (Oxford: Oxford University Press, 2015), 78.

[4] [1988] 2 SLR(R) 525 (Singapore Court of Appeal).

[5] Article 9(1) of the Singapore Constitution reads: 'No person shall be deprived of his life or personal liberty save in accordance with law.'

[6] Article 12(1) of the Singapore Constitution reads: 'All persons are equal before the law and entitled to the equal protection of the law.'

Constitution.[7] This decision proved to be sufficiently disquieting to the Executive, and subsequent amendments restricted judicial review in ISA cases to only narrow procedural grounds.[8]

It is noteworthy that the Singapore judiciary has had the opportunity to review a challenge to the nation's electoral process only once since the country gained independence. *Vellama d/o Marie Muthu* v. *Attorney General* (2013)[9] will go down in history as a 'constitutional moment'[10] in Singapore as its Court of Appeal affirmed for the first time that the Prime Minister had a constitutional duty under Article 49 of the Constitution[11] to call for a by-election when a casual vacancy arises. Such a judicial pronouncement would be a non-event in any other liberal constitutional democracy; but in Singapore, the decision is especially groundbreaking because the Court of Appeal has *never* in the country's history deemed a single statutory provision unconstitutional. Therefore, any rebuke of the government on constitutional grounds constitutes a watershed event in Singapore.

Vellama and the Constitutional Duty to Fill a Vacancy

In *Vellama*, a resident voter of the Hougang Single Member Constituency (SMC) instituted judicial review proceedings on 14 February 2012 for a

[7] One must however note that the Court of Appeal had merely quashed the detention order on a technicality and did not actually objectively review the Minister's exercise of his statutory powers of detention. The appeal primarily turned on the Court's interpretation of Section 8(1) of the ISA, which authorised the Minister of Home Affairs to issue a detention order if the President of Singapore was satisfied that this was necessary to prevent that person from acting in any manner prejudicial to the security of Singapore. On the facts, the detention orders were signed only by the Permanent Secretary of Home Affairs and the affidavit he signed merely testified to the fact that the government was satisfied that the detention orders were necessary. The Court held unanimously that this recital was insufficient. Instead, the Court opined that, in the absence of direct evidence from the President, the Cabinet or the authorised Minister must provide evidence that the Cabinet (or the authorised Minister) and the President, after receiving the government's advice, were satisfied that these measures were necessary.

[8] Since 1968, the PAP has controlled over 90% of the elected seats in Parliament. An adverse constitutional decision by the courts can be easily reversed with a constitutional amendment, which only requires the concurrence of two-thirds of the total number of the elected legislators. See Article 5(2) of the Singapore Constitution.

[9] *Vellama d/o Marie Muthu* v. *Attorney General* [2013] SGCA 39, [2013] 4 SLR 1 (Singapore Court of Appeal).

[10] See Kevin Tan and Thio Li-ann, *Singapore: 50 Constitutional Moments that Defined a Nation* (Singapore: Marshall Cavendish, 2015).

[11] Article 49(1) of the Singapore Constitution reads: 'Whenever the seat of a Member, not being a non-constituency Member, has become vacant for any reason other than a dissolution of Parliament, the vacancy shall be filled by election …'

mandatory order requiring the Prime Minister to advise the President to issue a writ of election for the electoral ward when her Member of Parliament resigned from office. By the time the applicant's case came before the Court of Appeal, the by-election that she had sought had already been held on 26 May 2012. Hence, the applicant's case was dismissed by the Court of Appeal on the ground that she lacked the standing to seek declaratory relief as the facts underpinning her original application had been rendered moot. And the Court of Appeal could have left the matter as that. But, curiously, the Court proceeded to decide the substantive constitutional issue raised by the appeal anyway.

Even more interestingly, the Court of Appeal rejected the government's argument that the Prime Minister had an unfettered discretion to decide whether to call for a by-election when a vacancy arose. Instead, the Court imposed a constitutional duty on the Prime Minister to fill a casual vacancy within a 'reasonable time'.[12]

In view that Article 49 of the Singapore Constitution states that a 'vacancy *shall* be filled by election', the Court of Appeal held that there was a constitutional imperative on the Prime Minister to fill a vacancy. As observed by the Court:

> *The implication of a less definitive and directory rather than mandatory verb where the word 'shall' is used, and where its ordinary sense is not open to question, is simply unwarranted.*[13]

In so doing, the Court of Appeal overruled the High Court's conclusion that the Prime Minister had an unfettered discretion as 'the phrase "shall be filled by election" in Art 49(1) referred to the process whereby vacated seats of elected Members are to be filled … and not the event of election'.[14]

Moreover, according to the Court of Appeal, the absence of a time-limit clause governing a by-election in the Constitution does not mean that 'the Prime Minister is thereby completely free to do as he pleases',[15] because Section 52 of the Interpretation Act provides that 'where no time is prescribed… that thing shall be done with all convenient speed'; and in the Court's view, this statutory provision basically enshrines the 'common law concept of a reasonable time'.[16] *A fortiori*, when a vacancy arises, the Prime Minister has a constitutional duty to call for a by-election within a reasonable time.

[12] *Vellama* (n 9) [84].
[13] *Ibid.* [77].
[14] *Vellama* v. *Attorney General* [2012] 4 SLR 698 [80] (High Court of Singapore).
[15] *Vellama* (n 9) [78].
[16] *Ibid.* [84].

Unfortunately, the Court reduced the force of this decision by conceding that the Prime Minister 'could justifiably take into account matters relating to policy … [and] it is impossible to lay down the specific considerations or factors which would have a bearing on the question as to whether the Prime Minister had acted unreasonably for not, to date, calling for a by-election to fill a vacancy',[17] such that 'no pre-determination of the Prime Minister's considerations would be warranted'.[18] Therefore, so long as the Prime Minister does not openly reject the possibility of a by-election, it would appear that there are no other constitutional limits laid down by the Court on the ministerial exercise of this discretion.

This deferential stance taken by the Court of Appeal is emblematic of the judicial ethos in Singapore that 'matters of public policy are the proper remit of the Executive'[19] and that courts should not be seen as 'the first line of defence against administrative abuses of power: instead, control can and should come internally from Parliament and the Executive itself in upholding high standards of public administration and policy'.[20] If so, as admitted by the Court, judicial intervention in election cases in Singapore would only occur in the most 'exceptional cases';[21] and in almost all cases, any such review would be a mere chimera.

While the Singapore Court of Appeal may not have been as bold in *Vellama* as it could have been, this ground-breaking case remains a monumental decision for Singapore. Insofar as the Court of Appeal recognised that there was a constitutional duty on the Prime Minister to call for an election when a vacancy arose, it has reaffirmed the 'basic proposition of the rule of law that all discretionary power is subject to legal limits'.[22]

More importantly, the pronouncement by the Court of Appeal in *Vellama* is an oblique repudiation of the PAP's practice of *not* calling for by-elections when vacancies arose in SMCs, a practice which began ever since the ruling party lost one parliamentary seat, a first since the country's independence, in a 1981 by-election.[23] In 1986, both the Anson and Geylang West SMCs were vacated by the incumbents but no by-elections were held. With regard to the Anson SMC, its (Opposition) Member of

[17] *Ibid.* [85].

[18] *Ibid.*

[19] *Ibid.* [34].

[20] Chan Sek Keong, 'Judicial Review – From Angst to Empathy' (2010) 22 *Singapore Academy of Law Journal* 469, 480.

[21] *Vellama* (n 9) [85].

[22] *Ibid.*

[23] The PAP lost the Anson SMC in a by-election held in 1981.

Parliament was disqualified from office after he was convicted of financial accounting irregularities;[24] and the Geylang West SMC became vacant after a PAP minister committed suicide whilst he was being investigated for corruption. No by-elections were held for either vacated seat, and their constituents had no elected representatives in Parliament for almost two years until the next general election was held in 1988. In the 1988 general election, the single wards of Anson and Geylang West were erased from the electoral map as they were merged with other PAP constituencies. It is thus of great significance that, since *Vellama*, the PAP government has called for a by-election within 6 months of a vacancy arising in a SMC.[25]

In a most interesting postscript, the Court of Appeal in *Yong Vui Kong* v. *Public Prosecutor* (2015)[26] made a couple of fascinating observations about the citizenry's right to vote in a completely unrelated constitutional challenge to the legality of the judicial corporal punishment regime in Singapore. While upholding the constitutionality of judicial caning *inter alia* on the basis that the prohibition against torture does not form part of the basic structure of the Singapore Constitution, the Court nevertheless suggested that the right to vote could 'possibly'[27] form part of the 'basic structure of the Constitution',[28] and thus 'may not be amended even by a validly passed constitutional amendment'.[29]

But one must note that the right to vote is not expressly protected in the Singapore Constitution at all. (A Constitutional Commission had proposed to the government in 1966 to amend the Constitution and expressly enshrine the right to vote;[30] but this proposal has never been taken up by the PAP.) In *Yong Vui Kong* (2015), the Court not only recognised that the right to vote is an *implied* constitutional right, it further suggested that this *implied* right formed part of Singapore's *unwritten* basic structure of the Constitution such that it may not even be removed by a constitutional amendment. By sheer judicial fiat, the Court has elevated an unwritten right to a super-right, one that can even trump a constitutional amendment.

24 For an overview of this political saga, see 'J.B. Jeyaretnam', Lawyers' Rights Watch Canada, 26 March 2012 <http://www.lrwc.org/j-b-jeyaretnam> accessed 1 February 2017.

25 In 2013 and 2016, the Prime Minister called for by-elections when the PAP Members of Parliament in two SMCs resigned from office on grounds of personal indiscretion.

26 *Yong Vui Kong* v. *Public Prosecutor* [2015] SGCA 11 (Singapore Court of Appeal).

27 *Ibid.* [69].

28 *Ibid.*

29 *Ibid.* [72].

30 *Report of the Constitutional Commission* 1966 (Singapore: Government Printer, 1966) [43].

Systemic Deficiencies in Singapore's Electoral System

The constitutional potential of the Court of Appeal's pronouncement in *Yong Vui Kong* would have been truly breath-taking if the Singapore courts were in the position to enforce it in practice.

However, since 1968, the PAP has controlled over 90% of the elected seats in Parliament. An adverse constitutional decision by the courts can be easily reversed with a constitutional amendment, which only requires the concurrence of two-thirds of the total number of the elected legislators.[31] Even if the Court of Appeal decides to take on the hyper-dominant party by actually invalidating a constitutional amendment, it is not inconceivable that the government may respond by ousting the 'errant' judges.

But this is not to say that the Court of Appeal should therefore just capitulate completely to the whims of the ruling regime. Instead, the path forward for the judiciary is to explore dialogic pathways and implement doctrines that allow courts to protect electoral rights with some 'bite', whilst preserving a substantial degree of legislative flexibility for the government to respond in disagreement if it so chooses, without the need to amend the Constitution or, worse, remove the judges.[32]

In essence, dialogic review allows courts, in the first instance, to reverse the political status quo such that a rights-friendly outcome *can* be enforced against the State; but the government is not disabled from reinstating its original views with a piece of ordinary legislation in Parliament. Dialogic doctrines impose enactment costs on the legislature if it disagrees with the judicial decisions, as the government must reclaim the field with the passage of a statute in Parliament.[33] To the extent that the Court has compelled Parliament to deliberate and openly debate the statutory reversal, the government would be forced to publicly defend its position, respond to objections raised by the opposition, and pay the political price. Dialogic review forces the government to be more transparent about its motivations and to take responsibility for its decision to depart from the judicial rules imposed by the Court. But insofar as the Court has not enforced a constitutional settlement of rights, the government is less likely to respond in kind by ousting judicial review with a constitutional amendment.

[31] Article 5(2) of the Singapore Constitution.

[32] Yap (n 3), 78.

[33] *Ibid.*, 104.

Two features of Singapore's electoral system are particularly disconcerting and would be ripe for such dialogic judicial review and intervention. First, the potential abuse of the multi-member group constituencies, known as the Group Representative Constituencies (GRCs); and the second, the gerrymandering of electoral boundaries by the incumbent ruling regime before every general election. Both issues will be explored in turn.

Group Representation Constituencies (GRCs)

Singapore has a unicameral legislature. Currently, its Parliament is composed of 89 elected members returned, on a first-past-the-post basis, at general elections that have to be held at least every five years.[34] Singapore's electoral system is unique insofar as it provides for both single-member constituencies (SMCs) and multi-member group constituencies in the parliamentary elections. Such multi-member group constituencies are known as Group Representative Constituencies (GRCs) and each GRC is formed by merging several single wards into one mega-constituency; all the electoral candidates in a GRC currently contest in teams composed of four to six persons and each elector would cast one vote for the team he or she supports. The GRC model was first introduced, following a constitutional amendment, in 1988, ostensibly to ensure racial diversity in Parliament as at least one team member must be an ethnic minority. Initially, each GRC would be composed of only three members. But in 1991, this was increased to four; and later, in 1996, the ceiling was raised to six.[35] While the entrenchment of minority representation in Parliament is a laudable political end, the integrity of this justification is undercut by the expansion of the GRC size. In fact, the GRC system is widely perceived to be merely an electoral mechanism for the ruling PAP to ensure the election of new promising but unknown candidates with ministerial calibre by fielding them in GRC teams alongside party stalwarts with mass electoral appeal. Currently, there are 13 SMCs and 16 GRCs in Singapore.

[34] Article 65(4) of the Singapore Constitution.

[35] Article 39A(1) of the Singapore Constitution reads: 'The Legislature may, in order to ensure the representation in Parliament of Members from the Malay, Indian and other minority communities, by law make provision for – (a) any constituency to be declared by the President, having regard to the number of electors in that constituency, as a group representation constituency to enable any election in that constituency to be held on a basis of a group of not less than 3 but not more than 6 candidates....'

In the last general election, held in 2015, the PAP won 83 of the 89 elected seats, and 15 out of 16 of the GRCs.

Gerrymandering of Electoral Boundaries

Gerrymandering is a 'pathology of democracy'[36] whereby the political incumbent is able to strategically skew the political competition in its favour by re-drawing pre-existing electoral boundaries. Voting blocs unsympathetic to the incumbent can be carved up and diffused into other pro-incumbent constituencies, such that the weight of the opposition votes can be diluted into political irrelevance.

In Singapore, the electoral boundaries are redrawn before every general election; and the redrawing exercise is performed by the Electoral Boundaries Review Committee (EBRC), a committee which usually comprises five civil servants and is headed by the Secretary to the Prime Minister.[37] While the EBRC acknowledges that it takes into consideration the pre-existing configurations of the constituencies, population shifts, and housing developments since the last boundary delineation exercise, it does not disclose the specific reasons for the creation, elimination, or reconfiguration of any constituency.[38] There are no public hearings of the delimitation exercise, the minutes of meetings are not made available to the public, and the public is not consulted on the recommendations proposed by the EBRC. In 2015, the EBRC released its proposed electoral boundary revisions only a month before the election was called thereby giving the opposition very limited time to react to the changes. According to Section 8(1) of the Parliamentary Elections Act, the legislature does not even need to debate and approve these changes to the electoral divisions; the law merely requires that the Minister, 'by notification in the Gazette, specify the names and boundaries of the electoral divisions of Singapore'.[39]

[36] Martin Shapiro, 'Gerrymandering, Fairness, and the Supreme Court' (1985) 33 *UCLA Law Review* 227, 239.

[37] 'Electoral Boundaries Drawn for Next General Election', *Channel News Asia*, 24 July 2015 <http://www.channelnewsasia.com/news/singapore/electoral-boundaries/2005186.html> accessed 1 February 2017.

[38] The Electoral Boundaries Review Committee, *Report of the Electoral Boundaries Review Committee 2015*, 24 July 2015 <http://www.eld.gov.sg/pdf/White%20Paper%20on%20the%20Report%20of%20the%20Electoral%20Boundaries%20Review%20Committee%202015.pdf> accessed 1 February 2017.

[39] Section 8 of the Parliamentary Elections Act (Chapter 218).

With regard to the most recent delimitation exercise that took place prior to the 2015 General Election, the Joo Chiat SMC – which the opposition narrowly lost by about 1% of the votes in the previous 2011 election – was erased from the electoral map and the constituency was instead absorbed into a neighbouring GRC. No reasons were given by the incumbent party for this curious elimination.[40] SMCs are generally more attractive to opposition candidates as the hurdles for parties intending to contest such single seats are significantly lower; therefore, it is no surprise that the slate of SMCs up for grabs are always changing before every election, thereby preventing the opposition from gaining a foothold in any single ward controlled by the PAP. But in fairness to the incumbent ruling party, since 1991, it has always retained the same electoral boundaries for constituencies *won* by the opposition party in the preceding election.[41]

Enforceable Constitutional Conventions and the Constitutional Right to Vote

In view of the fact that the citizenry's right to vote has been recognised by the Court of Appeal in *Yong Vui Kong* (2015) as implicitly protected in the Constitution, one can certainly argue that the GRC electoral system and the gerrymandering of electoral boundaries before every election undermine this fundamental liberty.

The GRC electoral system disadvantages political outsiders as they have to scramble to find between three and six electable candidates, including an ethnic minority, to contest on the same ticket in a larger multi-member electoral ward. The current Prime Minister Lee Hsien Loong himself has conceded that the GRC system favours the incumbent party.[42] This systemic electoral disadvantage that the opposition experiences when contesting in large wards, in turn, impacts adversely on the citizenry's right to vote the opposition into office.

[40] Netina Tan, 'Pre-electoral Malpractice, Gerrymandering and its Effects on Singapore's 2015 GE', in Terence Lee and Kevin YL Tan (eds), *Change in Voting: Singapore's 2015 General Election* (Singapore: Ethos Books, 2016), 180.

[41] In the 1988 general election, the Anson SMC, which was won by the opposition in the 1984 election, was abolished and the constituency was merged with a neighbouring PAP stronghold.

[42] 'PM Lee Hsien Loong at the debate on President's Address on 27 January 2016', 27 January 2016 <http://www.pmo.gov.sg/mediacentre/pm-lee-hsien-loong-debate-presidents-address-27-january-2016> accessed 1 February 2017.

In the same vein, the gerrymandering of electoral boundaries undercuts the right to vote by potentially allowing the incumbent party to diffuse votes for the opposition into political irrelevance, such that the government could win an overwhelming number of the elected seats in Parliament, even though a significant number of the electorate did not vote for them. In the 2011 General Election, the PAP won 60.1% of the popular vote but secured 81 out of 87 of the elected seats. Similarly, in the most recent 2015 general election, the PAP won 83 out of 89 of the elected seats with 69.9% of the popular vote.

Nevertheless, whilst a strong case can be made that the GRC electoral system and the electoral boundaries delimitation by the political incumbent violate one's right to vote, it would be imprudent for the Court of Appeal, at the outset, to invalidate either or both practices. The GRC system is expressly enshrined in the Singapore Constitution[43] and it would be unthinkable for the Court of Appeal to invalidate a feature explicitly provided for in the Constitution when it has never even struck down a single piece of ordinary legislation in its history. On the other hand, while the delimitation exercise by the incumbent is merely authorised by legislation,[44] the per se invalidation of this practice would only trigger an immediate constitutional amendment to reverse the decision, as the PAP government is so reliant on this practice to maintain its hyper-incumbency that it would absolutely not tolerate any judicial intervention of this nature.

The dialogic path forward for the Singapore judiciary is to ameliorate the constitutional concerns raised by both electoral features by recognising and enforcing *against* the government constitutional conventions that have been accepted tacitly and practised by the ruling party itself.

Constitutional conventions are norms that have evolved from political practices and customs that complement and contextualise the constitution;[45] and, as Dicey described them, they are 'rules for determining

[43] Article 39A(1)(a) of the Singapore Constitution reads: 'The Legislature may, in order to ensure the representation in Parliament of Members from the Malay, Indian and other minority communities, by law make provision for any constituency to be declared by the President, having regard to the number of electors in that constituency, as a group representation constituency to enable any election in that constituency to be held on a basis of a group of not less than 3 but not more than 6 candidates.'

[44] Section 8(1) of the Parliamentary Elections Act (Chapter 218) states: 'The Minister may, from time to time, by notification in the Gazette, specify the names and boundaries of the electoral divisions of Singapore for purposes of elections under this Act.'

[45] James W.J. Bowden and Nicholas A. MacDonald, 'Writing the Unwritten: The Officialisation of Constitutional Convention in Canada, the United Kingdom, New Zealand and Australia' (2012) 6 *Journal of Parliamentary and Political Law* 365, 367.

the mode in which the discretionary powers'[46] of the State ought to be exercised. While constitutional conventions are rarely enforceable by the courts,[47] it is untrue that common law courts never legally enforce conventions. A more accurate characterisation would be that a constitutional convention can be enforced when the courts, having successfully identified a convention, interpret or apply a pre-existing legal rule that renders the convention legally obligatory.[48] In other words, a constitutional convention can be enforced judicially when it implements a pre-existing legal right or duty, and not independently as a free-standing cause of action.

In *Attorney General* v. *Jonathan Cape*,[49] the English Court recognised a constitutional convention of ministerial collective responsibility whereby ministers do not disclose the opinions of individual ministers expressed during Cabinet meetings; and the Court was willing to enforce the convention insofar as it applied and implemented the common law tort of breach of confidence. On the facts of the case, an injunction against the publication of a former minister's diary disclosing Cabinet discussions was *only* refused because the grounds for granting injunctive relief were not satisfied.[50]

Turning to Singapore, two constitutional conventions pertinent to our discussion can be identified. First, the Singapore Government has never created more than 5 six-member GRCs since this multi-member electoral system was conceived. In fact, since 2011, there have been only 2 six-member GRCs. Second, the PAP has, for nearly three decades, always retained the same electoral boundaries for constituencies won by the opposition party in the preceding election. Both long-standing political practices have been observed by the ruling government and can be enforced by the Singapore Court of Appeal as constitutional conventions

46 A.V. Dicey and J.W.F. Allison (eds), *The Law of the Constitution* (Oxford: Oxford University Press, 2013), 188; see also Brian Galligan and Scott Brenton (eds), *Constitutional Conventions in Westminster Systems: Controversies, Changes and Challenges* (Cambridge: Cambridge University Press, 2015), 18–19.

47 *Reference re Secession of Quebec* [1998] 2 SCR 217 [98] (Supreme Court of Canada).

48 N.W. Barber, 'Laws and Constitutional Conventions' (2009) 125 *Law Quarterly Review* 294, 297.

49 [1976] QB 752 (Queen's Bench Division, High Court of England & Wales).

50 *Ibid.*, 770–771. For the injunction against the publication to be granted, the Court held that it must be shown that (a) the publication would be a breach of confidence; (b) the public interest requires the publication be restrained; (c) there are no other facts of the public interest contradictory of and more compelling than that relied upon; and the Court will closely examine the extent to which relief is necessary to ensure that restrictions are not imposed beyond the strict requirement of public need.

that vindicate, apply, and implement the constitutional right to vote. If so, the Electoral Boundaries Review Committee (EBRC), staffed by civil servants that report directly to the Prime Minister, can be disempowered by the courts from creating more six-member GRCs and gerrymandering with the electoral boundaries of opposition-held constituencies when performing its delimitation exercise before each election.

The judicial enforcement of such constitutional conventions would likely fall within the ruling government's 'tolerance interval'[51] as it merely crystallises as law political customs that the PAP has chosen to observe of its own accord for decades. In other words, the Court would not upset the political status quo, but would merely nudge the political branches to stay the course. At the same time, such 'soft' constitutional hand-cuffs are not useless constraints as they deter the Executive branch, in a moment of panic before a general election, from allowing six-member GRCs to dominate the electoral map and/or carving up opposition-held wards and merging them with neighbouring PAP strongholds. In this way, the EBRC would not be allowed to repeat what it did with the Anson SMC in the 1988 election, which was to merge the said electoral ward won by the opposition in the preceding 1984 election with another PAP-held constituency. But such a judicial ruling remains dialogic as the ruling government may still overturn these constitutional conventions if it so chooses, but it can only do so by introducing a bill in Parliament, having it debated publicly, voted upon, and passed into law. As Justice Brandeis once eloquently wrote, 'If the broad light of day could be let in upon men's actions, it would purify them as the sun disinfects'.[52] By enforcing constitutional conventions in these instances, all that the judges would have done is to prevent stealth electoral changes by executive fiat.[53]

Conclusion

Elections in Singapore are not a farce. The PAP government does not resort to corruption or ballot-rigging to win. But in its zeal to retain

[51] Lee Epstein, Olga Shvetsova and Jack Knight, 'The Role of Constitutional Courts in the Establishment and Maintenance of Democratic Systems of Government' (2001) 35 *Law and Society Review* 117, 128; David Landau, 'A Dynamic Theory of Judicial Role' (2014) 55 *Boston College Law Review* 1501, 1541.

[52] Louis D. Brandeis, *Letters of Louis D. Brandeis: Volume III, 1913–1915: Progressive and Zionist* (New York: State University of New York Press, 1973), 100.

[53] For a general discussion on stealth authoritarianism, see Ozan Varol, 'Stealth Authoritarianism' (2015) 100 *Iowa Law Review* 1673.

hyper-incumbency, the ruling regime constantly re-configures the electoral rules *ex ante* to stave off the opposition or arrest declining vote share.[54] In 1988, the GRC electoral system was introduced after the PAP failed to win *all* of the seats in Parliament in the preceding 1984 election – the first 'loss' it had suffered in a general election after the country's independence.[55] (They had only lost 2 out of 79 elected seats in the 1984 general election.) When the PAP lost 4 out of 81 elected seats in the 1991 general election, it amended the Constitution in 1996 to allow for six-member GRCs to be created, just before the 1997 general election. Alongside these unfair electoral rules that are deliberately designed to impede the prospects of the opposition winning elected seats in Parliament, the government also imposes short campaigning periods[56] and restrictive constraints on the distribution of political films[57] and electoral advertising;[58] such ostensibly party-neutral rules have a disproportionate adverse impact on the opposition parties, who do not enjoy the same coverage in the mainstream media controlled by the PAP.[59]

Where the leviathan state is a semi-permanent feature of Singapore's political landscape, and strong-form judicial review has not taken root in the country, the path forward for the Singapore Court of Appeal is to avoid dismantling the abovementioned 'cartel regulations'[60] entrenched by the political incumbent at the outset, but to enforce the constitutional conventions on electoral practices that the PAP has itself willingly observed for decades.

[54] Netina Tan, 'Manipulating Electoral Laws in Singapore' (2013) 32(4) *Electoral Studies* 632, 634.

[55] The PAP lost one elected seat in the 1981 Anson SMC by-election.

[56] Section 34(6) of the Parliamentary Elections Act (Chapter 218) restricts the campaigning period to between 9 and 56 days.

[57] See Section 33 of the Films Act (Chapter 107).

[58] See Parliamentary Elections (Electoral Advertising) Regulations.

[59] In Singapore, the Newspaper and Printing Presses Act (Chapter 206) requires a person to first obtain a licence before he or she can print, publish, or circulate a newspaper in Singapore and this licence can be refused or withdrawn by the Minister of Communications and Information at his or her discretion. Furthermore, any newspaper that publishes in Singapore must create two classes of shares, an ordinary share and a management share. Each management shareholder has 200 times the voting rights of an ordinary shareholder over any resolution relating to the appointment/dismissal of a director or any staff member of the newspaper company, and the former share type can only be owned by Singapore citizens or corporations that have been approved by the same Cabinet Minister.

[60] Pippa Norris, 'All Elections Are Not the Same: Why Power-sharing Elections Strengthen Democratisation', in Staffan I Lindberg (ed.), *Democratisation by Elections: A New Mode of Transition* (Baltimore: John Hopkins University Press, 2009), 152–153.

In the wake of the 2011 General Election, where the PAP lost 6 elected seats for the first time since the country's independence, including 1 five-member GRC, and failed to reclaim them in the 2015 General Election, Singapore's political scene is slowly becoming more pluralistic and competitive.[61] With the rise of an electorate that has become more educated, more demanding, and that seeks more political diversity and accountability than ever before,[62] the judicial enforcement of conventions that the PAP has abided by would have a significant impact on the country's democratic consolidation, as it deters a future Prime Minister, in a moment of folly, from reversing the status quo and upsetting the gains made by the opposition in the previous election. But so far as the Court of Appeal is merely enforcing practices that the PAP itself has observed for decades, and in the face of increasing public demand for electoral diversity, such a judicial manoeuvre will most likely be tolerated by the ruling PAP, as it would not want to pay the political price of openly reversing such decisions by legislation in Parliament. Such modest decisions, as *Vellama* was, may prove to be the most enduring judgments ever handed down by the Singapore Court of Appeal.

[61] Kenneth Paul Tan, 'Singapore in 2014: Adapting to the "New Normal"' (2015) 55(1) *Asian Survey* 157, 157.

[62] Chan Heng Chee, 'The Strategic Voter in the "New Normal"', *Straits Times*, 19 September 2015 <http://www.straitstimes.com/opinion/the-strategic-voter-in-the-new-normal> accessed 1 February 2017.

3

Malaysian Courts and Electoral Fraud

The hegemonic Barisan Nasional (BN) political coalition has been ruling Malaysia since the country gained independence in 1957.[1] In the last general election in 2013, BN suffered its worst electoral result, but it still retained 133 out of the 222 House of Representative seats, notwithstanding actually losing the popular vote.[2]

BN's resilience primarily hinges on its ability to manipulate the apportionment of electoral constituencies before each election. Electoral redistricting in Malaysia is performed by the Election Commission, staffed by government appointees[3] that report directly to the Prime Minister.[4] In the 2013 election, the average population size of constituencies won by BN was 40% smaller than those won by Pakatan Rakyat (PR) – the opposition coalition.[5] Tellingly, these small constituencies are mainly found in rural and poorer areas in Malaysia – BN's traditional strongholds – and were 'carefully carved out to boost incumbent support'.[6] Alongside this direct electoral impediment to political competition, BN further disadvantages the opposition by imposing short campaign periods,[7] limiting

1 Prior to 1973, the BN coalition was known as the Alliance coalition. See also Bridget Welsh, 'Elections in Malaysia: Voting Behaviour and Electoral Integrity', in Meredith L. Weiss (ed.), *Routledge Handbook of Contemporary Malaysia* (London: Routledge, 2015), 11; Edmund Terence Gomez, 'Resisting the Fall: The Single Dominant Party, Policies and Elections in Malaysia' (2016) 46 *Journal of Contemporary Asia* 570.

2 The BN only won 47.4% of the popular vote in the 2013 General Election. See Andreas Ufen 'The 2013 Malaysian Elections: Business as Usual or Part of a Protracted Transition?' (2013) 32 *Journal of Current Southeast Asian Affairs* 3.

3 The Members of the Election Commission are appointed by the King, after consultation with the Conference of Rulers, and on the advice of the Cabinet of Ministers. See Article 114(1) of the Federal Constitution, read with Article 40(1) of the Federal Constitution.

4 See 13th Schedule of the Federal Constitution.

5 Bridget Welsh, 'Malaysia's Elections: A Step Backward' (2013) 24 *Journal of Democracy* 136.

6 *Ibid.*, 146.

7 *Findings of the People's Tribunal on Malaysia's 13th General Elections*, 25 March 2014, 32 <http://www.bersih.org/wp-content/uploads/2014/03/Peoples-Tribunal-on-GE13-Findings-Report.pdf> accessed 1 February 2017; Lian Cheng, 'Minimum Campaign

their access to mainstream media,[8] and enforcing repressive sedition laws against dissidents.[9]

Unsurprisingly, the Malaysian courts have also done little to countermand BN's hegemony. Election petitions have been routinely tossed out on the ground that the applicants had not pleaded particularised material facts to justify relief.[10] Judges have also refused to compel the government to allow detainees[11] and citizens residing overseas[12] to vote as absentee voters. As it is typical of courts operating within dominant-party democracies, the judiciary acquiesces to governmental demands as the ruling regime can easily display its displeasure either by ousting judicial review or even the judges themselves.[13] In fact, it is noteworthy that the Federal Court of Malaysia – the nation's court of final resort – has only invalidated one statutory provision after three of its judges, including the Lord President, were impeached and removed on the basis of trumped-up charges in 1988.[14] With a dominant coalition in control of Parliament,

Period Now 11 Days', *Borneo Post*, 21 March 2013 < http://www.theborneopost.com/2013/03/21/minimum-campaign-period-now-11-days/> accessed 1 February 2017.

8 Tessa Houghton and Zaharom Nain, 'Watchdogs or Lapdogs? Monitoring Malaysia's Media Coverage of GE2013', in Johan Saravanamuttu, Lee Hock Guan and Mohamed Nawab Mohamed Osman (eds), *Coalitions in Collision: Malaysia's 13th General Elections* (Singapore: Institute of Southeast Asian Studies, 2015), 159–180.

9 Amnesty International, 'Malaysia Must End Unprecedented Crackdown on Hundreds of Critics through Sedition Act', 25 January 2016 <http://www.amnestyusa.org/news/press-releases/malaysia-must-end-unprecedented-crackdown-on-hundreds-of-critics-through-sedition-act> accessed 1 February 2017.

10 *Zaaba bin Ibrahim* v. *Hj Abdul Ghazali bin Karim* [2013] 10 MLJ 825 (High Court); *Ustaz Akmal bin Hj Kamaruddin* v. *Dato' Mohamad Daud bin Mohd Yusoff* [2014] 9 MLJ 841 (High Court).

11 *Yazid bin Sufaat* v. *Suruhanjaya Pilihanraya Malaysia* [2009] 6 MLJ 152 (Federal Court of Malaysia).

12 *Teo Hoon Seong & Ors.* v. *Suruhanjaya Pilihanraya Malaysia* [2012] 4 MLJ 245 (High Court).

13 Po Jen Yap, *Constitutional Dialogue in Common Law Asia* (Oxford: Oxford University Press, 2015), 78.

14 The Malaysian judicial crisis of 1988 was sparked by a letter. Tun Salleh, the Lord President of the Supreme Court of Malaysia (now re-titled Chief Justice of the Federal Court of Malaysia), wrote to the King on 26 March 1988 about the judiciary's concern over its deteriorating relationship with the government. (Specifically, back in 1987, the Malaysian Prime Minister, Mahathir Mohammad, had expressed his displeasure, on several occasions, within and outside Parliament, over various decisions of the Malaysian courts.) Unfortunately, the King took offence at the letter as he believed that the royalty would be drawn into a conflict with the government if he had intervened on the judiciary's behalf. On 1 May 1988, in an audience with the Prime Minister, the King conveyed his displeasure about the letter and asked for appropriate action to be taken against the Lord President. This eventually led to the impeachment and removal of the Lord President and

the government may retaliate to a robust judicial interpretation of the Constitution by deploying constitutional or unconstitutional means to discipline the courts. In Malaysia, where a constitutional amendment is currently out of reach for the dominant coalition in government,[15] at least without the consent of the opposition parties, the relative attraction of an extra-legal response, like the ouster of judges, may grow.[16]

Where BN's party dominance is reinforced by formal law – as we see with the web of regulations that perpetuate electoral malapportionment, disenfranchise unpopular voter groups, and stifle political speech – it may be understandable if Malaysian judges prefer to look the other way. But, in recent years, there have been very disconcerting reports that segments within the Malaysian government have been engaging in electoral fraud. Human rights groups have alleged that, in the 2013 General Election, the electoral roll included 'phantom' voters who were deceased or did not exist,[17] non-citizens were allowed to cast votes for the incumbent in close races,[18] and the 'indelible' ink used to identify voters who had already voted proved to be not so 'indelible'.[19] No one really knows how prevalent these electoral irregularities were, or whether they were the consequence of incompetence or corruption, as the government had expectedly

another Supreme Court judge. For a fuller discussion, see Andrew Harding, 'The 1988 Constitutional Crisis in Malaysia' (1990) 39 *International and Comparative Law Quarterly* 57; H.P. Lee, *Constitutional Conflicts in Contemporary Malaysia*, 2nd edn. (Oxford University Press, 2017). The only exception was the extraordinary decision by the Federal Court of Malaysia in *Semenyih Jaya v Pentadbir Tanah Daerah Hulu Langat* (20 April 2017) to invalidate a constitutional amendment introduced in June 1988 – and at height of the judicial crisis – to clip the wings of the judiciary. Prior to the amendment, Article 121 (1) of the Constitution read as follows: 'The judicial power of the Federation shall be vested in a Supreme Court and such inferior courts as may be provided by federal law.' The 1988 constitutional amendment removed the term 'judicial power'. In this same decision, the Federal Court also invalidated Section 40D of the Land Acquisition (Act A999), which had authorised government-appointed assessors – in lieu of judges – to conclusively determine the amount of compensation to be awarded when private land was compulsorily acquired by the government.

15 Constitutional amendments, in general, may only be passed in Malaysia with the support of at least two-thirds of the total number of members in each House of Parliament. See Article 159 of the Federal Constitution. Since the 2008 general election, BN has consistently failed to win two-thirds of the elected seats in the lower house.

16 Yap (n 13), 78.

17 Malaysian Electoral Roll Analysis Project, 2013 <http://malaysianelectoralrollproject.blogspot.sg/> accessed 1 February 2017.

18 *Findings of the People's Tribunal on Malaysia's 13th General Elections* (n 7), 31.

19 Pemantau Pilihan Raya Rakyat, *Clean & Fair? An Election Observation Report of the 13th Malaysian General Election*, March 2014, iv <http://www.bersih.org/wp-content/uploads/2013/09/Pemantau-Report-English-Final.pdf> accessed 1 February 2017.

refused to conduct any independent inquiries. It is one thing for the Malaysian courts to enforce the unfair electoral rules formally passed by BN to entrench its own incumbency; it is another matter altogether if the judiciary were to allow the government to break their own laws to steal elections. Condoning the latter would mean the demise of the rule of law.

Therefore, even in a dominant-party democracy, the courts must prevent elections from being stolen. Furthermore, they *can* succeed and get away with this as the stealing of elections would typically arouse greater public wrath than the formal fiddling with electoral laws,[20] such that even a hegemonic government seeking validation at the polls would hesitate to punish their judges for uncovering or pre-empting electoral fraud. And there are two less confrontational ways by which the judiciary can facilitate 'cleaner' elections in Malaysia: (1) ensure that the integrity of the electoral roll is upheld; and (2) issue declaratory orders against the Election Commission for any regulatory non-compliance. Both issues will be explored in turn.

Integrity of the Electoral Roll

The integrity of the election register is a perennial concern in Malaysia. In a post-mortem of the 2013 general election, human rights groups have documented thousands of suspicious entries in the electoral roll, which included non-citizens, deceased individuals, persons who had *not* registered as voters, an inexplicably high number of centenarians, multiple voters with identical names and dates of birth, and incomplete entries.[21] The opposition believes that these 'phantom' voters are the Trojan horses by which the BN government seeks to artificially shore up its support in tight races. Inaccurate entries are rarely expunged from the roll before an election as objections to these entries are only entertained if they are raised within a week from the date the electoral roll is made available for inspection.[22] Also, once the electoral roll is certified by the Election Commission and gazetted, Section 9A of the Election Act provides that the register 'shall be deemed to be final and binding and shall not be questioned or appealed against in, or reviewed, quashed or set aside by, any court'.[23]

[20] Sarah Birch, *Electoral Malpractice* (Oxford: Oxford University Press, 2011), 61.

[21] Pemantau Pilihan Raya Rakyat (n 19), 26.

[22] See Section 15(2) of the Elections (Registration of Electors) Regulations 2002. See also Welsh (n 5), 141.

[23] The ouster clause was introduced in 2002 after an Election Court in 2001 invalidated the election result in one constituency on the basis that the electoral roll for that constituency included thousands of dubious entries and these irregularities were not investigated by the

Genuflecting to the ouster clause, the Federal Court of Malaysia has affirmed that in an election petition submitted after an election, the courts would not inquire into the validity of the electoral roll when it had already been certified and gazetted, regardless of the irregularities raised.[24] Even if the election register was challenged by way of judicial review *before* an election had been held, the courts have equally refused to expunge dubious entries from the roll after it has been certified by the Commission.[25]

But it is noteworthy that common-law courts have traditionally been hostile to complete ouster clauses.[26] In England, since the landmark House of Lords decision in *Anisminic* v. *Foreign Compensation Commission*,[27] the courts have consistently 'read down' the restrictive effects of ouster clauses, such that the judiciary is not precluded from reviewing decisions made by inferior tribunals when they act unlawfully.

In Malaysia, *Anisminic* has been accepted as good law but, oddly enough, only in employment disputes governed under the Industrial Relations Act. Section 33B of the Industrial Relations Act (IRA) provides that a decision or order of the Industrial Court 'shall be final and conclusive, and shall not be challenged, appealed against, reviewed, quashed or called in question in any court'. The Federal Court has declared that such clauses do not 'have the effect of ousting the inherent supervisory power of the High Court to quash the decision of the Industrial Court by certiorari proceedings if it had acted without jurisdiction or in excess of the limits

Election Commission when objections were raised. See *Harris Mohd Salleh* v. *Ismail bin Majin* [2001] 3 MLJ 433 (High Court).

24 *Muhammad Sanusi* v. *Mohd Tajuddin Abdullah* [2009] 1 CLJ 1 (Federal Court of Malaysia).

25 *Charles Anthony Santiago* v. *Suruhanjaya Pilihan Raya* [2014] 7 MLJ 271 (High Court).

26 Clive Lewis, *Judicial Remedies in Public Law*, 4th edn. (London: Sweet & Maxwell, 2009), 315–316.

27 [1969] 2 AC 147 (House of Lords). The Foreign Compensation Commission was established to distribute compensation, paid by the Egyptian government to the UK government, for British property requisitioned during the Suez Crisis. To establish a successful claim, the applicant must either be the owner of the property or the successor-in-title of the owner; and the owner and any person who became successor-in-title of the owner must be British. The Commission denied Anisminic's claim for compensation on the basis that Anisminic, though British, had a successor-in-title which was Egyptian. Notwithstanding an ouster clause which provided that the Commission's determination shall not be questioned in any court of law, the House of Lords held that it had the jurisdiction to review the Commission's determination if that determination was a nullity. On the facts, the House of Lords decided that the phrase 'any person who became successor in title to such person' was inapplicable if the claimant was the original owner of the requisitioned property. Hence, insofar as the Commission had refused compensation on the basis of the foreign citizenship of Anisminic's ostensible successor in title, it had taken into account an irrelevant consideration, and its determination was therefore a nullity.

of its jurisdiction or if it has done or failed to do something in the course of the inquiry which is of such a nature that its decision is a nullity.'[28] The Court of Appeal – albeit in another employment dispute governed under the IRA – has further extended this principle by stating unequivocally that '[a]n inferior tribunal or other decision-making authority, whether exercising a quasi-judicial function or purely an administrative function, has no jurisdiction to commit an error of law'[29] and its decisions 'will not be immunised from judicial review by an ouster clause however widely drafted.'[30] While awards handed down by the Industrial Court are routinely reviewed by the High Court,[31] ouster clause notwithstanding, the Malaysian judiciary has capitulated to the privative clauses imposed in all other regulatory contexts, e.g. extradition proceedings,[32] immigration matters,[33] to name a couple.

Going forward, to ensure cleaner elections in Malaysia, the judiciary must also apply the *Anisminic* principle to the Election Act and circumscribe the unfettered discretion that the Election Commission currently has over the compilation of the electoral roll. Accordingly, while the courts should not micro-manage the affairs of the Election Commission, as long as applicants in an election petition or judicial review proceeding can adduce compelling evidence that the electoral roll has included inaccurate entries, the Court must have the right to expunge the errors, notwithstanding the Commission's certification. Where the electoral roll is so tainted that the election held in any particular constituency is suspect, the courts must also have the concomitant power to overturn the election results and call for new elections. Naturally, the latter power should be exercised sparingly, and only when it is demonstrated that the number of false entries is so large that it would have impacted the election result.[34]

[28] *Hotel Equatorial* v. *National Union of Hotel, Bar & Restaurant Workers* [1984] 1 MLJ 363, 368–369 (Federal Court of Malaysia).

[29] *Syarikat Kenderaan Melayu Kelantan* v. *Transport Workers Union* [1995] 2 MLJ 317 [49] (Court of Appeal).

[30] *Ibid.* [51].

[31] *Sabah Forest Industries* v. *Industrial Court Malaysia* [2013] 2 MLJ 410 (Court of Appeal).

[32] *Public Prosecutor* v. *Ottavio Quattrocchi* [2004] 3 MLJ 149 (Federal Court of Malaysia).

[33] *Pihak Berkuasa Negeri Sabah* v. *Sugumar Balakrishnan* [2002] 3 MLJ 72 (Federal Court of Malaysia).

[34] Section 32 of the Election Offences Act (Act 4) provides that an election shall be declared void when 'general bribery, general treating or general intimidation have been so extensively prevailed that they may be reasonably supposed to have affected the result of the election' or when 'non-compliance with the provisions of any written law relating to the conduct of any election... affected the result of the election.'

If the rule of law is to remain one of Malaysia's most basic political commitments,[35] the courts must introduce a set of legality principles that structures and constrains the administrative practices of the Election Commission. The rise of the 'administrative common law'[36] ameliorates the constitutional tensions of a burgeoning bureaucratic state as courts are empowered to superintend the operation and review the decisions of the executive's ministries and agencies. Rights-based administrative review, imbued with constitutional ideals, is also dialogic and prudential so far as the public agencies are not foreclosed from pursuing the legislative goals they are statutorily tasked to pursue, but are merely compelled to observe certain fundamental procedural or substantive norms that promote good governance and fair play before they so act.[37]

Declaratory Orders and the Use of Indelible Ink

To detect voters who have already voted in an election, and to prevent those people from voting again, electoral law requires the Election Commission to use indelible ink to mark the finger of every voter after he or she is issued with a ballot paper.[38] But in the last 2013 general election, human rights groups have complained that the ink used could be removed easily, thereby raising the risk of electoral fraud.[39]

The Pakatan Rakyat – a coalition of opposition parties – even went to court, seeking judicial review and requesting the Court to invalidate the entire 2013 general election on the basis that the Election Commission had been derelict in its constitutional duty to manage the election by failing to use indelible ink as statutorily required. Unsurprisingly, the lawsuit was struck out at the leave stage.

In *Parti Islam Se-Malaysia* v. *Tan Sri Dato' Seri Abdul Aziz*,[40] the Court of Appeal struck out the claim primarily on the basis that an election result could only be challenged by way of an election petition, and the applicants could not call into question election results in a judicial review

35 For a general discussion of rule of law principles for administrative governance, see Kevin M. Stack, 'An Administrative Jurisprudence: The Rule of Law in the Administrative State' (2015) 115 *Columbia Law Review* 1985.

36 Gillian Metzger, 'Embracing Administrative Common Law' (2012) 80 *George Washington Law Review* 1293.

37 Yap (n 13), 92–93.

38 Elections (Conduct of Elections) Regulations, Regulation 19(4).

39 See *Findings of the People's Tribunal on Malaysia's 13th General Elections* (n 7), 27; and Pemantau Pilihan Raya Rakyat (n 19), iv.

40 [2015] 4 MLJ 439 (Court of Appeal).

action. Leaving aside the politics, as a matter of law, this decision was also inevitable. Article 118 of the Malaysian Constitution expressly provides that '[n]o election to the House of Representatives… shall be called in question except by an election petition presented to the High Court'. One should note that the applicants would not have succeeded in their claims even if they had submitted an election petition instead. Section 32(b) of the Election Offences Act provides that any non-compliance with an electoral law would not render the election result in question void unless the 'non-compliance affected the result of the election'.[41] The Federal Court had emphasised that the onus was on the petitioner to prove to the satisfaction of the election judge that the non-compliance had affected the election result.[42] Therefore, previously in *Dato' Ismail bin Kamus* v. *Pegawai Pengurus Pilihan Raya*,[43] even though the Election Commission conceded that it had wrongfully extended the polling hours beyond the stipulated time period and had used the wrong electoral rolls in two polling stations, the petitioners failed to overturn the election as they simply could not prove that the irregularities had affected the results. In the same vein, election petitions submitted after the 2013 Election were practically all rejected on the basis that the applicants were unable to traverse 'the net of technicalities'[44] that was deliberately cast to impede a successful claim.[45]

Interestingly, the applicants in *Parti Islam Se-Malaysia* had also asked, in the alternative, for the Court to issue a general declaration that the Election Commission had failed in the discharge of its constitutional duty, without seeking any further consequential relief. Specifically, the applicants sought to rely on *R Ramachandran* v. *Industrial Court*,[46] an industrial dispute, where the Federal Court declared that it had the power to directly award compensation to an employee who was wrongly dismissed, in lieu of remitting the case to the Industrial Court for an assessment of damages. While the operative statute in question – the Industrial Relations Act – did not *expressly* authorise the Federal Court to award damages, the Court noted that Paragraph 1 of the Schedule to the Courts of Judicature Act

41 The only exceptions are bribery, general intimation, and corruption. See Section 32(a),(c),(d) of the Election Offences Act (Act 5).

42 *Dato' Ismail bin Kamus* v. *Pegawai Pengurus Pilihan Raya* [2005] 3 MLJ 193, [21] (High Court).

43 *Ibid.*

44 *Zaaba bin Ibrahim* (n 10) [24].

45 See r 4(1)(b), r 4(4)(3), r 15 of Election Petition Rules 1954. See also *Ustaz Akmal bin Hj Kamaruddin* (n 10).

46 [1997] 1 MLJ 145 (Federal Court of Malaysia).

1964 conferred on the judiciary significant latitude in crafting additional remedies.[47] Therefore, according to the Federal Court in *Ramachandran*, unless there was an express statutory provision that prohibited the grant of a specific remedy,[48] the Court was free to 'mould the relief in accordance with the demands of justice'.[49]

Nevertheless, by a majority of two to one, the Court of Appeal in *Parti Islam Se-Malaysia* swiftly dismissed the applicability of *Ramachandran*. According to the majority, the Federal Court decision simply did not apply as the courts herein did not 'have the jurisdiction to hear the matter'.[50] The Court of Appeal's reasoning is problematic on two counts. First, in *Ramachandran*, the operative Industrial Relations Act also included a statutory clause that ousted judicial review,[51] but the Federal Court intervened nonetheless. Second, there was no jurisdictional bar – constitutional or otherwise – that would expressly prohibit the courts from issuing a general declaration that was *not* coupled with any further consequential relief. Article 118 of the Federal Constitution requires election results to be challenged only by way of election petitions. But if the applicants were merely seeking a declaration that the Election Commission had failed in the discharge of its constitutional duty, and the electoral results were not being challenged in any way, Article 118 would simply not be engaged. This was the precise point raised by Prasad Abraham JCA, who dissented in part. While accepting that the election results could only be reviewed in an election petition, he took the view that a stand-alone declaratory order, without more, was not barred by Article 118 of the Constitution, and could be sought in a judicial review proceeding.[52] Echoing an earlier Federal Court decision in *Pengarah Tanah dan Galian, Wilayah Persekutuan* v. *Sri Lempah Enterprise*,[53] Prasad Abraham

47 Paragraph 1 of the Schedule of the Courts of Judicature Act 1964 provides for the Additional Powers of the High Court, which include the 'power to issue to any person or authority directions, orders or writs, including writs of the nature of habeas corpus, mandamus, prohibition, quo warranto and certiorari, or any others, for the enforcement of the rights conferred by Part II of the Constitution, or any of them, or for any purpose.'

48 [1997] 1 MLJ 145 (Federal Court of Malaysia) [37].

49 *Ibid.* [43].

50 *Parti Islam Se-Malaysia* (n 40) [69].

51 Section 33B of the Industrial Relations Act (IRA) (Act 177) provides that a decision or order of the Industrial Court 'shall be final and conclusive, and shall not be challenged, appealed against, reviewed, quashed or called in question in any court'.

52 *Parti Islam Se-Malaysia* (n 40) [81].

53 [1979] 1 MLJ 135. On the facts, the Federal Court of Malaysia held that, in a planning permission dispute between a land developer and the government, the Court was entitled

JCA emphasised that 'the existence of a statutory remedy is no bar to an action for a declaration'[54] as the 'jurisdiction of the High Court is not to be taken away without express words'.[55]

In *Parti Islam Se-Malaysia*, the opposition coalition's claim against the Election Commission was struck out at the leave stage, such that the Court never had the opportunity to assess the evidence relating to its alleged mismanagement of the 2013 general election. But, going forward, this decision must be reconsidered. The issue of stand-alone declaratory orders against the Election Commission may be the only effective and dialogic means for the Malaysian judiciary to address electoral fraud in the country. In this way, the courts can draw public attention to any perceived electoral irregularities and compel the Commission to comply with the very laws Parliament has passed, whilst not rousing any additional ire as it preserves the circumscribed election petition as the only means by which an election result can be challenged.

Conclusion

In 2015, news broke of a US $681 million transfer from a troubled state-owned investment fund, 1 Malaysia Development Berhad (1MDB), into Prime Minister Najib Razak's personal bank accounts. A political firestorm ensued, but Najib has hitherto successfully outmanoeuvred all his critics. Deputy Prime Minister Muhyiddin Yassin, a fierce critic of Najib's role in the 1MDB fund, was sacked; the Attorney General Abdul Gani Patail, who was on the verge of bringing official criminal charges against the Prime Minister, was forcibly retired for 'health' reasons.[56] The Malaysian Anti-Corruption Commission and the replacement Attorney General, Apandi Ali, have since cleared Najib of all wrongdoing by confirming that the funds were a political donation from the royal family in Saudi Arabia. It is noteworthy that Malaysia does not limit who or how much a person, foreign or local, can donate to a party or a politician, nor does the law require any disclosure of the donation

to issue a declaration that the government had imposed an invalid condition on the use of the developer's land.

54 *Parti Islam Se-Malaysia* (n 40) [85].

55 *Ibid.*

56 Dhirenn Nair, 'Malaysia's Defiant Prime Minister: The 1MDB Purge', *The Diplomat*, 9 August 2016 <http://thediplomat.com/2016/08/malaysias-defiant-prime-minister-the-1mdb-purge/> accessed 1 February 2017.

source.[57] As the BN rank-and-file and the government machinery close ranks around Najib, the High Court has unsurprisingly refused to nullify the entire 2013 general election on the basis of the Prime Minister's donation scandal.[58]

The opposition parties have also been unable to capitalise on Najib's missteps due to internal bickering. The PR opposition coalition collapsed in 2015 after the exit of the Parti Islam Se-Malaysia (PAS), the leading Islamist party in Malaysia. The PAS furthered splintered when a more progressive 'rebel' wing left to form a new political party – Amanah. With the opposition in disarray, BN won handily in the Sarawak state elections and in two by-elections, all of which were concluded in mid-2016.[59]

On the back of BN's latest electoral wins, speculations are growing that Najib would be calling for new elections soon, especially before the new opposition party Parti Pribumi Bersatu Malaysia – founded by strident Najib critic and former premier Mahathir Mohammad – gains traction. The Election Commission has already published its latest changes to electoral districts and, in this latest redistricting exercise, while new parliamentary seats have not been created, twelve pre-existing ones were renamed.[60] The opposition have decried the revisions as another attempt by the ruling BN regime to skew the political competition to its advantage.

As the dominant BN coalition controls 'all the commanding heights of government power'[61] in Malaysia, the courts are inevitably marginalised as policy-makers. But even if the judges are powerless to countermand the formal rules enacted by the BN to entrench its incumbency, if the rule of law is to mean anything at all in Malaysia, the courts must

57 Andreas Ufen, 'Laissez-faire versus Strict Control of Political Finance: Hegemonic Parties and Developmental States in Malaysia and Singapore' (2015) 47 *Critical Asian Studies* 564, 574–575.

58 'High Court strikes out PKR's civil suit against Malaysia's PM Najib', *Straits Times*, 21 January 2016, <http://www.straitstimes.com/asia/se-asia/high-court-strikes-out-pkrs-civil-suit-against-malaysias-pm-najib> accessed 1 February 2017.

59 Rashaad Ali, 'Malaysian By-Elections: Najib's Winning Ways', *RSIS Commentary*, 30 June 2016 <https://www.rsis.edu.sg/wp-content/uploads/2016/07/CO16165.pdf> accessed 1 February 2017.

60 'Election Commission changes names for 12 parliamentary, 34 state seats', *Malaymail*, 15 September 2016 <http://www.themalaymailonline.com/malaysia/article/election-commission-changes-names-for-12-parliamentary-34-state-seats> accessed 1 February 2017.

61 Tom Ginsburg and Robert A Kagan, 'Institutionalist Approaches to Courts as Political Actors', in Tom Ginsburg and Robert Kagan (eds), *Institutions and Public Law: Comparative Approaches* (New York: Peter Lang, 2005), 6.

at the very least ensure that the government abide by the very laws they pass. Apropos of elections, the judiciary has to impose a set of legality principles that constrains the administrative practices of the Election Commission. If the judges are averse to unseating elected officials *ex post*, the imposition of mandates on the Election Commission *ex ante* may plausibly be the most dialogic way for the courts to compel the Commission to faithfully discharge its statutory duties and deliver clean elections in Malaysia.

4

Hong Kong Courts and Constitutional Contradictions

Since China's resumption of sovereignty over Hong Kong on 1 July 1997 and the concomitant establishment of the Special Administrative Region (HKSAR) under the sacred but elusive principle of 'One Country, Two Systems', the Hong Kong judiciary has had the unenviable task of safeguarding the constitutional liberties enshrined under the Basic Law whilst tending to the political sensitivities of the central government in Beijing.[1] This is no menial feat as it requires the preservation of Hong Kong's robust common law traditions within the confines of an essentially Chinese civil law instrument.

Unsurprisingly, in the electoral challenges that have come before the Hong Kong courts, a distinct contradiction has been discerned.[2] Hong Kong's traditionally active judiciary has been willing to extend voting rights writ small to disenfranchised prisoners,[3] and allow those who have been convicted of minor offences to stand for elections;[4] but the courts have been reluctant to make major systemic electoral changes[5] or intervene in the high-stakes Hong Kong Chief Executive Elections[6] that could erode China's political control over the HKSAR. The political reality in Hong Kong is that Beijing has devised an electoral system that is intended to entrench its control over the HKSAR government.

First, the head of the HKSAR government – the Chief Executive – is currently elected by an Election Committee composed of only 1200 members, with 300 members fielded from each of the following four sectors.

[1] Po Jen Yap, '10 Years of the Basic Law: The Rise, Retreat and Resurgence of Judicial Power' (2007) 36 *Common Law World Review* 166, 167.

[2] Simon N.M. Young, 'Judicial Review of Elections in Hong Kong: Resolving a Contradiction', in Po Jen Yap (ed.), *Judicial Review of Elections of Asia* (London: Routledge, 2016), 11.

[3] *Chan Kin Sum* v. *Secretary for Justice* [2009] 2 HKLRD 166 (Court of First Instance).

[4] *Wong Hin Wai* v. *Secretary for Justice* [2012] 4 HKLRD 70 (Court of First Instance).

[5] *Chan Yu Nam* v. *Secretary for Justice* [2010] HKEC 1893 (Court of Appeal).

[6] *Re Ho Chun Yan Albert* [2012] 15 HKCFAR 686 (Court of Final Appeal); *Leung Chun Ying* v. *Ho Chun Yan Albert* [2013] 16 HKCFAR 735 (Court of Final Appeal).

These sectors are: (1) the industrial, commercial and financial sectors, (2) the professions, (3) labour, social services, religious, and other sectors; and (4) members of the Legislative Council, representatives of district-based organisations, Hong Kong deputies to the National People's Congress, and representatives of Hong Kong members of the National Committee of the Chinese People's Political Consultative Conference.[7] An overwhelming majority of the Election Committee members are pro-Beijing, thereby ensuring that only a pro-Beijing candidate can be elected as Chief Executive.[8]

Second, the Chinese Central Government, vis-à-vis Hong Kong's Legislative Council, has deliberately retained the Functional Constituencies (FCs) electoral method, a system in which the right to vote depends upon a person's membership or registration in a recognised social, economic, industrial, commercial, political advisory, or professional body represented in the legislature. In many of these FCs, e.g., Insurance, Transport, Tourism, Finance, Labour, it is not the individuals working in these professions who are eligible to vote; instead, it is only the recognised corporate bodies operating in these professions that can vote. It is significant that, since the establishment of the HKSAR, the pro-Beijing/pro-establishment camp has relied on these 'corporate' votes to dominate the FC elections, such that the pro-establishment camp is able to command an overall majority of the seats in the Legislative Council, even though it lags behind in the Geographical Constituencies (GCs) elections that are constituted via universal suffrage.[9] One may note that since the Hong Kong executive government is heavily reliant on the support of the pro-establishment camp in the legislature for the passage of its bills, unrestricted elections by universal suffrage for all of the seats in the Legislative Council would unlikely be allowed until the pro-establishment camp is able to form a clear majority in the Legislative Council, without the use of the FC system as a political crutch.

[7] Nevertheless, Article 45 of the Basic Law provides that the ultimate aim in Hong Kong's political transition is for the Chief Executive to be elected by universal suffrage upon nomination by a broadly representative nominating committee in accordance with democratic procedures.

[8] Simon Young and Richard Cullen, *Electing Hong Kong's Chief Executive*, (Hong Kong: Hong Kong University Press, 2010) 79, 91.

[9] Currently, 35 seats in the Legislative Council are constituted via universal suffrage in Geographical Constituencies (GC) elections whilst another 35 seats are constituted via Functional Constituencies (FC) elections.

The Hong Kong judiciary is also not spared from Beijing's oversight. The Standing Committee of the National People's Congress (NPCSC) is empowered under the Basic Law to overrule any constitutional decision of the Court of Final Appeal (CFA) by a Legislative Interpretation.[10] In fact, the NPCSC has chastised the CFA by overturning its very *first* constitutional decision handed down post-handover.[11]

With a Goliath poised to countermand any perceived aggressive moves by the Hong Kong judiciary, it is unsurprising that the local judges have become more cognisant of the potential political fall-outs from their decisions. But this is not to say that the courts have become politically irrelevant in Hong Kong's constitutional landscape. Unlike Singapore, the Hong Kong judiciary has built up a history of invalidating legislation since the Bill of Rights Ordinance (Chapter 383) (BORO) was enacted in the territory in 1991.[12] Like all political practices, judicial practices are path-dependent,[13] such that Hong Kong judges can appeal to history and *stare decisis* for continuing the practice of enforcing human rights against the Hong Kong government.[14] Furthermore, Beijing cannot and will not reverse every decision by the CFA as it does not want to appear to be rescinding from its commitment to allow the HKSAR to 'exercise a high degree of autonomy and enjoy ... independent judicial power',[15] as this would adversely impact on Hong Kong's long-term viability as

[10] Article 158 of the Basic Law reads: When the Standing Committee makes an interpretation of the provisions concerned, the courts of the Region, in applying those provisions, shall follow the interpretation of the Standing Committee.

[11] On 26 June 1999, the NPCSC issued its First Interpretation under the Basic Law and overruled the CFA's decision in *Ng Ka Ling v. Director of Immigration* (1999) 2 HKCFAR 4 that exempted Mainland children born to Hong Kong permanent residents from obtaining the requisite immigration permits before they could acquire the right of abode in Hong Kong.

[12] Yash Ghai, 'Sentinels of Liberty or Sheep in Woolf's Clothing? Judicial Politics and the Hong Kong Bill of Rights' (1997) 60 *Modern Law Review* 459.

[13] Alec Stone Sweet, 'Path Dependence, Precedent, and Judicial Power', in Martin Shapiro and Alec Stone Sweet (eds), *On Law, Politics, and Judicialisation* (New York: Oxford University Press, 2002), 112.

[14] Article 8 of the Basic Law reads: 'The laws previously in force in Hong Kong, that is, the common law, rules of equity, ordinances, subordinate legislation and customary law shall be maintained, except for any that contravene this Law, and subject to any amendment by the legislature of the Hong Kong Special Administrative Region.' Article 39 of the Basic Law reads: 'The provisions of the International Covenant on Civil and Political Rights, the International Covenant on Economic, Social and Cultural Rights, and international labour conventions as applied to Hong Kong shall remain in force and shall be implemented through the laws of the Hong Kong Special Administrative Region.'

[15] Article 2 of the Basic Law.

an international financial centre and China's own long-term goal of re-unifying Taiwan.

The HKSAR government is similarly unable to reverse every adverse decision handed down by the courts. For the FC electoral seats, the individual legislators are only accountable electorally to the voters in their specific sectoral constituencies; for the GC seats, the use of proportional representation has led to the electoral success of multiple small parties and individual law-makers.[16] As the Chief Executive is not drawn from any political party, and with the presence of multiple political parties, independents, and FC representatives in the Legislative Council, the HKSAR government has to constantly broker different interests among competing political forces when it seeks to pass legislation.[17] While this is not difficult when the government is whipping up support for legislation that Beijing considers imperative, the pro-Beijing[18] lawmakers' interests often diverge from the HKSAR government's on issues that are not fundamental to Beijing; and, in such cases, these lawmakers would break ranks with the local government to accommodate their own constituents. This fragile coalition between the HKSAR executive government and the pro-Beijing lawmakers therefore limits the former's ability to command a legislative majority on *non-core* socio-political issues; and the political impasse in turn provides the Hong Kong judiciary with significant leeway to rule against the government on a modest scale.

Therefore, while major electoral systemic overhauls or the overturn of the high-stakes Chief Executive election results are off-limits to the courts, the judges can and have ushered in modest changes to Hong Kong's restrictive electoral regime. But even as the courts rule against the government, insofar as the judges provide decisional space for the government to craft an independent, considered response in their remedial legislation, the courts can promote a constitutional dialogue between the judiciary and the government on electoral rights in Hong Kong.

[16] Siu-kai Lau, 'Hong Kong's Partial Democracy under Stress', in Yue-man Yeung (ed.), *New Challenges for Development and Modernisation* (Hong Kong: The Chinese University Press, 2002), 186.

[17] Brian Fong, 'Executive-Legislative Disconnection in Post-colonial Hong Kong' (2014) 1 *China Perspectives* 5, 12. See also Stephen Gardbaum, 'Political Parties, Voting Systems, and the Separation of Powers' (2017) 65 *American Journal of Comparative Law* (forthcoming).

[18] Pro-Beijing lawmakers in the Legislative Council include both fiscally conservative business elites and socialist leftists.

Judicial Extension of Electoral Rights

Village Representative Elections

In the New Territories, a rural part of Hong Kong, only an indigenous inhabitant – defined as 'a person who was in 1898 a resident of an established village in Hong Kong or who is descended through the male line from that person'[19] – was traditionally entitled to vote and stand as a candidate in the Village Representatives (VRs) election. In *Secretary for Justice* v. *Chan Wah*,[20] non-indigenous villagers challenged this electoral rule as it denied their right to participate in public affairs as protected under Article 21(a) of the BORO.[21]

Given that VRs 'represent the village as a whole (comprising both the indigenous and the non-indigenous villagers)'[22] in liaising with the authorities on behalf of the village, and that their role extends up to the Legislative Council,[23] the CFA unanimously decided that the exclusion of non-indigenous inhabitants from such village elections was an unreasonable violation of their right to participate in public affairs.[24]

This decision would have been completely unassailable but for Article 40 of the Basic Law, which provides that the lawful traditional rights and interests of the indigenous inhabitants of the New Territories shall be protected by the HKSAR. The indigenous villagers argued that the political rights at issue were derivative rights that were implicitly protected under Article 40 and therefore could prevail over any inconsistencies with the BORO.[25]

While the CFA did not reject the possibility that political rights could be 'derived if they are *necessarily implicit* within the rights and interests expressly protected by art. 40',[26] the Court would only deduce such implicit rights if 'the traditional rights and interests [protected by art. 40] cannot be *adequately* protected without the political rights contended for'.[27] Curiously, however, the CFA went on to conclude that the traditional rights

[19] Section 2 of Government Rent (Assessment and Collection) Ordinance (Cap. 515).

[20] (2000) 3 HKCFAR 459 (Court of Final Appeal).

[21] Article 21 of the BORO reads: 'Every permanent resident shall have the right and the opportunity ... and without unreasonable restrictions: (a) to take part in the conduct of public affairs, directly or through freely chosen representatives.'

[22] *Chan Wah* (n 20), 474F.

[23] *Ibid.*, 473G-I.

[24] *Ibid.*, 474G.

[25] *Ibid.*, 477B-C.

[26] *Ibid.*, 477G.

[27] *Ibid.*, 477H.

of the indigenous villagers were sufficiently protected by pre-existing legislation on rent control and there was no justification for further deriving the political rights they were contending for.[28] Unfortunately, the CFA did not explain how the indigenous villagers' exemption from Government rent and rates thereby foreclosed their right to also preserve their village electoral arrangements. What is evidently clear is that the CFA was too eager about promoting political equality to be fettered by legal niceties.

This decision left the government in a quandary as they had to assuage the concern from the indigenous villagers that their interests would not be undermined if the non-indigenous villagers were allowed to vote and stand for the VRs elections.[29] In the end, the government reconciled the interests of all parties by devising a dual system in which two VRs are elected in each village, one representing only the indigenous residents and one for everyone in the village.[30] One must note that this twin-track electoral framework did not feature in the CFA's judgment in *Chan Wah* at all; but the introduction of this electoral scheme underscores the distinctive roles that the judiciary and the lawmakers can play in facilitating a constitutional conversation on rights.[31]

Prisoners' Voting Rights

Traditionally, prisoners were prohibited from voting in Legislative Council elections in Hong Kong.[32] Furthermore, remanded persons, in custody awaiting trial, were also not given access to voting, even though they were not statutorily disqualified. In *Chan Kin Sum* v. *Secretary for Justice*,[33] the applicants challenged this blanket disenfranchisement of prisoners and remanded persons as an unreasonable restriction of their right to vote.

28 *Ibid.*, 477H-J.

29 Legislative Council Secretariat, *Paper for the Bills Committee on Village Representative Election Bill*, 18 November 2002, LC Paper No. LS 15/02-03, para. 12.

30 Rural Representative Election Ordinance (Cap. 576).

31 Swati Jhaveri and Anne Scully-Hill, 'Executive and Legislative Reactions to Judicial Declarations of Constitutional Invalidity in Hong Kong: Engagement, Acceptance or Avoidance?' (2015) 13 *International Journal of Constitutional Law* 507, 519.

32 Section 53(5)(a) and (b) of the Legislative Council Ordinance (Cap. 542) read: 'An elector is also disqualified from voting at an election if the elector (a) has, in Hong Kong or any other place, been sentenced to death or imprisonment (by whatever name called) and has not either (i) served the sentence or undergone such other punishment as a competent authority may have substituted for the sentence; or (ii) received a free pardon; or (b) on the date of the election, is serving a sentence of imprisonment.'

33 *Chan Kin Sum* (n 3).

The Court of First Instance (CFI) accepted in principle that the electoral disenfranchisement of prisoners could prevent crime by sanctioning the conduct of convicted prisoners and providing incentives for the citizenry to exercise civic responsibility. Notwithstanding the legitimate aims that the government was seeking to pursue, the Court noted that the impugned legislative ban was disproportionate as all prisoners were barred from voting, regardless of the nature and severity of the offences or even the length of the custodial sentences.[34] Even prisoners on suspended sentences or released on parole were barred from voting. Nevertheless, the Court was willing to suspend its declaration of invalidity for about seven months as the learned judge considered that the legislature would 'legitimately require and deserve a reasonable period of time to work out a replacement arrangement, whatever it may be'.[35] On the facts, the Court refused to determine what type of voting restrictions would pass constitutional muster or 'where the cut-off line should be drawn and how it should be drawn'[36] as it is the function of the legislature and not 'the function of the courts to say what would constitute reasonable restrictions in Hong Kong'.[37] This decision was therefore dialogic as the Court had remanded the electoral issue to the legislature such that it could 'reply to the court's decision with one of a wide range of constitutional options available to it'.[38]

As for remanded persons awaiting trial, the Court emphasised that they were not statutorily disqualified from voting at all. There were merely no arrangements made to allow them to vote whilst they were in remand. In a gentle rebuke to the government, the Court so observed:

> *In my view, the authorities cannot have it both ways. They cannot, on the one hand, detain a remanded person in a place of detention on election day thereby preventing him from physically attending a normal polling station to cast his vote (if he so wishes), yet argue, on the other hand, that they are, nonetheless, under no duty, in those circumstances, to make special arrangements in the place of detention (or elsewhere) so as to enable the remanded person to exercise his constitutional right to vote. The lack of special arrangements available to those on remand to enable them to vote on election day is indefensible.*[39]

34 *Ibid.* [112] [116].

35 *Chan Kin Sum v. Secretary for Justice* [2009] HKEC 393 [79] (Court of First Instance).

36 *Chan Kin Sum* (n 3) [165].

37 *Ibid.*

38 Kent Roach, 'Remedial Consensus and Dialogue under the Charter: General Declarations and Delayed Declarations of Invalidity' (2002) 35 *University of British Columbia Law Review* 211, 219.

39 *Chan Kin Sum* (n 3) [184].

Accordingly, the Court declared that the Electoral Affairs Commission would be imposed with the responsibility of putting in place a mechanism for allowing remanded persons to vote.[40]

What is particularly noteworthy about this decision is that the government had attempted to justify the disenfranchisement of the prisoners on the basis that Hong Kong's 'peculiar political, social, cultural and historical background'[41] exempted the government from practising universal suffrage in the same way as Western societies. In response, the Court conceded that the BORO does not require Hong Kong to have a fully-elected Chief Executive or Legislative Council. But the Court went on to make the following observations:

> *In so far as universal suffrage is already allowed in the election of LegCo [Legislative Council] members for geographical constituencies, the presumption must be in favour of inclusion and the aim must be directed at identifying the will of people through universal suffrage. One could indeed argue that, where only 50% of the LegCo members are elected by universal suffrage, that makes the right to vote doubly important and precious.*[42]

In short, whilst the Court accepted the legality of the core institutional framework that preserves China's fundamental interests, this was not a *carte blanche* to justify all types of restrictive electoral practices that were currently in place.

After the CFI's judgment in *Chan Kin Sum* was handed down, the government decided not to appeal the decision. After a series of public consultations and deliberations, the Legislative Council responded in 2009 by repealing all restrictions on prisoners' right to vote, thus achieving a result that went beyond what was mandated in *Chan Kin Sum*.

Convicted Persons' Right to Stand for Elections

The applicants in *Wong Hin Wai* v. *Secretary for Justice*[43] were on bail pending appeal against their convictions and sentences of imprisonment for public order offences they had committed. Under section 39(1)(b)(i) of the Legislative Council Ordinance (LCO) (Chapter 542),[44] they were

[40] *Ibid.* [186–187].
[41] *Ibid.* [105].
[42] *Ibid.* [106].
[43] *Wong Hin Wai* (n 4).
[44] Section 39(1)(b)(i) of the LCO read: 'A person is disqualified from being nominated as a candidate at an election, and from being elected as a Member, if the person has, in Hong

disqualified from standing for the Legislative Council election unless they had finished serving their sentences before the end of the nomination period. The central issue of the case turned on whether this electoral restriction constituted an unlawful curtailment of the applicants' right to stand for election, as protected under Article 21 of the BORO.[45]

It is important to note that this blanket ban was actually introduced in 1997 by the Provisional Legislative Council (PLC).[46] (The PLC had a limited term of one year and it was tasked by China to take charge of Hong Kong's legislative affairs until the first Legislative Council was elected in 1998.) Before 1997, electoral disqualification was only applicable to a person whose unserved prison sentence exceeded three months.[47] The rationale for the change was disclosed in the Memorandum on Review of the Electoral Provisions Ordinance prepared by the Constitutional Affairs Bureau in 1997, which suggested that this '3-month threshold' should be tightened so as to prevent escaped convicts from holding office in the legislature.[48]

In view of this rationale, the CFI held that there was no rational connection between barring escaped convicts from elections and banning all persons with unserved jail terms from electoral office. The electoral

Kong or any other place, been sentenced to death or imprisonment (by whatever name called) and has not either served the sentence or undergone such other punishment as a competent authority may have been substituted for the sentence.'

45 Article 21 of the BORO reads: 'Every permanent resident shall have the right and the opportunity … and without unreasonable restrictions: (a) to take part in the conduct of public affairs, directly or through freely chosen representatives; (b) to vote and to be elected at genuine periodic elections which shall be by universal and equal suffrage, and shall be held by secret ballot, guaranteeing the free expression of the will of the electors.'

46 When the Preparatory Committee was preparing for the establishment of the first HKSAR Government after the handover, it decided that the first session of the Legislative Council should not be convened with those existing members under the British administration. The PLC was set up with members appointed by China in December 1996 and came into operation in 1997 to review and enact legislation (electoral law included) for the transition towards the handover. See generally, Johannes Chan, 'From Colony to Special Administrative Region', in Johannes Chan and CL Lim (eds), *Law of the Hong Kong Constitution*, 2nd edn. (Hong Kong: Sweet & Maxwell, 2015), 5.

47 The disqualification provision for candidates in the Legislative Council elections before 1997 was stipulated under section 21(1)(c) of the now-repealed Legislative Council (Electoral Provisions) Ordinance 1985, which read: 'A person shall be disqualified from being nominated as a candidate in an election or holding office as an elected Member if he has in Hong Kong or any other place been sentenced to death or imprisonment (by whatever name called) for a term exceeding three months and has not either suffered the punishment to which he was sentenced or such other punishment as may by competent authority have been substituted therefor or received a free pardon.'

48 *Wong Hin Wai* (n 4) [57].

restriction was so overbroad that it targeted not only escaped convicts, as originally intended by the government, but also the applicants who were on bail pending their appeals.[49] Therefore, the law was deemed so disproportionate that it could not pass constitutional muster. But one must also note that the scope of this ruling was sufficiently circumscribed as the Court did *not* require the government to allow all persons with unserved jail sentences to stand for election. Instead, the Court actually accepted implicitly that the pre-1997 statutory disqualification for persons with unserved sentences of three months (or more) was constitutional:

> *In the absence of any suggestion that the previous balance struck ... did not adequately serve the interest of Hong Kong, with the progressive developments of political maturity in Hong Kong since 1985, I do not see how the change in 1997 can be said to be a proportionate measure to address the aim of having suitable candidates.*[50]

After this decision, the Hong Kong government conducted a public consultation and explored various options for electoral reform.[51] In particular, the Court had also raised concerns, though it did not decide this point, that section 39(1)(d) of the LCO[52] was also constitutionally problematic. In essence, this law bars politicians who are in jail on nomination or election day from being nominated and elected as a member of the Legislative Council, even if they would be released by the time the new term of the Legislative Council commences; and the Court openly raised in *obiter* the following constitutional issues for further legislative deliberation:

> *Whilst each candidate would have different limitations in terms of resources and manpower to conduct his or her own campaign, a candidate serving a*

49 *Ibid.* [59].

50 *Ibid.* [99].

51 Constitutional and Mainland Affairs Bureau, 'Consultation Paper on Disqualification of Candidates with Unserved Prison Sentences and other Related Matters', 21 July 2014, Chapter 3–4. In the consultation, the government suggested that electoral disqualification would only apply to (i) a person who is currently serving a sentence of imprisonment, unless and until he or she is subsequently granted bail pending appeal and/or (ii) an escaped convict, irrespective of whether he or she is waiting for the determination of an appeal from being nominated in the Legislative Council election. To clarify what constitutes imprisonment, it was proposed that a convicted person who is released under supervision of the detention and/or rehabilitation centres is not an imprisoned person and thus should not be disqualified.

52 Section 39(1)(d) of the LCO reads: 'A person is disqualified from being nominated as a candidate at an election, and from being elected as a Member, if the person on the date of nomination, or of the election, is serving a sentence of imprisonment.'

> *prison sentence would be subject to a greater disadvantage. Does it mean that such a candidate should be allowed time out from imprisonment to conduct a campaign? Has this question been considered in other jurisdictions? How should this be balanced against the public interest in the effectiveness of our criminal justice system in terms of punishment by prison sentence? How about security issues if such a candidate is allowed to have time out? All these questions have to be addressed in the assessment of the overall reasonableness of s.39(1)(d).*[53]

At the time of writing, legislative reform is still pending and, with the invalidation of section 39(1)(b)(i) of the LCO, all persons on bail pending appeal against their convictions and sentences now have the right to run for office.

Judicial Preservation of the Electoral Status Quo

Corporate Voting in Legislative Council Elections

Corporate voting is a fundamental feature of the Functional Constituencies (FC) electoral method. Currently, there are 28 FCs represented in the Legislative Council, which include the Legal, Financial Services, and Insurance FCs. Each FC is allowed to return one FC legislator, except for the Labour FC, which is permitted to return three members, and the two District Council FCs, which return six members.[54] In 10 of the FCs, e.g. Insurance, Transport, Tourism, Finance Services, Labour, it is not the individuals working in these professions who are eligible to vote; instead, it is *only* the recognised corporate bodies operating in these professions

[53] *Wong Hin Wai* (n 4) [111]. After consultation and deliberation, the government has expressed its intention to retain section 39(1)(d) of the LCO for three reasons, notwithstanding the CFI decision in *Wong Hin Wai*. First, the government is of the view that allowing an imprisoned person time out of prison to conduct election campaigns would give rise to operational, logistics, manpower resource, and security problems, which would put that person in a privileged position compared with other prisoners. Secondly, removing this restriction may result in an abuse of the system that would undermine the public interest in the integrity of the custodial sentence and the criminal justice system. Finally, such a restriction indeed still exists in many jurisdictions such as Canada and New Zealand. For details, see Constitutional and Mainland Affairs Bureau, 'Results of the Public Consultation on Disqualification of Candidates with Unserved Prison Sentences and other Related Matters and Proposed Way Forward', 17 November 2014, LC Paper No. CB(2)267/14–15(03) [7–9].

[54] See Legislative Council Ordinance; Hong Kong Electoral Affairs Commission, Report on the 2012 Legislative Council Election Held on 9 September 2012, 131–132 <http://www.legco.gov.hk/yr12-13/english/panels/ca/papers/ca1217cb2-306-e.pdf> accessed 1 February 2017.

that are eligible to vote,[55] and they would select their authorised representatives to vote as their proxies. For 8 other FCs, e.g., Real Estate and Construction, Catering, Information Technology, corporate voters co-exist with individual electors.[56]

The FC system was first introduced by the British government in 1985 as part of an overall plan to develop representative government in Hong Kong. The aims of such FC elections were to allow the economic and professional sectors to be well-represented in the legislature and to maintain Hong Kong's stability and prosperity after the handover. After the handover in 1997, the pro-Beijing/pro-establishment camp has relied on these corporate votes to dominate the FC elections, such that the pro-establishment camp is able to command an overall majority of the seats in the Legislative Council, even though it lags behind in the Geographical Constituencies (GC) elections that are constituted via universal suffrage.[57] Therefore, it is highly unlikely that China will allow the FC system and/or corporate voting to be abolished in the near future as this would erode its political control over the affairs of the Hong Kong legislature.

Unsurprisingly, the Hong Kong judiciary has acquiesced to the constitutionality of corporate voting. In *Chan Yu Nam* v. *Secretary for Justice*,[58] the Court of Appeal rejected the argument that corporate voting was inconsistent with Article 26 of the Basic Law.[59] Given that 'functional constituencies, embracing corporate voting, have played a central role'[60] in Hong Kong's political development since 1985, it was inconceivable that China had intended to 'endorse a change as fundamental as the abolition … of corporate voting for functional constituencies'[61] by a side-wind when its repeal was neither provided for in the Basic Law nor reflected in the 'history and the policy which created it'.[62] Furthermore, the Basic Law

[55] Hong Kong Electoral Affairs Commission, *Report on the 2012 Legislative Council Election Held on 9 September 2012*, 22 November 2012, 135 <http://www.legco.gov.hk/yr12-13/english/panels/ca/papers/ca1217cb2-306-e.pdf> accessed 1 February 2017.

[56] *Ibid.*

[57] Ma Ngok, 'Political Parties and Elections', in Wai-man Lam, Percy Luen-tim Lui, Wilson Wong and Ian Holliday (eds), *Contemporary Hong Kong Politics: Governance in the Post-1997 Era* (Hong Kong: Hong Kong University Press, 2007), 131–132. See also Sonny Lo, *Competing Chinese Political Visions* (Santa Barbara: Praeger, 2010), 130–131.

[58] *Chan Yu Nam* (n 5).

[59] Article 26 of the Basic Law reads: 'Permanent residents of the Hong Kong Special Administrative Region shall have the right to vote and the right to stand for election in accordance with law.'

[60] *Chan Yu Nam* (n 5) [81].

[61] *Ibid.* [85].

[62] *Ibid.*

implicitly condones the participation of corporate voters in Legislative Council elections insofar as Annex II states that 'the delimitation of functional sectors and *corporate bodies*, their seat allocation and election methods; and the method for electing members of the Legislative Council ... shall be specified by an electoral law'.

Chief Executive Elections

The Chief Executive is the head of the HKSAR government and he or she is elected by a 1200-member Election Committee. As discussed earlier, it is noteworthy that an overwhelming majority of the members sitting on the Election Committee are pro-Beijing delegates, and pro-democracy candidates therefore have no real chance of winning this election. Furthermore, this small-circle but high-stakes election excludes the direct participation of over 90% of registered voters in Hong Kong.[63]

The validity of CY Leung's election as Hong Kong's third Chief Executive came before the CFA in 2012. A pro-democracy Chief Executive election candidate, Albert Ho, challenged the election result on the basis that CY Leung had violated the Elections (Corrupt and Illegal Conduct) Ordinance (ECICO)[64] when he allegedly made two materially false and misleading statements prior to the election. In the first statement, CY Leung allegedly told journalists that he did not have any unauthorised building structures in his home. In the second statement, CY Leung had publicly accused Henry Tang, another Chief Executive candidate, of concealing from the public the existence of illegal structures at the latter's residence. One may note that Henry Tang was a pro-Beijing candidate and he was widely tipped to be the next Chief Executive. But when local reporters revealed that Tang had unauthorised structures in his basement, the tide of public opinion turned against him; and it is believed that Beijing, in response to public opinion, influenced the delegates on the Election Committee to vote for CY Leung instead. In an interesting twist to the tale, *after* CY Leung was elected as Chief Executive, the local press uncovered that Leung too had unauthorised structures in his home.

[63] Young and Cullen, *Electing Hong Kong's Chief Executive* (n 8), 1.

[64] Section 26(2) of the Elections (Corrupt and Illegal Conduct) Ordinance (Chapter 554) reads: 'A candidate engages in illegal conduct at an election if the candidate publishes a materially false or misleading statement of fact about the candidate or candidates with whom the candidate is associated, or about another candidate or other candidates, for the purpose of: (a) promoting the election of the candidate or candidates with whom the candidate is associated; or (b) prejudicing the election of the other candidate or candidates.'

This revelation drove Albert Ho, the only pro-democracy candidate in the Chief Executive race, to lodge an election petition that CY Leung was not duly elected, in view of his alleged misrepresentations that constituted a violation of ECICO.[65]

The CFA in *Re Ho Chun Yan Albert*[66] swiftly rejected the crux of the electoral challenge. In essence, the CFA agreed with the lower court that the first statement was allegedly made by CY Leung *before* he had publicly declared his candidacy for Chief Executive, and the ECICO only regulated statements made by persons who had been nominated or had publicly declared their candidacy.[67] Therefore, while the first statement has proved to be untrue, there was no violation of the electoral law at issue. In the Court's view, there was no legal duty on the candidate to publicly retract any false statements he made prior to his candidacy.[68] As for the second statement, the CFA also agreed with the lower court that it could not be established that the statement was materially false or misleading merely because 'Mr CY Leung was susceptible to the very same attack which he was making on Mr Tang'.[69] In short, hypocrisy is not a lie. Accordingly, the CFA refused to grant leave to hear the *substance* of the electoral challenge.

Nevertheless, the Court granted leave to hear an important *procedural* issue. Under the Chief Executive Election Ordinance (CEEO), a failed candidate in the Chief Executive race has only seven days to lodge an election petition after the result is declared.[70] The lower court had found this time limit to be excessively short and applied a remedial interpretation to the electoral law so as to confer upon the Court a discretion to extend time, where necessary.[71] One must note that regardless of how the CFA ruled on this *procedural* issue, Leung's position was secured when the CFA refused leave to hear the *substantive* merits of the electoral dispute.

65 Section 32(1)(a)(iv) of the Chief Executive Election Ordinance (Chapter 569) reads: 'An election may be questioned only by an election petition on the ground that ... the person declared by the Returning Officer ... as elected was not duly elected because ... he engaged in corrupt conduct or illegal conduct at the election.'

66 *Re Ho Chun Yan Albert* (n 6).

67 Section 2 of the ECIO reads: '"candidate" (a) means a person who stands nominated as a candidate at an election; and (b) also means a person who, at any time before the close of nominations for an election, has publicly declared an intention to stand as a candidate at the election'.

68 *Re Ho Chun Yan Albert* (n 6) [26].

69 *Ibid.* [39].

70 Section 34(1) of the Chief Executive Election Ordinance (Chapter 569) reads: 'An election petition questioning an election must be lodged within 7 working days after the day on which the result of the election is declared.'

71 [2012] 5 HKLRD 149 [125] (Court of First Instance).

By clarifying the exact terms of the appeal, the CFA made it abundantly clear to Beijing that it was not going to unseat its choice.

Interestingly, in *Leung Chun Ying* v. *Ho Chun Yan Albert*,[72] the CFA also upheld the constitutionality of the seven-day statutory limit and thus overruled the lower's court decision to read-in a judicial discretion to extend time. In the lower court, the seven-day limit was deemed unconstitutional as the government could not discharge its burden of justifying how a short time bar as such was proportionate. Specifically, the lower court applied *Mok Charles* v. *Tam Wai Ho*,[73] a prior CFA decision, which invalidated a statutory restriction that barred the CFA from hearing any appeal over Legislative Council electoral disputes. In disagreement with the lower court, the CFA in *Leung Chun Ying* insisted that its prior *Charles Mok* decision could be distinguished:

> *No useful guidance can be obtained from Charles Mok ... In that case, the court was faced with a total absence of any appeal in election petition proceedings ... This is not the same situation in the present case where a comparison had to be made between time limits.*[74]

While the CFA is certainly right that *Charles Mok* can be distinguished on the basis that the Court was therein addressing a statutory clause that ousted the CFA's jurisdiction completely, it is important to note that, in *Charles Mok*, the Court required the government to demonstrate how the legislative restriction at issue was proportionate, in particular how it was 'no more than is necessary'[75] to accomplish the legitimate aims of the electoral law. To be consistent, the CFA in *Leung Chun Ying* should have required the government to prove how this tight seven-day time limit was necessary, especially since counsel for Albert Ho pointed out that returns for election expenses in the Chief Executive elections do not have to be lodged until 30 days after the publication of the election result, and it would be well past the seven-day deadline before any such illegal conduct could be discovered and raised in a timely election petition.[76]

However, in *Leung Chun Ying*, the CFA did *not* mention, let alone apply, the proportionality analysis! Instead, the proportionality test applied in *Charles Mok* was turned on its head when the CFA herein decided to accord significant deference to the legislative choice, instead of

[72] (2013) 16 HKCFAR 735 (Court of Final Appeal).
[73] (2010) 13 HKCFAR 762 (Court of Final Appeal).
[74] *Leung Chun Ying* (n 72) [47].
[75] *Charles Mok* (n 73) [28].
[76] *Leung Chun Ying* (n 72) [48].

requiring the government to justify on a balance of probability the rights-derogation at issue:

> *Elections, however, also involve political and policy considerations and it is in these areas where the legislature is involved. The determination that seven days is the appropriate limit for the lodging of election petitions is one that does involve considerations other than legal ones. A due margin of appreciation should be accorded in the present case.*[77]

By sweeping aside the proportionality analysis, the CFA was thus free to downplay the excessiveness of the seven-day time limit:

> *First, where a line is drawn, it is inevitable that there may be hard cases that would arise when persons fall within the wrong side of the line. Secondly, it must be borne in mind in the present context that if a situation were to arise where one or more of the grounds [for lodging an election petition] only came to light after the seven-day period, the election petition procedure does not provide the only means of redress.*[78]

In perhaps the most important part of this judgment, the CFA then suggested an alternate mode of electoral redress, i.e., persons who were *not* candidates in the Chief Executive Election, and hence unaffected by the seven-day time limit that applied only to the election candidates, could still launch separate judicial review proceedings against the election result.[79] In other words, while the candidates themselves were time-barred after seven days, their surrogates were free to seek judicial review and challenge the validity of the election after that. There is essentially no *substantive* difference in result between (a) allowing the Court to exercise a *discretion* to extend the seven-day time limit for candidates lodging election petitions and (b) authorising their third-party surrogates to *seek leave* to bring judicial review proceedings to litigate the very same electoral issue. But in ruling as it did, the CFA reached a decision that upheld the impugned law, whilst preserving its oversight over electoral matters, and thereby strategically avoided a potential conflict with Beijing over the validity of a law regulating the Chief Executive election, a central concern of the Chinese government.

In 2014, the NPCSC issued its Decision on electoral reform. Specifically, Beijing authorised the election of the Chief Executive by the people from 2017 onwards; but there can be only two or three

[77] *Ibid.* [45].
[78] *Ibid.* [49].
[79] *Ibid.*

candidates for the people to choose from, and each candidate must be first approved by more than half of all of the members on a nominating committee.[80] The composition and formation method of this nominating committee would be the same as that for the current Chief Executive Election Committee. In essence, the current Election Committee would transition into a nominating committee, and all registered Hong Kong voters would be able to vote on candidates who have been pre-screened by the pro-Beijing delegates on this nominating committee. Consequently, the Hong Kong government published various proposals on how the HKSAR could introduce electoral reform in accordance with the NPCSC Decision.[81]

A pro-democracy activist (and law undergraduate) was dissatisfied with the democratic reforms sanctioned by the NPCSC Decision and the constitutional proposals introduced, and she took the Hong Kong government to court. But, unsurprisingly, the CFI swiftly refused to grant her leave to seek judicial review. The CFI held definitively that 'a decision of the NPCSC … is not subject to review by the court[s] in Hong Kong';[82] and since the NPCSC had the 'ultimate authority to disapprove'[83] any constitutional proposals endorsed by the Hong Kong legislature, the local government was under no legal duty to consult the people on 'non-viable options'[84] that would contradict the NPCSC's stipulated framework for electoral reform. In any case, since the local legislature had not endorsed any proposal for electoral reform, the Court held that it was premature to intervene in a 'pre-enactment challenge'.[85]

[80] Decision of the Standing Committee of the National People's Congress on Issues Relating to the Selection of the Chief Executive of the Hong Kong Special Administrative Region by Universal Suffrage and on the Method for Forming the Legislative Council of the Hong Kong Special Administrative Region in the Year 2016 <http://www.2017.gov.hk/filemanager/template/en/doc/20140831b.pdf> accessed 1 February 2017.

[81] See *Consultation Report and Proposals on the Method for Selecting the Chief Executive by Universal Suffrage*, April 2015 <http://www.2017.gov.hk/filemanager/template/en/doc/report_2nd/consultation_report_2nd.pdf> accessed 1 February 2017. The HKSAR government's eventual proposal for electoral reform was rejected by the Hong Kong Legislative Council on 18 June 2015. See Albert Chen, 'Law and Politics of the Struggle for Universal Suffrage in Hong Kong, 2013–15' (2016) 3 *Asian Journal of Law and Society* 189, 197.

[82] *Leung Lai Kwok Yvonne* v. *Chief Secretary for Administration* [2015] HKEC 1034 [30] (Court of First Instance).

[83] *Ibid.* [33].

[84] *Ibid.*

[85] *Ibid.* [40].

Constitutional Dead-ends and Dialogue

The above discussion reveals a distinct contradiction in the Hong Kong judiciary's approach to electoral rights-adjudication. While the courts have enhanced the access of prisoners, persons convicted of minor offences, and non-indigenous villagers to the electoral process, they have steered away from confronting Beijing on corporate voting in functional constituencies and the regulatory restrictions in the Chief Executive Election.[86] The latter systemic issues directly impact Beijing's retention of control over Hong Kong's legislative or executive branches of the government, and there is no way that China would acquiesce to any significant judicial overhaul. These major systemic deficiencies are basically constitutional no-go zones for the courts and the judges know it.

Simon Young has, however, raised the following concern:

> *If the relevant political actors are unable to realise the aim of universal suffrage [in Hong Kong], why should the courts continue to hold rights in abeyance and tolerate deficient institutions while waiting for a political process that may never bear fruit?*[87]

In turn, Young advocates for the Hong Kong judiciary to give the people 'the *full measure* of their political rights by considering [such] rights challenges with the *same intensive scrutiny* applied in previous cases concerned the fundamental freedoms of expression, assembly, and association'.[88]

With respect, Young's position is untenable. If the Hong Kong courts were to apply rigorous review and dismantle the inherent institutional inequalities preserved by the Basic Law, such as the per se invalidation of corporate voting or the qualifying conditions on becoming Chief Executive, this would only prove to be a Pyrrhic victory, as China would simply respond with an NPCSC Interpretation that reverses the judicial decision swiftly and definitively. One may note that in the very first constitutional decision issued by the CFA post-handover in *Ng Ka Ling v. Director of Immigration*,[89] where the Court overreached and conferred the constitutional right of abode in Hong Kong to children born in the

[86] Young (n 2), 25.
[87] *Ibid.*, 27.
[88] *Ibid.*, 30.
[89] (1999) 2 HKCFAR 4 (Court of Final Appeal).

Mainland to Hong Kong permanent residents, the decision was reversed by the NPCSC within six months.[90] It is not inconceivable that China would respond even more ferociously than it did in *Ng Ka Ling* when the stakes herein for Beijing are even higher. The clipping of judicial wings, or even the ouster of judges, is not a fanciful scenario.

When Hong Kong's political reform trajectory has hit a hard wall, the progressive and pragmatic response for the Court is neither to capitulate completely to the powers-that-be nor to punch back harder. Instead, the judiciary should explore *modest* and *dialogic* solutions that ameliorate the inherent institutional inequalities whilst consciously providing ample legislative space for the local legislature to use the *ordinary* political process to respond to the Court's decision.[91] Even if China is not thrilled by a judicial decision, insofar as the Court has created space for continued independent legislative policy-making and does not mandate the details of subsequent statutory sequels, Beijing may decide to stay its hand. This way, the HKSAR government may be allowed to address the judicial decision *on its own* with the passage of an *ordinary* law, and Hong Kong can avoid an NPCSC Interpretation or constitutional amendment[92] that is directly foisted upon the city from Beijing. Such political reprisals would only do more long-term harm to Hong Kong.

By prescribing interstitial rules that accommodate space for legislative deliberation and modification, the Court would be opening up a channel of dialogue on electoral rights with the Hong Kong government. So far as the narrow judicial rulings are tolerated and implemented, even minimally, by the powers-that-be, a modest step forward on political reform would have been taken.

Consequently, if the Hong Kong judiciary is willing to pursue such a constitutional conversation with the local legislature on political rights, two specific electoral issues in Hong Kong are ripe for dialogic redress by the courts and they will be explored in turn.

[90] The Interpretation by the Standing Committee of the National People's Congress of Articles 22(4) and 24(2)(3) of the Basic Law of the Hong Kong Special Administrative Region of the People's Republic of China (Adopted at the Tenth Session of the Standing Committee of the Ninth National People's Congress on 26 June 1999) <http://www.basiclaw.gov.hk/en/basiclawtext/images/basiclawtext_doc17.pdf> accessed 1 February 2017.

[91] See generally Po Jen Yap, *Constitutional Dialogue in Common Law Asia* (Oxford: Oxford University Press, 2015).

[92] See Article 159 of the Hong Kong Basic Law.

Disparity of Voting Power within the Functional Constituencies (FCs)

While any legal argument to invalidate corporate voting per se in FC elections is dead on arrival before the courts, this does not mean that other related problems pertaining to the FC system cannot be successfully litigated and mitigated. In particular, the disparity of voting power within the FCs is a real concern in Hong Kong and it adversely impacts FC elections in two ways.

First, the size of the constituency base in each FC differs such that the relative voting power of an *individual* elector in a small FC would be far greater than that of another *individual* voter in a large FC. The FC with the smallest electorate base is the Heung Yee Kuk, a statutory body that represents the indigenous inhabitants of New Territories in advising the government on socio-economic matters pertaining to their welfare, and it had an electoral base of 147 registered individual electors in 2016.[93] On the other hand, the Education FC had an electoral base of 88,185 registered individual electors in 2016.[94] The variation in constituency size thus invariably affects the relative weight that each vote carries in determining the voter's preferred candidate in the relevant FC.

Second, there is the problem of 'packing' in FC elections, a common practice amongst large corporations. Currently, conglomerates with several subsidiaries and associate companies are able to 'pack' a single or even a few FCs with multiple corporate electors that are subject to the singular control of the parent company. (The full extent to which 'packing' takes place in the FCs is practically impossible to verify as the recording or copying of any information from the public register of FC electors for research purposes is prohibited by law.[95]) By 'packing' the same or different FCs, large corporations, through the multiple subsidiaries they control, can cast more votes in FC elections than small corporate bodies.

One must note that, whilst the Basic Law expressly allows corporate bodies to participate in FC elections, the text of the Basic Law itself does not explicitly authorise 'packing' by large conglomerates nor does it

93 The Government of the Hong Kong Special Administrative Region, 'Voter Registration Statistics: Functional Constituency' <http://www.voterregistration.gov.hk/eng/statistic20163.html> accessed 1 February 2017.

94 *Ibid.*

95 Simon Young and Anthony Law, 'Privileged to Vote: Inequalities and Anomalies of the FC System', in Christine Loh (ed.), *Functional Constituencies: A Unique Feature of the Hong Kong Legislative Council* (Hong Kong: Hong Kong University Press, 2006), 98.

condone the drastic disparity of voting power between *individual* electors in different FCs. All of these electoral anomalies are merely the consequence of the LCO,[96] an ordinary statute.

In lieu of invalidating corporate voting per se, the more dialogic path forward for the Hong Kong judiciary is to question the disparity of voting power between individual electors inter se and review how 'packing' disadvantages smaller corporate bodies by allowing large conglomerates to cast more votes though their subsidiaries. Naturally, at the outset, the Court should avoid dictating the appropriate size of the electoral base for individual electors in each FC, nor should it ban corporate 'packing' completely. But insofar that it can be demonstrated that the pool of individual electors in some FCs is tiny (e.g., 147 individuals in Heung Yee Kuk FC) compared to the electoral base in other FCs (e.g., 88,185 individuals in the Education FC), or that certain large conglomerates have 'packed' dozens or hundreds of votes in multiple FCs, the Court can establish an electoral right[97] and/or equal protection[98] violation and require the government to ameliorate these constitutional concerns.

More importantly, instead of invalidating the impugned electoral law with immediate effect, the Court should issue a suspension order, as it did in the prisoners' voting right case of *Chan Kin Sum*, and grant the Hong Kong government 'an opportunity to engage in policy-making, by deciding which of a range of multiple constitutional options would be implemented in light of the court's ruling'.[99] A suspended declaration gives the legislature, rather than the courts, the opportunity to make the initial selection on how best to comply with the constitutional mandates among those competing alternatives available, such that due deference is paid to the primacy of the legislature's law-making role.[100] As long as the Court does not dictate the specific content and details of the legislative replies, e.g. the population ratio of the smallest FC electoral base (for individual electors) to the largest one or the maximum number of subsidiaries' votes parent companies can control, the Hong Kong government may

96 Legislative Council Ordinance (Chapter 542).

97 Article 21 of the BORO reads: 'Every permanent resident shall have the right and the opportunity ... (a) to take part in the conduct of public affairs, directly or through freely chosen representatives; (b) to vote and to be elected at genuine periodic elections which shall be by universal and equal suffrage and shall be held by secret ballot, guaranteeing the free expression of the will of the electors.'

98 Article 25 of the Basic Law reads: 'All Hong Kong residents shall be equal before the law.'

99 Roach (n 38), 212.

100 See Bruce Ryder, 'Suspending the Charter' (2003) 21 *Supreme Court Law Review* (2d) 267, 285.

very plausibly acquiesce and introduce some form of remedial legislation that improves upon the electoral status quo,[101] as they did in *Chan Wah* and *Chan Kin Sum* when the Court ruled against them in modest ways. In essence, by doing less, the Court can often achieve more.

Resignation of Legislators and By-elections

Currently, when a legislator resigns from his or her seat in the Legislative Council, he or she is disqualified from running again for the by-election held to fill the said vacancy.[102] The law was passed in October 2012 after five pro-democracy legislative councillors from different Geographical Constituencies (GC), as a collective act of political protest, resigned mid-term in 2010 to trigger city-wide by-elections for their seats. (Given that electoral seats in the GCs are awarded on a proportional basis, their re-election was virtually guaranteed; and their resignation and re-election was pure political posturing.)

The constitutionality of this law was challenged but upheld by the Court of Appeal in *Kwok Cheuk Kin* v. *Secretary for Constitutional and Mainland Affairs*.[103] The focus of the electoral challenge centred on whether the electoral restriction was proportionate, in particular whether it served a legitimate aim. The Court unanimously agreed that it should defer to the government on their 'assessment as to whether there is a need to discourage resignations with a view to trigger by-elections',[104] especially since this (somewhat unnecessary) political exercise cost HK$126 million in public expenditure.[105]

[101] In land-scarce Hong Kong, the Heung Yee Kuk's controversial practice of selling their traditional land rights to rich developers has angered the general public and the Hong Kong government, and a judicial ruling against the Heung Yee Kuk FC may even give the Hong Kong government the political leverage it needs to reduce the Kuk's political influence in the Legislative Council. See Ng Kang Chung, 'Hong Kong Development Minister Slams Heung Yee Kuk Stance on Trading Small House Rights', *South China Morning Post*, 25 January 2016 <http://www.scmp.com/news/hong-kong/politics/article/1905250/hong-kong-development-minister-slams-heung-yee-kuk-stance> accessed 1 February 2017.

[102] Section 39(2A) of the LCO reads: 'A person is also disqualified from being nominated as a candidate at a by-election if –

(a) within the 6 months ending on the date of the by-election –
(i) the person's resignation under section 14 as a Member took effect; or
(ii) the person was taken under section 13(3) to have resigned from office as a Member; and
(b) no general election was held after the relevant notice of resignation or notice of non-acceptance took effect.'

[103] [2015] 5 HKLRD 881 (Court of Appeal).

[104] *Ibid.* [62].

[105] *Ibid.* [13].

Unfortunately, while the government may have been pursuing a legitimate aim when crafting a law of this nature, the Court of Appeal erred insofar as it also decided that the electoral restriction was 'no more than necessary to address those concerns'.[106] Specifically, counsel had raised concerns that the law was overbroad insofar as inter alia it had also barred legislative councillors who resigned after being convicted of a criminal offence but had their convictions quashed on appeal after their resignations and before the resulting by-election.[107]

Oddly, the Court of Appeal only had this pithy reply:

> *With respect, they are fanciful suggestions and we do not find those to be a concrete basis for upsetting the balance struck by the legislature in the form of a modest restriction.*[108]

One wonders why the suggestion was particularly 'fanciful', especially since many (somewhat unruly) pro-democracy legislators are regularly convicted of minor public order offences in Hong Kong,[109] and their right to stand for elections, pending appeal, notwithstanding has been vindicated by the lower court in *Wong Hin Wai*.[110]

The tenor of the Court's judgment was summed up by Chief Judge of the High Court, Andrew Cheung, in his concurring opinion:

> *Generally speaking, the court is neither constitutionally positioned nor institutionally equipped to deal with a political issue, that is, an issue essentially involving political rather than legal judgment … This is so regardless of whether the right sought to be restricted is a fundamental right, and also whether the issue is encountered at the first limb or the third limb of the proportionality test. For good reasons, the court should, generally speaking, accord the government/ legislature a broad margin of appreciation regarding their discretionary judgment on such an issue.*[111]

While the government might have resisted the Court's decision if it had attempted to invalidate completely this electoral prohibition, there are other dialogic progressive paths the Court could have pursued, in lieu of either invalidating or upholding the impugned law completely. Trimming has been defended by Cass Sunstein as a heuristic for judges to

[106] *Ibid.* [65].
[107] *Ibid.* [67].
[108] *Ibid.* [68].
[109] *Leung Kwok Hung & Others* v. *HKSAR* (2005) 8 HKCFAR 229 (Court of Final Appeal); *HKSAR* v. *Wong Yuk Man* [2015] 1 HKLRD 132 (Court of First Instance).
[110] *Wong Hin Wai* (n 4).
[111] *Kwok Cheuk Kin* (n 103) [6].

attend carefully to competing positions and attempt to steer between the poles when reaching a particular legal result.[112] And judges 'trim' either by striking a middle path or preserving what is most essential to competing reasonable positions, so that political conflict is reduced and people who hold competing positions do not feel humiliated or excluded by the outcome.[113]

In this case, the Court could have effectively trimmed and scaled back the scope of the law by declaring that a blanket ban was *unnecessary* as it also bars (i) lawmakers who resign after being convicted of a criminal offence but have their convictions quashed on appeal after their resignations and before the resulting by-election; and (ii) legislators who resign to attend to ailing family members but whose family situations are resolved before the by-election,[114] both valid concerns raised by the counsel for the applicant. Such a judicial declaration, coupled with the use of a suspension order, preserves the core of the government's objection to the *costly* grand-standing by the pro-democracy legislators, while giving time to the legislature to pass remedial legislation that addresses concerns that a blanket ban would unfairly affect lawmakers with more legitimate reasons for their resignations.

As a result, the issue of a delayed declaration of invalidity would facilitate a 'remedial dialogue'[115] between the courts and the legislature, and broker a compromise in this instance between the rivalling political factions in Hong Kong.

Oath-taking and the Ouster of Legislators

At the time of writing, a new political storm is brewing in Hong Kong. In the wake of the 2014 Umbrella Movement that paralysed the financial district in Hong Kong for 79 days, Hong Kongers have thumbed their noses at Beijing by voting a slew of young pro-democracy street protestors into the Legislative Council in 2016. More significantly, six of the newly elected lawmakers have either openly advocated Hong Kong's independence from China or defended Hong Kong's right to democratic self-determination.[116]

[112] Cass Sunstein, 'Trimming' (2009) 122 *Harvard Law Review* 1049, 1051.

[113] *Ibid.*

[114] *Kwok Cheuk Kin* (n 103) [67].

[115] Roach (n 38) 221.

[116] Gary Cheung and Jeffie Lam, 'Rise of Localists in Hong Kong Polls Set to Bring Headaches for Beijing, Analysts Say', *South China Morning Post*, 5 September 2016.

Less compromising and more confrontational, these newly elected lawmakers openly derided China at their swearing-in ceremony on 12 October 2016 and a pair of them (Sixtus Leung and Yau Wai-ching) even referred to China as 'Sheen-na' – a derogatory term used by the Japanese on the Chinese during the Second World War – and pledged allegiance to the 'Hong Kong nation' instead. Unsurprisingly, the President of the Legislative Council did not accept the validity of the pair's oaths but nevertheless allowed them to retake their oaths at the next Legislative Council meeting.

However, before Leung and Yau could retake their oaths, the Hong Kong government swiftly went to court and sought a declaration that the pair had been disqualified from their office on 12 October 2016 when they had declined to take the requisite legislative oath and that the Legislative Council President was therefore disempowered from re-administering their oaths. Furthermore, before the CFI could hand down its ruling, China intervened. On 7 November 2016, the NPCSC handed down an Interpretation of Article 104[117] of the Basic Law, which unequivocally stated the following:

> *An oath taker is disqualified forthwith from assuming the public office specified in the Article if he or she declines to take the oath. An oath taker who intentionally reads out words which do not accord with the wording of the oath prescribed by law, or takes the oath in a manner which is not sincere or not solemn, shall be treated as declining to take the oath. The oath so taken is invalid and the oath taker is disqualified forthwith from assuming the public office specified in the Article ... If the oath taken is determined as invalid, no arrangement shall be made for retaking the oath.*[118]

Capitulating to Beijing, the CFI on 15 November 2016 determined that Leung and Yau had intentionally declined to take the requisite oath of

<http://www.scmp.com/news/hong-kong/politics/article/2015349/rise-localists-hong-kong-polls-set-bring-headaches-beijing> accessed 1 February 2017.

[117] Article 104 of the Basic Law reads: 'When assuming office, the Chief Executive, principal officials, members of the Executive Council and of the Legislative Council, judges of the courts at all levels and other members of the judiciary in the Hong Kong Special Administrative Region must, in accordance with law, swear to uphold the Basic Law of the Hong Kong Special Administrative Region of the People's Republic of China and swear allegiance to the Hong Kong Special Administrative Region of the People's Republic of China.'

[118] See Paragraphs 2(3) and 2(4) of the Interpretation of Article 104 of the Basic Law of the Hong Kong Special Administrative Region of the People's Republic of China by the Standing Committee of the National People's Congress (7 November 2016).

office on 12 October 2016 and that they had therefore been automatically disqualified from assuming their office.[119] The CFI decision was affirmed by the Court of Appeal on 30 November 2016.[120]

According to the Court of Appeal, the abovementioned NPCSC Interpretation has conclusively set out the penalty of disqualification as the consequence of an oath-taker's refusal to take the relevant oath,[121] and the Court must therefore enforce the Interpretation and disqualify the errant lawmakers.[122]

With respect, there are two separate and conceptually distinct issues herein and the Court has conflated both. The first concerns the consequence for legislators if they intentionally decline to take the approved oath; the second pertains to which branch of government is tasked with enforcing any adverse consequence that follows from an invalid oath. The Interpretation has made it abundantly clear that the consequence of the abovementioned misconduct is disqualification; but one must note that the Interpretation is actually *silent* on whether the judiciary has to be the branch of government that disqualifies a lawmaker after his or her oath is deemed invalid. In fact, Albert Chen, an eminent pro-Beijing constitutional law scholar and member of Hong Kong Basic Law Committee – a political body that advises the NPCSC prior to the official issue of any Interpretation – has revealed publicly *prior to the CFI's ruling* that it was open to the Hong Kong courts to punt the issue over to the oath administrator at the Legislative Council.[123]

The Court of Appeal justified its right to disqualify the lawmakers on the basis that it was its constitutional duty to 'adjudicat[e] on the consequence of a failure to meet the constitutional requirement'[124] imposed under Article 104 of the Basic Law. As reasoned by the Court, Article 104 of the Basic Law requires key public officials to swear allegiance to the HKSAR before they can assume office, and since it is for the courts to determine whether a constitutional requirement has been met,[125] a

[119] *Chief Executive of the Hong Kong Special Administrative Region* v. *President of the Legislative Council* [2016] 6 HKC 417 (Court of First Instance).

[120] *Chief Executive of the Hong Kong Special Administrative Region* v. *President of the Legislative Council* [2016] 6 HKC 541 (Court of Appeal).

[121] *Ibid.* [29].

[122] *Ibid.* [42].

[123] Jeffie Lam and Joyce Ng, 'Hong Kong Courts Can Decide Fate of At Least 10 Lawmakers Despite Beijing Ruling', *South China Morning Post*, 11 November 2016 <http://www.scmp.com/news/hong-kong/politics/article/2045224/hong-kong-courts-can-decide-fate-least-10-lawmakers-despite> accessed 1 February 2017.

[124] *Chief Executive* (n 120) [31].

[125] *Ibid.* [32]

fortiori, it must be for the courts – and not the oath administrator – to determine whether a valid oath as required under Article 104 has been taken.[126] Otherwise, if a member of the Legislative Council is 'wrongly ruled by the Clerk or President [of the Legislative Council] to have failed to comply with article 104 and disqualified',[127] that member would have no relief.

With respect, the Court of Appeal's concerns are legitimate but misplaced. Undoubtedly, for the reasons given by the Court, the judiciary must be empowered under Article 104 to determine whether an oath taken is valid. If no judicial safeguards are in place, a delinquent and partisan oath administrator can unilaterally remove lawmakers duly elected by the people. Hence, in any dispute, upon a final judicial ruling that the oath taken is *valid*, the matter should rest henceforth, and that lawmaker must be permitted to assume office.

On the other hand, it is my view that if the Court decides that the oath taken is *invalid*, it should be left to the oath administrator to decide whether the lawmaker should be disqualified or given a second chance to retake the oath. (Naturally, if the legislator's conduct during oath-taking falls within the ambit of the Interpretation, the oath administrator would have no discretion and would be legally bound by the Interpretation to disqualify him/her.) Unfortunately, the Court of Appeal took the view that the disqualification of the said legislators was immediate and automatic, and it is to its reasons I now turn.

First, the Court of Appeal held that Paragraph 2(3) of the Interpretation '*automatically disqualified* [the pair of lawmakers] *forthwith* from assuming their offices'.[128] This is an unfortunate judicial sleight of hand. The term 'automatic' or 'automatically' is found nowhere in the Interpretation. The Interpretation only uses the term 'forthwith', which means 'without delay',[129] and it would not be inconsistent with the Interpretation for the Court of Appeal to punt the issue over to the oath administrator at the Legislative Council to proceed with the disqualification expeditiously. As discussed earlier, the Interpretation is actually *silent* on who should do the disqualifying. In fact, the courts are not even mentioned in the Interpretation at all.

126 *Ibid.* [33].

127 *Ibid.* [74] (Concurring Opinion by Vice President Lam).

128 *Ibid.* [42].

129 Catherine Soanes and Angus Stevenson (ed.), *Concise Oxford English Dictionary*, 11th edn. (Oxford: Oxford University Press, 2006), 560.

Second, the Court of Appeal held that Section 21 of the Oaths and Declarations Ordinance (Chapter 11) (ODO) provides that 'any person who declines … to take an oath duly requested … shall … if he has already entered on his office, vacate it, and if he has not entered on his office, be disqualified'. Therefore, the Court reasoned that Section 21 of the ODO not only did not allow the two lawmakers to retake their oaths,[130] their removal from office was automatic.[131] On the Court's reading of Section 21 of the ODO, any lawmaker who declines to take the oath shall be automatically disqualified or removed from office. If the Court was correct, this would mean that lawmakers who had declined to take the oath at the first available opportunity after being duly requested to do so, merely because they or their family members suddenly require emergency medical attention right before they were to be sworn in, those lawmakers too would be *automatically* disqualified from office. This surely cannot be right. More importantly, this would not even be what the ODO mandates. Section 19 of the ODO merely requires a member of the Legislative Council to take his/her oath 'as soon as possible' after the commencement of his/her term of office and Section 19 expressly provides that this oath can be taken at the first or 'at any other sitting of the Council'. Therefore, Section 21 of the ODO, which disqualifies a lawmaker for declining or neglecting to take the oath 'duly requested which he is required to take by this Part [IV of the ODO]', only takes effect when Section 19 – also in Part IV of the ODO – is flouted. This means that a lawmaker will only be disqualified after he or she declines or neglects to take the oath required by Section 19 of the ODO, i.e. he or she declines to take a valid LegCo Oath as soon as reasonably possible[132] after the commencement of his or her term of office, and not on the first occasion he or she first declined to take the

[130] *Chief Executive* (n 120) [42].

[131] *Ibid.* [43].

[132] In construing statutes, courts would avoid a construction that leads to an absurd result, since that is unlikely to be what the legislature intended: Francis Bennion and Oliver Jones (ed.), *Bennion on Statutory Interpretation: A Code*, 6th edn. (London: Sweet & Maxwell, 2013), 869. Moreover, common-law courts have often construed the phrase 'as soon as possible' to mean 'within a reasonable time': see *Hydraulic Engineering Co* v. *McHaffie Goslett & Co* (1878) 4 QBD 670, 673 (EWCA); *Vines* v. *Djordjevitch* (1955) 91 CLR 512, 522 (HCA); *R.* v. *Greenaway* (1994) 12 CRNZ 103, 106 (NZCA); *SWV Pty Ltd* v. *Spiroc Pty Ltd* (2006) 201 FLR 238, [58–59] (NSWSC). Therefore, 'as soon as possible' in s.19 ODO should mean 'as soon as *reasonably* possible', and therefore within 'a *reasonable* time'.

requisite oath. It is unfortunate that the Court of Appeal did not explore the interpretive effect Section 19 has on Section 21 and the interplay between both statutory provisions.

Admittedly, the political fates of the two juvenile lawmakers would have been sealed even if the Court of Appeal had passed the buck to the oath administrator in the Legislative Council. But by not participating in the legislators' inglorious removal from office, the Hong Kong courts would have preserved their image as the guardian of the city's civil liberties and warded off criticisms that it had now become an enabler of the executive government's unspeakable political agenda.[133] More importantly, one should note that this court victory has emboldened the Hong Kong government, which has now gone to court to seek the removal of four additional pro-democracy lawmakers.[134] By unilaterally disqualifying the lawmakers, the Hong Kong judiciary has unwittingly opened the floodgates to more (unnecessary) litigation and embroiled itself in more political controversy.[135]

[133] Audrey Eu, 'The Road of No Return Part 2: How the Courts could have Handled the Oaths Row', *Hong Kong Free Press*, 7 December 2016, <https://www.hongkongfp.com/2016/12/07/road-no-return-part-2-courts-handled-oaths-row/> accessed 1 February 2017.

[134] While these four lawmakers had intentionally slipped pro-democracy messages into their legislative oaths, their oaths were either approved by the oath administrator or were validly retaken when the first attempts were ruled invalid. See Chris Lau, 'Hong Kong Lawmakers Accused of Setting aside Solemnity in Taking Oaths', *South China Morning Post*, 2 December, 2016 <http://www.scmp.com/news/hong-kong/politics/article/2051266/hong-kong-lawmakers-accused-setting-aside-solemnity-taking> accessed 1 February 2017.

[135] See Chris Lau, Eddie Lee, and Tony Cheung et al., 'Veteran Hong Kong Taxi Driver Group Member asks Court to Invalidate Eight Legco Oaths', *South China Morning Post*, 10 November 2016, <http://www.scmp.com/news/hong-kong/law-crime/article/2044745/veteran-hong-kong-taxi-driver-group-member-asks-court> accessed 1 February 2017; Chris Lau and Eddie Lee, 'Did CY Leung Mess Up his own Oath? Legal Challenge over Hong Kong Leader's 2012 Swearing In', *South China Morning Post*, 11 November 2016 <http://www.scmp.com/news/hong-kong/law-crime/article/2045129/did-cy-leung-mess-his-own-oath-legal-challenge-over-hong> accessed 1 February 2017; Chris Lau and Eddie Lee, 'Pro-Beijing Group Member asks Hong Kong Court to Disqualify 11 Lawmakers over Legco Oaths', *South China Morning Post*, 14 November 2016 <http://www.scmp.com/news/hong-kong/law-crime/article/2045801/pro-beijing-group-member-asks-hong-kong-court-disqualify-11> accessed 1 February 2017; Chantal Yuen, 'Retired Photojournalist seeks Legal Challenge over Oaths of 14 Lawmakers and Chief Exec. CY Leung', *Hong Kong Free Press*, 17 November 2016 < https://www.hongkongfp.com/2016/11/17/retired-reporter-seeks-legal-challenge-over-oaths-of-14-lawmakers-and-chief-exec-cy-leung/> accessed 1 February 2017.

Conclusion

After China's resumption of sovereignty over Hong Kong in 1997, the fundamental jurisprudential conundrum confronting the CFA is how it can preserve the judiciary as a separate and independent branch of government, whilst quelling any concerns from the Mainland that Hong Kong courts, if left unleashed, would turn the city into another 'renegade province' in the South.

If the Hong Kong judiciary is too aggressive in enforcing electoral rights against the government, China would simply circumvent its judgments by routinely using NPCSC Interpretations (or even a Basic Law amendment) to censure the court and circumscribe its powers further. On the other hand, if the courts are too indulgent on the HKSAR government, the Basic Law would be reduced to a mere hollow shell that only protects electoral rights on paper, but not in practice. In light of these practical realities, it is imperative that judges make constitutional law in continuous dialogue with the political culture.[136]

As observed by Jamal Greene:

> *To say that constitutional argument must attend to politics is not to say, with the Critical Legal Studies movement, that all law is politics or that the language of law is false or self-contradictory.*[137]

Instead, we live in a pluralistic society whereby all participants in the legal discourse are competing to calcify their own political preferences within the contours of conventional constitutional argumentation,[138] which appeal to the constitutional text and structure, its history, judicial precedents, and the consequences of a particular result.[139] Where the interactions between the different types or 'modalities'[140] of constitutional arguments do not uniformly or overwhelmingly point in a particular interpretive direction, progressive and prudent judges would have the leeway to trim the impugned law in a way that accommodates political exigencies.

136 Jamal Greene, 'Selling Originalism' (2009) 97 *Georgetown Law Journal* 657, 716.

137 *Ibid.*, 719.

138 *Ibid.*

139 See Philip Bobbitt, *Constitutional Fate: Theory of the Constitution*, 1st edn. (New York: Oxford University Press, 1984); Po Jen Yap, 'A Typography of Constitutional Arguments in Hong Kong' (2014) 44 *Hong Kong Law Journal* 459.

140 *Ibid.*

Insofar as the judiciary continue to create dialogic opportunities for institutional collaboration with the Hong Kong government on electoral reform, the judicial enforcement of electoral rights can serve as a catalyst for Hong Kong's advancement, albeit slowly, towards universal suffrage. Indeed, this may be the only effective approach the courts can take as judicial abdication would only condone political stagnation, while intrusive judicial review would only lead to reprisals that threaten further political repression or regression.

PART II

Dynamic Democracies

5

The Supreme Court of India and Criminality in Politics

The Supreme Court of India is widely perceived to be the most activist judiciary in Asia. Since the early 1980s, and in the aftermath of Emergency rule in India, public interest litigation has become the means by which its Supreme Court has sought to secure observance of the law by state agencies and extend social justice to the large masses of underprivileged persons in the country.[1] With a litany of socio-economic problems – poverty, gender violence, child mortality – severely under-addressed even today, Indian judges perceive their role to be more 'managerial'[2] or 'catalytic'[3] as they actively engage in a 'day-to-day judicial control and correction'[4] of the political malaise in government.

The Indian Supreme Court in a Dominant-Party Democracy

But the Supreme Court did not start out this way. Like many courts in the world, its brand of activism also had very humble beginnings. In the 1950s and 1960s, the Court was highly deferential to governmental action.[5] However, the Court exercised a streak of independence vis-à-vis the Indian National Congress (Congress) government on land reform and regularly required the government to provide adequate compensation for compulsorily acquired property. But, at that time, in the face of a dominant Congress party that had ruled India continuously since the republic's first general election in 1952, the Court asserted itself

[1] Po Jen Yap, 'New Democracies and Novel Remedies' (2017) *Public Law* 30; Manoj Mate, 'The Rise of Judicial Governance in the Supreme Court of India' (2015) 33 *Boston University International Law Journal* 169.

[2] See Judith Resnik, 'Managerial Judges' (1982) 96 *Harvard Law Review* 374.

[3] Katherine Young, *Constituting Economic and Social Rights* (Oxford: Oxford University Press, 2012), 172–191.

[4] T.R. Andhyarujina, 'The Unique Judicial Activism of the Supreme Court of India' (2014) 130 *Law Quarterly Review* 53.

[5] *Ibid.*, 55.

gingerly, 'short of a frontal confrontation with the political branches'.[6] In *Golak Nath* v. *State of Punjab* (1967),[7] the Supreme Court held that Parliament could not pass constitutional amendments that violated the fundamental rights protected in the Constitution. But the Court also removed the sting from this decision by stating that its ruling would only apply prospectively to future constitutional amendments and not to those under challenge.

The Congress Party led by Indira Gandhi was not placated by this judicial concession. Following a landslide victory at the 1971 polls, the Congress Party passed the 24th Amendment to overrule *Golak Nath* by expressly asserting that Parliament had the unlimited power to amend all parts of the Constitution, including the enshrined fundamental rights. The 25th Amendment was also passed to insulate the State acquisition of private property and socialist policies that implement the Directive Principles from judicial review.[8]

[6] Rosalind Dixon and Samuel Issacharoff, 'Living to Fight Another Day: Judicial Deferral in Defence of Democracy' (2016) *Wisconsin Law Review* 683, 687.

[7] [1967] 2 SCR 762.

[8] The 25th Amendment of the Indian Constitution reads: '1. Short title.– This Act may be called the Constitution (Twenty-fifth Amendment) Act, 1971. 2. Amendment of article 31.– In article 31 of the Constitution, –

(a) for clause (2A), the following clause shall be substituted, namely: –

"(2) No property shall be compulsorily acquired or requisitioned save for a public purpose and save by authority of a law which provides for acquisition or requisitioning of the property for an amount which may be fixed by such law or which may be determined in accordance with such principles and given in such manner as may be specified in such law; and no such law shall be called in question in any court on the ground that the amount so fixed or determined is not adequate or that the whole or any part of such amount is to be given otherwise than in cash:

Provided that in making any law providing for the compulsory acquisition of any property of an educational institution established and administered by a minority, referred to in clause (1) of article 30, the State shall ensure that the amount fixed by or determined under such law for the acquisition of such property is such as would not restrict or abrogate the right guaranteed under that clause.";

(b) after clause (2A), the following clause shall be inserted, namely:–

"(2B) Nothing in sub-clause (f) of clause (1) of article 19 shall affect any such law as is referred to in clause (2)."

3. Insertion of new article 31C.– After article 31B of the Constitution, the following article shall be inserted, namely:–

"31C. Saving of laws giving effect to certain directive principles.– Notwithstanding anything contained in article 13, no law giving effect to the policy of the State towards securing the principles specified in clause (b) or clause (c) of article 39 shall be deemed to be void on the ground that it is inconsistent with, or takes away or abridges any of the rights conferred by article 14, article 19 or article 31; and no law containing a declaration that it is for giving effect to such policy shall be called in question in any court on the ground that it does not give effect to such policy:

In *Kesavananda Bharati* v. *Kerala* (1973),[9] the Supreme Court of India acquiesced and overruled *Golak Nath*. However, by a slender majority of seven to six judges, the Court held that while Parliament could amend any part of the Indian Constitution, including the enshrined provisions on fundamental rights, it could not amend the 'basic structure' of the Indian Constitution.

But the direct impact of the Court's ruling in *Kesavananda* was far more modest than its rhetoric. The 24th Amendment was upheld in its entirety. The 25th Amendment was also largely upheld, save a sub-section which provided that any law passed with a declaration that it was intended to give effect to the Directive Principles on the State's socio-economic policies could not be 'called in question in any court on the ground that it does not give effect to such policy.'[10] The majority judges argued that, by ousting judicial review altogether, the amendment violated an implied 'essential feature' of the Indian Constitution and was thus unconstitutional.[11] Therefore, in *Kesavananda*, the Court crafted a political compromise: it caved on Gandhi's socio-economic agenda – in view of her massive 1971 electoral win – but also warned Gandhi about the limits of her rule.[12]

Political tensions between the judiciary and the ruling Congress government escalated further in June 1975 when an Allahabad High Court judge convicted Gandhi of two electoral violations and disqualified her from office for six years. While the decision was stayed by the Supreme Court pending appeal, Gandhi responded by declaring a State of Emergency throughout India and passed a slew of statutory amendments to reverse the lower court's decision. In essence, Gandhi had tasked public servants to logistically support her 1971 re-election campaign, which was an electoral infraction. In response to the Allahabad High Court decision, the regulatory coverage of the electoral laws was amended to exclude election candidates who had *not* been officially nominated – Gandhi was *not* at the material time – and logistical assistance rendered by public servants would

Provided that where such law is made by the Legislature of a State, the provisions of this article shall not apply thereto unless such law, having been reserved for the consideration of the President, has received his assent."'

9 (1973) 4 SCC 225; AIR 1973 (SC) 1461.

10 See 25th Amendment of the Indian Constitution (n 8).

11 For extended discussions of the Supreme Court's decision in *Kesavananda*, see Granville Austin, *Working a Democratic Constitution: The Indian Experience* (New Delhi: Oxford University Press, 1999); C.C. Aikman, 'The Debate on the Amendment of the Indian Constitution,' (1978) 9 *Victoria University of Wellington Law Review* 357.

12 Rosalind Dixon and David Landau, 'Transnational Constitutionalism and a Limited Doctrine of Unconstitutional Constitutional Amendment' (2015) 13 *International Journal of Constitutional Law* 606.

also not constitute an electoral violation. All these statutory changes were also made retrospective, thereby absolving Gandhi from all criminal liability. But the passage of the statutory amendments did not satisfy Gandhi. Her pliant Parliament also passed the 39th Amendment, which insulated the Prime Minister's election from any judicial inquiry and rendered pending proceedings in respect of such elections null and void.

In *Indira Gandhi* v. *Raj Narain* (1975),[13] the Supreme Court once again forged a political compromise. Strategically, the Court unanimously upheld Gandhi's election. Parliament had made the statutory changes retrospective and the Court upheld its right to do so. But, by a majority of four judges to one, the Court also invalidated the 39th Amendment. For Chandrachud J, the constitutional amendment had negated the right to equality as it had discriminated in favour of the Prime Minister; Khanna J held that the constitutional amendment infringed upon the 'principle of free and fair elections';[14] and Mathew J opined that the impugned amendment had attempted to undermine 'the exercise of judicial power [to] ascertaining the adjudicative facts'.[15] Even Ray CJ – who had dissented in *Kesavananda* and had been specially picked to supersede three more senior judges as Chief Justice[16] – invalidated the amendment on the basis that it was not 'applying any law and it, therefore, offended the rule of law'.[17]

The 'basic structure' doctrine was first conceived and developed as a judicial response to the legislative excesses of the Congress government, which had relied on a supine Parliament to effect constitutional changes that the 'hyper-executive' government unilaterally wanted. However, in the face of a belligerent Prime Minister and her super-dominant government, the Supreme Court drew a symbolic line in the sand but largely acquiesced to their demands. The State of Emergency imposed in 1975 led to the suspension of fundamental rights and the detention of opposition politicians without trial. But the Supreme Court simply turned a blind eye.[18] Emboldened by this perceived judicial weakness, the Congress-led government passed the 42nd Amendment in 1976, which made nearly 60 significant changes to the Indian Constitution, including an express elimination of judicial review over constitutional amendments.[19]

13 [1976] 2 SCR 347.
14 *Ibid.* [215].
15 *Ibid.* [309].
16 Austin (n 11), 278–292.
17 [1976] 2 SCR 347 [59].
18 *ADM Jabalpur* v. *Shivkant Shukla* (1976) 2 SCC 521.
19 After the Janata Party won the general election in 1977, it passed the 44th Amendment to the Indian Constitution, which repealed several key provisions in the controversial 42nd

Indian Supreme Court in a Dynamic Democracy

The legislative excesses of the Gandhi government during the Emergency eventually led to her party's resounding defeat in the 1977 general election. The Janata Party's victory at the polls was a watershed event in India, as it marked the first time since independence that a non-Congress party took command. Even though the Janata Party's time in government was short-lived – as Congress prevailed once again in the 1980 election – Gandhi returned to power sufficiently humbled and subdued.

Gandhi's electoral defeat gave the Supreme Court a new lease of life. In the 1980s, the Supreme Court gradually expanded its jurisprudence on fundamental rights and became an active participant in the dispensation of social justice.[20] But it was only when electoral politics in India fragmented further in the 1990s that the Court gained more political space to address a major systemic issue in India's electoral system: material corruption.

Congress lost its majority in the Lok Sabha (Lower House of Parliament) in the 1989 election. More significantly, 1989 marked the rise of minority governments in India, which persisted till 2014 when the Bharatiya Janata Party (BJP) was returned to power with an absolute majority.[21] As the governance of the largest democracy in the world was stymied by unstable and fractious coalition governments – compounded by the ascendance of regional and caste-based parties in national politics[22] – the Supreme Court exploited its newfound 'policy' space to address systemic material corruption and criminality in Indian politics.[23]

Material corruption – the abuse of public office for personal financial gain – is pervasive in Indian politics.[24] Vast networks of criminal syndicates have built extensive linkages with governmental officials and bureaucrats.

Amendment. The ouster of any judicial review over constitutional amendments was also invalidated by the Supreme Court in *Minerva Mills* v. *Union of India* (1980) 3 SCC 625.

20 See Andhyarujina (n 4).

21 In the 2014 general election, BJP, on its own, won 282 of the 554 elected seats in the Lok Sabha.

22 Sanjay Kumar, 'A Shift towards Regionalisation of Indian Politics', in Sudha Pai (ed.), *Handbook of Politics in Indian States: Regions, Parties and Economic Reforms* (New Delhi: Oxford University Press, 2013), 148.

23 See Aditya Sondhi, 'Elections', in Sujit Choudhry, Madhav Khosla, and Pratap Bhanu Mehta (eds), *The Oxford Handbook of the Indian Constitution* (Oxford: Oxford University Press, 2016), and Surya Deva, 'Democracy and Elections in India: Reviewing the Role of the Election Commission and the Courts' in Po Jen Yap (ed.), *Judicial Review of Elections in Asia* (London: Routledge, 2016), 38–56.

24 Manoj Mate, 'High Courts and Election Law Reform in the United States and India' (2014) *Boston University International Law Journal* 267, 292–294.

In turn, the infiltration of billions of unregulated 'black' money into Indian politics has undermined the fairness of elections and impacted the nation's socio-economic development adversely.[25] Many criminals have in fact sought direct access to power by becoming legislators themselves.[26] Political parties are also attracted to rich candidates: they regularly allot a certain percentage of party tickets to candidates who can finance their own campaigns or compensate the parties financially.[27] Well-financed criminals have also been successful at the polls. Since official records were taken in 2004, at least 24% of the Members of Parliament in the Lok Sabha have declared criminal antecedents, and at least 12% of the legislators were involved in police probes relating to serious crimes.[28] In fact, in the current Lok Sabha, 34% of the elected parliamentarians have declared that they possessed criminal antecedents or have pending criminal charges against them.[29]

Common Cause v. *Union of India* (1996)[30] was the first significant decision handed down by the Supreme Court against systemic corruption in politics. Political parties are required by law to maintain accounts of their incomes and donations, and file annual tax returns. But, prior to *Common Cause*, none of the major parties – BJP, Congress, and Janata – complied with this legal requirement. Furthermore, individual lawmakers were circumventing the statutorily imposed campaign expenditure limits[31] by declaring that certain expenditures were incurred on their behalf by their political parties – a statutory exception.[32] The Supreme Court in *Common*

[25] Vohra Committee of the Government of India Ministry of Home Affairs, *Vohra Committee Report*, para. 6.2.

[26] Law Commission of India, *Electoral Disqualifications* (Report No. 244), February 2014, 15 <http://lawcommissionofindia.nic.in/reports/report244.pdf> accessed 1 February 2017.

[27] See Milan Vaishnav, 'The Market for Criminality: Money, Muscle and Elections in India', unpublished paper (2011) <https://casi.sas.upenn.edu/sites/casi.sas.upenn.edu/files/iit/Market%20for%20Criminality%20-%20Aug%202011.pdf> accessed 1 February 2017, and Niranjan Sahoo, 'Spectrum, Election and Corruption Conundrum', unpublished paper (2011) <http://www.orfonline.org/research/spectrum-election-and-corruption-conundrum> accessed 1 February 2017. In the 2014 Lok Sabha Election, 31% of the Members of Parliament declared that they did not receive any campaign funding from their respective political parties. See Association for Democratic Reforms, *Lok Sabha Election Watch 2014*, 327 <http://adrindia.org/sites/default/files/Lok_Sabha_Report_2014_compressed.pdf> accessed 1 February 2017.

[28] *Lok Sabha Election Watch 2014* (n 27), 47.

[29] *Ibid.*

[30] [1996] 3 SCR 1208.

[31] The limit results from the combined effect of Section 77(3) of the Representation of the People Act, 1951 and Rule 90 of the Conduct of Election Rules 1961.

[32] Explanation 1 to Section 77 of the Representation of the People Act, 1951 reads: 'Notwithstanding any judgment, order or decision of any court to the contrary, any

Cause astutely addressed both problems together. First, the Court cut down the scope of the statutory exception by stating that the onus was on the individual politician to prove that the expenditure was in fact incurred by his or her party and not by him or her.[33] More significantly, this burden of proof could only be discharged if the politicians' own parties had filed tax returns on their audited parties' accounts, and the disputed expenditure was in fact declared in those accounts.[34] Therefore, by tying the politicians' personal liability to their parties' regulatory compliance, the Supreme Court was able to compel the political parties and their politicians to be more transparent about the amount and source of their donations.

Next, in response to a petition alleging that India's Central Bureau of Investigation (CBI) had failed to investigate and prosecute various prominent politicians for graft, the Supreme Court in *Vineet Narain* v. *Union of India*[35] issued a series of directives that reorganised the CBI's administrative structure, and conferred the Central Vigilance Commission – India's anti-graft public agency – with the authority to oversee the CBI's operations.[36]

In 1999, the Law Commission of India recommended that legislation be passed to require all candidates contesting in Lok Sabha elections to declare their assets and criminal antecedents.[37] But Parliament refused. Dissatisfied with the state of affairs, the Court in *Union of India* v. *Association for Democratic Reforms* (2002)[38] held that the right to free expression[39] protected in the Indian Constitution would 'include casting of votes',[40] and for this purpose, 'information about the candidate to be selected is a must'.[41] Therefore, 'in the absence of suitable legislation',[42]

expenditure incurred or authorised in connection with the election of a candidate by political party or by any other association or body of persons or by any individual (other than the candidate or his election agent) shall not be deemed to be, and shall not ever be deemed to have been, expenditure in connection with the election incurred or authorised by the candidates or by his election agent for the purposes of this sub-section.'

33 [1996] 3 SCR 1208 [20].

34 *Ibid.* [19–20].

35 (1998) 1 SCC 226.

36 Po Jen Yap, 'New Democracies and Novel Remedies' (n 1).

37 Law Commission of India, *170th Report on Reform of the Election Law*, 1999 <www.lawcommissionofindia.nic.in/lc170.htm> accessed 1 February 2017.

38 [2002] 3 SCR 696.

39 Article 19(1)(a) of the Indian Constitution reads: 'All citizens shall have the right … to freedom of speech and expression.'

40 [2002] 3 SCR 696 [54(7)].

41 *Ibid.*

42 *Ibid.* [52].

the Court was empowered to direct the Election Commission to 'fill the void'[43] and mandate that each Lok Sabha candidate should declare in an affidavit his or her criminal antecedents, pending criminal charges, assets and liabilities, and educational qualifications.[44]

Displeased with the new disclosure requirements imposed by the Court, the Indian Parliament responded with a statutory amendment that partially reversed the ruling in *Association for Democratic Reforms*. The amended law required election candidates to declare their criminal antecedents and pending criminal charges, but not their assets and liabilities nor their educational qualifications. More significantly, Section 33B of the amended legislation stated that no candidate was required to furnish any additional information that was not statutorily imposed,[45] thereby overruling those additional disclosure requirements imposed in *Association for Democratic Reforms* that were not enshrined into law. But in *People's Union for Civil Liberties* v. *Union of India* (2003) (PUCL),[46] the Supreme Court fought back. In particular, the controversial Section 33B was unanimously invalidated by the Court. According to Justice Shah, who penned the leading opinion, the disclosure requirements imposed by the Court in *Association for Democratic Reforms* vindicated the citizenry's *constitutional* right to free expression, and therefore could not be overturned by a mere statute.[47] While the majority in *PUCL* (2003) expressly rejected Parliament's right to statutorily trim any disclosure requirements imposed by the Court, Justice Reddi, in a concurring opinion, held that Parliament could scale back on the judicially imposed requirements, so long as the legislative reply was 'reasonably adequate to secure the right of information available to the voter/ citizen'. In particular, Justice Reddi, unlike the majority, took the view that a candidate's education was 'not a vital and useful piece of information to the voter',[48] and he would therefore uphold Parliament's refusal to compel disclosure on a candidate's education qualifications.[49]

[43] *Ibid.*

[44] *Ibid.* [56].

[45] Section 33B of the Representation of the People Act read: 'Notwithstanding anything contained in any judgment, decree or order of any court or any direction, order or any other instruction issued by the Election Commission, no candidate shall be liable to disclose or furnish any such information, in respect of his election which is not required to be disclosed or furnished under this Act or the rules made thereunder.'

[46] [2003] 2 SCR 1136.

[47] *Ibid.* [83].

[48] *Ibid.* [132].

[49] *Ibid.* [133(3)].

But the Supreme Court was soon ready to go beyond the imposition of new disclosure requirements on election candidates. It was going to directly remove criminals from politics. Section 8(3) of the Representation of the People Act (RPA) provides that 'a person convicted of any offence and sentenced to imprisonment for not less than two years' shall be disqualified from public office. And the Court began its expansive reading of this penal law to drive criminals from elected office. First, in *BR Kapur* v. *State of Tamil Nadu* (2001),[50] the Supreme Court held that this statutory disqualification also applied to politicians who were granted a suspended sentence of more than two years, pending appeal. Next, in *K Prabhakaran* v. *P Jayarajan* (2005),[51] the Court held that this statutory bar also applied if a politician was convicted of multiple offences and the sentences ran consecutively such that the aggregate period of imprisonment exceeded two years, even if individually the term of imprisonment for each offence was less than two years.

In *K Prabhakaran*, the Supreme Court rejected the argument that penal provisions must always be interpreted strictly in the accused's favour. Instead, as observed by the Court:

> *Those who break the law should not make the law. Generally speaking, the purpose sought to be achieved by enacting disqualification on conviction for certain offences is to prevent persons with criminal background from entering into politics, and the House – a powerful wing of governance … The provision has to be so meaningfully construed as to effectively prevent the mischief sought to be prevented. The expression 'a person convicted of any offence' has to be construed as all offences of which a person has been charged and held guilty at one trial. The applicability of the expression 'sentenced to imprisonment for not less than 2 years' would be decided by calculating the total term of imprisonment for which the person has been sentenced.*[52]

More recently, in *Lily Thomas* v. *Union of India* (2013),[53] the Supreme Court invalidated a statutory exception – Section 8(4) of the RPA – that accorded preferential treatment to political incumbents by allowing them to remain in office, notwithstanding their convictions and sentences, until their appeals were disposed of judicially.[54] The Court held that the

50 (2001) 7 SCC 231.
51 (2005) 1 SCC 754.
52 *Ibid.* [69]-[70].
53 (2013) 7 SCC 653.
54 Section 8(4) of the RPA read as follows: '[A] disqualification … shall not, in the case of a person who on the date of the conviction is a member of Parliament or the Legislature of a State, take effect until three months have elapsed from that date or, if within that period an

Constitution expressly prohibits Parliament from deferring the date on which the statutory disqualification applied.[55] Specifically, Article 102(1)(e) of the Constitution provides that 'a person shall be disqualified for being chosen as, and for being a member of either House of Parliament … if he is so disqualified by or under any law made by Parliament'. While Section 8(4) of the RPA was one such law passed by Parliament, the Court adopted a strained interpretation of the Constitution by reading the clause 'under any law' in Article 102(1)(e) as imposing a constitutional mandate on Parliament to apply the *same* law on both new and incumbent legislators.[56] Arguably, the impugned statutory provision could have been invalidated as a violation of equal protection,[57] an argument raised by counsel but not addressed by the Court.

The Supreme Court's drive to enhance the quality of parliamentarians continued in *People's Union for Civil Liberties* v. *Union of India* (2013).[58] In this case, the Court invalidated an administrative rule that required a voter to publicly sign a declaration if he or she decided *not* to vote for any of the candidates contesting. But it is noteworthy that this decision was justified on the basis that the compromise of voter secrecy violated the electorate's constitutional right to expression.[59] Consequently, the Election Commission in collaboration with the federal Government was directed to implement a 'None of the Above' option in the Electronic Voting Machines, so that voters can vote anonymously against all the available choices.[60] This important systemic change – albeit modest as NOTA votes do not have an impact on election results – was justified by the Court on the following basis:

> *Giving right to a voter not to vote for any candidate while protecting his right of secrecy is extremely important in a democracy. Such an option gives the voter the right to express his disapproval with the kind of candidates that are being put up by the political parties. When the political parties will realise that a large number of people are expressing their disapproval with the*

appeal or application for revision is brought in respect of the conviction or the sentence, until that appeal or application is disposed of by the court.'

55 (2013) 7 SCC 653 [20].

56 *Ibid.* [16].

57 Article 14 of the Indian Constitution reads: 'The State shall not deny to any person equality before the law or the equal protection of the laws within the territory of India.'

58 (2013) 10 SCC 1.

59 *Ibid.* [24].

60 This judicial direction has been implemented by the Election Commission in 2013 and voters can now vote in secret against all contesting parliamentary candidates. See *Lok Sabha Election Watch 2014* (n 27), 39.

> *candidates being put up by them, gradually there will be a systemic change and the political parties will be forced to accept the will of the people and field candidates who are known for their integrity.*[61]

Interestingly, in *Manoj Narula* v. *Union of India* (2014),[62] the Supreme Court stayed its hand and held that there was no constitutional obligation on the Prime Minister against appointing Cabinet Ministers who had been charged with serious crimes. But one must note that the petition was first filed in 2006 against various controversial Ministerial appointments made by Prime Minister Manmohan Singh of the Congress Party. By the time the decision was handed down in 2014, Prime Minister Narendra Modi from the BJP had just taken office and the underlying controversy was rendered moot. Perhaps as a gesture of goodwill to a new Prime Minister, the Supreme Court emphasised that the RPA expressly disqualified persons after they had been convicted in court; and while the Indian Law Commission in 2014 had pressed for a statutory amendment to also disqualify persons charged with serious crimes,[63] such a 'disqualification cannot be added'[64] by the Court. Instead, the Court held that it should be 'left to the wisdom of the Prime Minister'[65] to 'liv[e] up to the trust reposed in him'[66] and not appoint such unsavoury characters to public office.

The lead opinion in *Manoj Narula* was penned by Justice Dipak Misra, who soon jettisoned his prior reluctance to legislate from the bench. Several months later, in *Krishnamoorthy* v. *Sivakumar* (2015),[67] Dipak Misra J, on behalf of the Supreme Court, held that an election candidate's failure to disclose criminal antecedents or pending serious criminal charges in his or her nomination form constituted a corrupt practice, and if he or she were elected, the election would be set aside. One may note that in the 244th Report (2014) referenced in *Manoj Narula*, the Indian Law Commission had expressly highlighted that false or inaccurate disclosures did not trigger any serious consequences for the errant candidates: non-disclosure of such material information neither constituted a corrupt practice nor was it a ground to void an election.[68] This time, in response to Parliament's failure to remedy this legislative lacuna, the Supreme Court decided to go about

[61] (2013) 10 SCC 1 [55].
[62] (2014) 9 SCC 1.
[63] *Electoral Disqualifications* (n 26), 50–54.
[64] (2014) 9 SCC 1 [86].
[65] *Ibid.*
[66] *Ibid.*
[67] (2015) 3 SCC 467.
[68] *Electoral Disqualifications* (n 26), 48.

it on its own. The Court held that the failure to disclose one's criminal antecedents – including pending cases where serious criminal charges had been framed – constituted an act of 'undue influence' under Section 123(2) of the RPA.[69] Since 'undue influence' amounted to a 'corrupt practice' under the RPA, the election of the perpetrator could be set aside. But one must note that 'undue influence' in the RPA is merely defined in Section 123(2) as any direct or indirect interference with a person's exercise of any electoral right. Notwithstanding this, in an expansive reading of the term, the Court held that the concealment of any material information relating to the candidate's criminal antecedents deprived the voters of 'an informed and advised choice'[70] such that this practice should equally constitute an indirect interference with the voters' electoral rights.

More recently, in 2017, the Supreme Court in *Abhiram Singh* v. *C.D. Commachen & Others*[71] expanded the regulatory ambit of Section 123(3) of the RPA[72] and decided that the stipulated legislative provision also prohibited electoral candidates from referencing the religion, caste, community, or language of the *voters* during their campaigns. It is noteworthy that, on a literal reading of the law, the said provision only deemed as a corrupt practice any reference by electoral candidates to the religion, caste, community, or language of the candidates themselves and not the voters. For years, the BJP has been contesting elections on a Hindu nationalist agenda and party members have regularly stoked anti-Muslim sentiments to win votes, and this important ruling was handed down on the heels of a then-pending state election in Uttar Pradesh – India's most populous state – where religion and caste had dominated the campaigns.[73]

69 Section 123(2) of the RPA reads: 'Corrupt practices.– The following shall be deemed to be corrupt practices for the purposes of this Act: –
(2) Undue influence, that is to say, any direct or indirect interference or attempt to interfere on the part of the candidate or his agent, or of any other person [with the consent of the candidate or his election agent], with the free exercise of any electoral right.'

70 (2015) 3 SCC 467 [86].

71 Civil Appeal No. 37 of 1992 (Supreme Court of India).

72 Section 123(3) of the RPA reads: 'The following shall be deemed to be corrupt practices for the purposes of this Act: … The appeal by a candidate or his agent or by any other person with the consent of a candidate or his election agent to vote or refrain from voting for any person on the ground of his religion, race, caste, community or language or the use of, or appeal to religious symbols or the use of, or appeal to, national symbols, such as the national flag or the national emblem, for the furtherance of the prospects of the election of that candidate or for prejudicially affecting the election of any candidate.'

73 'Indian Court Bans Politicians from Using Religion, Caste to Win Votes', *Reuters*, 4 January 2017 <http://in.reuters.com/article/uk-india-law-religion-idINKBN14O1CO> accessed 1 February 2017.

By prohibiting as a corrupt practice the appeal to voters on religious/ethnic grounds, the Supreme Court was attempting to force politicians to abandon their divisive communalist electoral strategy in upcoming state and national elections.

As the Supreme Court combats corrupt parliamentarians, its animus toward criminals in politics has had an unfortunate spill-over effect on the voting rights of convicts. Since *People's Union for Civil Liberties* v. *Union of India* (2013), the Supreme Court has recognised that the right to vote constituted a form of political expression protected under the Constitution. But it has also consistently rejected the proposition that this right extended to convicts. In *Anukul Chandra Pradhan* v. *Union of India*,[74] the Supreme Court made the following observation:

> *If the object [of the law] is to keep persons with criminal background away from the election scene, a provision imposing a restriction on a prisoner to vote cannot be called unreasonable.*[75]

In its zeal to 'prevent [the] criminalisation of politics and maintain probity in elections',[76] the Court has regularly acquiesced to Parliament's blanket ban on all prisoners from voting in parliamentary elections, regardless of the severity of their offences. The Court reaffirmed this regressive position again in *Chief Election Commissioner* v. *Jan Chaukidar (Peoples Watch)* (2013).[77] A more nuanced and proportionate response would be for the Court to allow detainees convicted only of minor offences to vote, such that the State can still exclude persons imprisoned for offences relating to violent crimes, corruption, and major electoral infractions from the political process.

Conclusion

Between 1989 and 2014, no political party in India was able to win a majority of the seats in the Lok Sabha, and successive minority governments had to rely on the support of regional and caste-based parties to govern. With this fragmentation of political power, the Supreme Court of India gained 'policy' space and power to address on its own the socio-political woes that plague the nation.

[74] (1997) 6 SCC 1.
[75] *Ibid.* [6].
[76] *Ibid.* [4].
[77] [2013] 10 SCR 1163.

The Supreme Court's expansive reading of the RPA and its embrace of a positive right to information are judicial attempts to combat corruption in Parliament by ousting criminals from politics and promoting informed voting amongst the electorate.[78] But one must note that India's brand of judicial activism is not confined to its anti-corruption drive. The Court's valiant effort to rein in systemic corruption is merely part of its wider intervention in all spheres of India's public life.[79] In response to the perceived intransigence, incompetence, or inattentiveness of the political branches,[80] the Court has chosen to issue detailed judicial directives on a litany of common-place social woes in India: sexual harassment in the workplace,[81] garbage disposal,[82] traffic control,[83] and even ragging in universities.[84] In short, the Supreme Court of India has become – as some critics call it – an all-in-one governance agency.[85]

Even as the BJP was returned to power in 2014 with an absolute majority in Parliament – a first for any party in 25 years – early signs indicate that the Court will not be relinquishing its managerial role anytime soon. Most recently, the Court invalidated a constitutional amendment that revamped judicial appointments to the Supreme Court and High Courts – judges would be appointed by a six-member National Judicial Appointments Commission (chaired by the Chief Justice)[86] in lieu of the prior judge-led collegium system where the judges themselves had

[78] See Manoj Mate, 'India's Participatory Model: The Right to Information in Election Law' (2016) 48 *Georgetown Washington International Law Journal* 377, 435.

[79] But one should note that the Supreme Court which is staffed by about 31 judges usually resolves disputes in panels of two or three judges, and these small-panel decisions can be reconsidered by benches of five or more judges. See Chintan Chandrachud, 'Measuring Constitutional Case Salience in the Indian Supreme Court' (2014) 6 *Journal of Indian Law and Society* 42.

[80] Kent Roach and Geoff Budlender, 'Mandatory Relief and Supervisory Jurisdiction: When is it Appropriate, Just and Equitable?' (2005) 122 *South African Law Journal* 325; Young (n 3), 189.

[81] *Vishaka* v. *State of Rajasthan* (1997) 6 SCC 241.

[82] *BL Wadehra* v. *Union of India* (1996) 2 SCC 594.

[83] *MC Mehta* v. *Union of India* (1997) 8 SCC 770.

[84] *Vishwa Jagriti Mission* v. *Central Government* (2001) 6 SCC 577.

[85] Surya Deva, 'Public Interest Litigation in India: A Quest to Achieve the Impossible?' in Po Jen Yap and Holning Lau (eds), *Public Interest Litigation in Asia* (London: Routledge, 2010), 57.

[86] See *Supreme Court Advocates-on-Record* v. *Union of India*, Writ Petition (Civil) No. 13 of 2015. The six members on the Commission would have been the Chief Justice, two most senior judges on the Supreme Court, the Law Minister, and two persons appointed by a Committee composed of the Chief Justice, the Prime Minister, and the Leader of the Opposition in Lok Sabha.

near-complete control over the appointment process.[87] By declaring the constitutional amendment to be a violation of the basic structure doctrine, the Court swiftly restored the status quo.

Confronted with a government/bureaucracy that is beset by inertia, the Supreme Court of India has taken upon itself the responsibility of compelling action when the political branches are in serious and chronic default.[88] For better or worse, judges of the Indian Supreme Court have taken the failures of the existing democratic institutions as a mandate for them to 'replace these institutions and carry out some or all of their tasks'.[89]

[87] For a critique of the Supreme Court decision, see Chintan Chandrachud, 'Debating the NJAC Judgment of the Supreme Court of India: Three Dimensions', *UK Constitutional Law Association Blog*, 3 November 2015 <https://ukconstitutionallaw.org/2015/11/03/chintan-chandrachud-debating-the-njac-judgment-of-the-supreme-court-of-india-three-dimensions/> accessed 1 February 2017.

[88] See Manoj Mate, 'Public Interest Litigation and the Transformation of the Supreme Court of India', in Diana Kapiszewski, Gordon Silverstein and Robert Kagan (eds), *Consequential Courts: Judicial Roles in Global Perspective* (Cambridge: Cambridge University Press, 2013), 262–288.

[89] David Landau, 'A Dynamic Theory of Judicial Role' (2014) 55 *Boston College Law Review* 1501, 1534.

6

The Constitutional Court of Taiwan and Calibrated Judicial Review

The Republic of China (ROC), or Taiwan, as it is more commonly known, is currently governed under an amended version of the ROC Constitution drafted by the Kuomintang (KMT) government and made operative across China in 1947. As war was waged between the KMT and the Chinese Communists, the Temporary Provisions Effective During the Period of Communist Rebellion (TP) were introduced by the KMT in 1948 to grant the ROC President extensive emergency powers.[1] Martial law was declared in May 1949 and, following the KMT's defeat on the mainland, President Chiang Kai-shek's regime retreated to Taiwan in December 1949.

Taiwan's Constitutional Court within a Dominant-Party Democracy

Authoritarian rule by the KMT persisted in Taiwan until the mid-1980s when Chiang Kai-shek's son and successor, President Chiang Ching-kuo, decided to initiate democratic reform within Taiwan. First, the KMT acquiesced to the establishment of the Democratic Progressive Party (DPP), an opposition party, in 1986. The following year, in 1987, martial law was finally lifted in Taiwan. With Chiang Ching-kuo's death in 1988, his successor, President Lee Teng-hui, accelerated the pace of constitutional reforms, and the Council of Grand Justices of the Judicial Yuan played an equally indispensable role in this regard.

The Council of Grand Justices or, as it is more commonly known today, the Constitutional Court of Taiwan, was established in 1948 pursuant to the ROC Constitution and the Judicial Yuan Organisation Act.

[1] For a fuller discussion, see Tom Ginsburg, *Judicial Review in New Democracies: Constitutional Courts in Asian Cases* (Cambridge: Cambridge University Press, 2003), 111–119. See also F. Fraser Mendel, 'Judicial Power and Illusion: the Republic of China's Council of Grand Justices and Constitutional Interpretation' (1993) 2 *Pacific Rim Law & Policy Journal* 157, 162.

Unsurprisingly, while Taiwan remained under martial law, the Council was largely a handmaiden of the KMT regime. Specifically, in 1954, the Council ruled that, in view of the 'severe calamity' that the country was experiencing, Legislative Yuan elections were to be suspended and lawmakers elected in 1948 could continue in office until the next election was called.[2] This Interpretation No. 31 (1954) essentially authorised for the national representatives elected in Mainland China to remain in power in Taiwan for decades.

By the late 1980s, these geriatric legislators had become a huge liability for Lee Teng-hui's KMT government. There was overwhelming public consensus in favour of retiring these old guards, and the KMT elites, too, wanted them gone. But it was awkward for the KMT administration to force their own senior colleagues to retire.[3] Therefore, the Council was invited to resolve this conundrum and it obliged.

In Interpretation No. 261 (1990), the Court held that neither its Interpretation No. 31 nor the TP was 'intended to permit the indefinite exercise of powers by the first-term Legislators'.[4] As the 'periodic election of representatives is an essential avenue for reflection of the will of the people',[5] the Court held that those national representatives who had not been re-elected since 1948 would have to leave office by 31 December 1991, and new elections had to be called to re-elect the lawmakers.

This decision marked a milestone in Taiwan's constitutional development. But it was one that had the approval of the reform faction within the KMT, led by President Lee. Without this decision, Lee might never have consolidated his position within the KMT and pursued his democratisation agenda.[6] Following Interpretation No. 261, constitutional reforms were passed in 1991 to allow for political parties to be represented in Taiwan's Legislative Yuan in proportion to the popular votes that the parties won in the legislative election; and these party representatives would serve alongside the lawmakers directly elected in the individual geographical districts. Taiwan's first post-democratisation legislative election

[2] JY Interpretation No. 31, 29 January 1954 (Constitutional Court, Taiwan) <www.judicial.gov.tw/constitutionalcourt/en/p03_01.asp?expno=31> accessed 1 February 2017.

[3] See Chien-Chih Lin, 'Majoritarian Judicial Review: The Case of Taiwan' (2014) *National Taiwan University Law Review* 103, 119.

[4] JY Interpretation No. 261, 21 June 1990 (Constitutional Court, Taiwan) <www.judicial.gov.tw/constitutionalcourt/en/p03_01.asp?expno=261> accessed 1 February 2017.

[5] *Ibid.*

[6] See Ginsburg, *Judicial Review in New Democracies* (n 1), 146–147.

was held in 1992 and the KMT won 95 out of the 161 seats.[7] In 1996, the first direct presidential election was held and Lee Teng-hui won handily with 54% of the popular vote.[8]

Even as Taiwan transitioned to a competitive-party system in the 1990s, it is noteworthy that the KMT remained in power, albeit now with a mandate from the people. Operating within a dominant-party democracy where the KMT controlled both the Presidency and the Legislative Yuan, the Constitutional Court responded to its environment by exercising low-equilibrium judicial review of legislation. In the same vein as Interpretation No. 261, the Constitutional Court issued electoral decisions during this period that dovetailed with the interests of the KMT elites. In Interpretation No. 290 (1992), the Constitutional Court upheld an electoral law that required electoral candidates to possess certain minimum education qualifications and working experience before they could run for public office.[9] Next, in Interpretation No. 331 (1993), the Constitutional Court held that voters could not recall legislators who were nominated by their political parties to fill the party seats in the Legislative Yuan; these party representatives could only be removed from office by their respective parties.[10]

Similarly, the Constitutional Court in Interpretation No. 468 (1998) upheld two electoral provisions that required every potential Presidential candidate to garner endorsements from at least 1.5% of the total number of electorates and provide a security deposit of one million NT dollars, before he or she is statutorily eligible to run for office. According to the Court, these restrictions were not unreasonable as the law sought to prevent 'the people from needlessly participating in presidential and vice presidential elections, thus wasting social resources'.[11]

[7] Jiunn-rong Yeh, *The Constitution of Taiwan: A Contextual Analysis* (Oxford: Hart Publishing, 2016), 103.

[8] Zhao Suisheng, 'Reunification Strategy: Beijing Versus Lee Teng-hui', in Bruce J. Dickson and Chien-min Chao (eds), *Assessing the Lee Teng-hui Legacy in Taiwan's Politics: Democratic Consolidation and External Relations* (Armonk, New York: M.E. Sharpe, 2002), 230.

[9] JY Interpretation No. 290, 24 January 1992 (Constitutional Court, Taiwan) <www.judicial.gov.tw/constitutionalcourt/en/p03_01.asp?expno=290> accessed 1 February 2017.

[10] JY Interpretation No. 331, 30 December 1993 (Constitutional Court, Taiwan) <www.judicial.gov.tw/constitutionalcourt/en/p03_01.asp?expno=331> accessed 1 February 2017.

[11] JY Interpretation No. 468, 22 October 1998 (Constitutional Court, Taiwan) <www.judicial.gov.tw/constitutionalcourt/en/p03_01.asp?expno=468> accessed 1 February 2017. In fact, in the 1990s, the Constitutional Court had invalidated only one electoral law. In Interpretation No. 340 (1994), the Court quashed a law that disadvantaged independents (without party affiliation) from running for public office. All candidates seeking to run for public office had to pay a guarantee deposit but independents without party affiliation had to pay twice the sum required of a candidate sponsored by a political

Equally significant was Interpretation No. 419 (1996), where the Court had to decide whether (1) President Lee Teng-hui, just elected by the people in Taiwan's first direct Presidential election, could have his Vice President-elect, Lien Chan, concurrently stay on as his Premier, a post the latter held prior to the Presidential election; and (2) the incumbent Premier was required to resign prior to the inauguration of the newly elected President and be re-confirmed by the Legislative Yuan again.[12] President Lee had wanted Vice President Lien to concurrently stay on as Premier as the former wanted to avoid an acrimonious legislative re-confirmation. While the KMT had control of the Legislative Yuan, filibusters and violent fights, instigated by the opposition parties, had disrupted the legislative agenda for months.[13]

Fascinatingly, the Constitutional Court held that whilst the Constitution prohibited the President from concurrently serving as the Premier, there was nothing in the Constitution that expressly barred the Vice President from concurrently serving as Premier. However, with the same person holding both political offices, issues on power succession would arise if the position of President was vacated. Therefore, whilst such a concurrent appointment was not unconstitutional, the Court held that it was 'not completely in conformity with the Constitution's objective'.[14] Furthermore, the Court also held that there was no 'constitutional obligation'[15] on the incumbent Premier to resign and be re-appointed following a presidential election as this matter fell within the President's discretion, and was not subject to review by the Court. In response, the KMT-controlled government passed a constitutional amendment in 1997 to confer upon the President the *exclusive* right to appoint the Premier, but Vice President Lien Chan also resigned as Premier after the constitutional reforms were passed.[16]

party. See JY Interpretation No. 340, 25 February 1994 (Constitutional Court, Taiwan) <www.judicial.gov.tw/constitutionalcourt/en/p03_01.asp?expno=340> accessed 1 February 2017.

12 JY Interpretation No. 419, 31 December 1996 (Constitutional Court, Taiwan) <www.judicial.gov.tw/constitutionalcourt/en/p03_01.asp?expno=419> accessed 1 February 2017.

13 Jiunn-rong Yeh, 'Presidential Politics and the Judicial Facilitation of Dialogue between Political Actors in New Asian Democracies: Comparing the South Korean and Taiwanese Experiences' (2010) 8(4) *International Journal of Constitutional Law* 911, 933.

14 See JY Interpretation No. 419 (n 12).

15 *Ibid.*

16 Article 3 of the Additional Articles of the Constitution of the Republic of China (Taiwan) <http://english.president.gov.tw/Page/95> accessed 1 February 2017.

As discussed above, while Taiwan remained a dominant-party democracy, the Constitutional Court exercised low-octane review over the electoral practices of the incumbent KMT government. But it is of note that during this transitional period, the Court attempted to engage in 'soft' review by making non-binding recommendations or gently admonishing the political actors when their practices seemed constitutionally troubling.[17]

In Interpretation No. 290 (1992), while the Court upheld the electoral law that imposed minimum education qualifications and working experience on electoral candidates, it also suggested that 'as the pursuit of education grows even more popular and voters' ability to make informed choices becomes better, whether such restrictions should be maintained should be considered in light of the examples of other democracies'.[18] Similarly, in Interpretation No. 419 (1996), though the concurrent appointment of the Vice President as Premier was not declared invalid and void ab initio, the Court also observed that this was also 'not completely in conformity with the Constitution'.[19] Finally, in Interpretation No. 468 (1998), while the statutory barriers of entry imposed on potential Presidential candidates were upheld, the Court suggested that 'review and improvement should, of course, be conducted in due time as social conditions and political environments change, so as to conform to the constitutional intent to safeguard the people's suffrage'.[20]

Taiwan's Constitutional Court within a Dynamic Democracy

On 18 March 2000, Chen Shui-bian from the DPP won the Presidential election. This was a watershed event as Chen's election put an end to the KMT's uninterrupted rule over Taiwan. As Taiwan transitions into a dynamic democracy, where opposing parties are able to take turns in government, the Constitutional Court – no longer at the sufferance of one dominant party – also gains more 'policy' space to make systemic changes to the electoral system. Indeed, the judges did not wait very long before they re-calibrated and began to engage in high-equilibrium review.

17 See Neal Kumar Katyal, 'Judges as Advicegivers' (1998) 50 *Stanford Law Review* 1709; Po Jen Yap, *Constitutional Dialogue in Common Law Asia* (Oxford: Oxford University Press, 2015), 86.

18 JY Interpretation No. 290, 24 January 1992 (Constitutional Court, Taiwan) <www.judicial.gov.tw/constitutionalcourt/en/p03_01.asp?expno=290> accessed 1 February 2017.

19 See JY Interpretation No. 419 (n 12).

20 See JY Interpretation No. 468 (n 11).

Less than a week after Chen's victory at the presidential polls, the Constitutional Court issued Interpretation No. 499 (2000), which invalidated two major constitutional amendments passed by the National Assembly in 1999. (Prior to 2005, the National Assembly was the legislative body that was exclusively responsible for the passage of constitutional amendments.) In essence, delegates on the National Assembly had attempted to extend their existing term of office by over two years and also allow political parties and independents with seats in the Legislative Yuan (Taiwan's primary legislative chamber) to appoint delegates to the said Assembly, in proportion to the votes they won in the preceding Legislative Yuan election.[21]

By a majority of 13 to 4, the Constitutional Court invalidated the impugned constitutional amendments on the basis that their passage was procedurally flawed. For the majority, where procedural flaws in question were 'clear and gross',[22] the impugned constitutional amendments would be invalidated. It is noteworthy that, on the facts, the amendments had been voted on by the delegates anonymously, and the majority judges held that this violated the 'principles of openness and transparency'.[23] The Court held that, for constitutional amendments, 'open balloting' was necessary to allow the public to know how their elected representatives discharged their duties.[24]

Eleven out of the 13 judges unequivocally signed the majority opinion. Two judges, however, issued separate concurring opinions.[25] For Justice Lin Young-mou, while he agreed that the constitutional amendments should be invalidated on the basis that their passage was procedurally flawed, he argued that the 'clear and gross flaw' test was too deferential to the political branches, and he preferred a more rigorous standard of review. On the other hand, Justice Sun Sen-yen preferred to decide the procedural issue more narrowly. For him, the Constitution was silent on whether anonymous voting was permitted. But since internal regulations on National Assembly proceedings required an open vote when one third of the delegates requested for one, and since anonymous voting took place

[21] Yeh (n 7), 45.

[22] JY Interpretation No. 499, 24 March 2000 (Constitutional Court, Taiwan) <http://www.judicial.gov.tw/constitutionalcourt/en/p03_01.asp?expno=499> accessed 1 February 2017.

[23] *Ibid.*

[24] *Ibid.*

[25] *Ibid* (Concurring and dissenting opinions are only available in the Chinese language) <http://www.judicial.gov.tw/constitutionalcourt/p03_01.asp?expno=499> accessed 1 February 2017.

notwithstanding that a third of the delegates had made such a request, Justice Sun would invalidate the amendments on this narrow ground of procedural non-compliance.

On the other hand, 3 judges (Justice Su Jyun-hsiung, Justice Lai In-jaw, and Justice Chen Chi-nan) dissented on the procedural ground.[26] For them, the majority's opinion was flawed as the Constitution did not explicitly require constitutional amendments to be passed by an open vote, and the Court should therefore not interfere with the National Assembly's own internal proceedings.

With the constitutional amendments invalidated, the Constitutional Court could have left the matter at that. But, fascinatingly, the Court decided to proceed and address the issue of whether the two amendments were *substantively* invalid. More interestingly, by a majority of 15 to 2, the Court invalidated the amendments on substantive grounds. The two concurring judges (Justices Lin and Sun) and two of the judges (Justices Lai and Chen) who dissented on the procedural issue actually agreed with the majority that the substance of the amendments was unconstitutional.

According to the majority, there was a 'built-in, self-defensive mechanism'[27] in the Constitution which barred any constitutional amendment that violated 'basic principles of constitutional freedom and democratic rule of law' – implicit substantive constraints on constitutional change. This was so even though the Constitution did not 'expressly identify those unchangeable provisions'.[28] In the present case, as the delegates to the National Assembly had the supreme power to amend the Constitution, their appointment by political parties and independent legislators – in lieu of a vote by universal suffrage – violated 'the constitutional order of democracy'.[29] Furthermore, the unilateral extension of the delegates' existing term of office by over two years violated the 'principle of democratic constitutional rule of law'[30] and was also deemed invalid.

Finally, it is noteworthy that for the two judges who voted to uphold the constitutional amendments, neither of them disagreed with the majority that there were implied substantive limits on constitutional revisions in Taiwan. However, for Justice Su Jyun-hsiung, courts should exercise judicial

26 *Ibid.*
27 See JY Interpretation No. 499 (n 22).
28 *Ibid.*
29 *Ibid.*
30 *Ibid* (Concurring and dissenting opinions are only available in the Chinese language) <http://www.judicial.gov.tw/constitutionalcourt/p03_01.asp?expno=499> accessed 1 February 2017.

restraint when adjudicating over the propriety of constitutional reforms and should generally defer to public consensus.[31] He would also have preferred to decide the constitutionality of the term-extension amendment only after the delegates' term of office actually ceased. On the other hand, Justice Tseng Hua-sun argued that the entire constitutional petition should be dismissed on the ground that the dispute was not ripe for adjudication – the impugned amendments in question had not taken effect.

The National Assembly delegates were outraged by Interpretation No. 499 (2000) and they perceived this as an outrageous act of judicial activism. But as the public was very supportive of this decision and the KMT was politically weakened by its unprecedented loss of the Presidency, the National Assembly acquiesced. In 2000, a constitutional amendment was passed whereby the National Assembly was reduced to an ad-hoc institution, with its delegates elected from a party-list and only called into session when there was a constitutional amendment to be voted on. But the delegates also decided to 'punish' Constitutional Court judges who were non-career judges, as those drawn directly from academia were perceived to be more activist. For Constitutional Court justices who were previously *not* career judges, their pensions were no longer constitutionally guaranteed.[32]

The National Assembly was eventually abolished in 2005. Alongside its abolition, another major electoral reform via constitutional amendment was introduced. The number of electoral seats in the Legislative Yuan seats was reduced from 225 to 113. More importantly, 73 seats would be (geographical) district seats, with each city/county guaranteed a seat, regardless of its population size; and 34 seats would be reserved for political parties.[33] Each voter would have two votes, one to be cast for an individual contesting in his or her district, and one for his or her preferred political party. The 'party' seats would be awarded to the parties in proportion to the votes they win, but only if the party in question gained at least 5% of the total votes cast. It is noteworthy that this constitutional reform was agreed to by both the KMT and the DPP, as it helped consolidate the electoral strength of bigger political parties over smaller fringe ones.[34]

31 *Ibid.*

32 Article 5 of the Additional Articles of the Constitution of the Republic of China reads: 'The provisions of Article 81 of the Constitution and pertinent regulations on the lifetime holding of office and payment of salary do not apply to grand justices who did not transfer from the post of a judge.'

33 Article 4 of the Additional Articles of the Constitution of the Republic of China.

34 All of these constitutional changes introduced in 2005 were part of the 7th round of constitutional revisions to the Constitution of the Republic of China. In this same round, Article 12 of the Additional Articles of the Constitution of the Republic of China was

Unsurprisingly, smaller political parties, now disadvantaged at the polls, sought to invalidate these constitutional amendments. But in Interpretation No. 721 (2014), the Constitutional Court demurred and reaffirmed its central holding in Interpretation No. 499:

> *Unless its process of amendment contains clear and gross flaws or its content involves a breach of the constitutional democratic order, an amendment to the Constitution shall be respected (with reference to J.Y. Interpretation No. 499). In other words, so long as an amendment to the Constitution does not contradict the principle of the democratic republic and the principle of sovereignty of and by the people, or does not involve alteration to the core contents of fundamental rights of people or the principle of checks and balances of governmental powers, such an amendment does not breach the constitutional democratic order.*[35]

But, in this instance, the Court was unconvinced that the impugned amendments were substantively invalid. Although the 5% threshold would prevent a few political parties from gaining seats in the Legislative Yuan, the Court upheld its constitutionality on the basis that 'its purpose is to ensure the efficiency of legislative operations and the smooth interaction between the executive branch and the Legislature is not impeded by a clustering of small parties and fragmentation of the political party system'.[36] This is not an unreasonable ruling, as it is common amongst many modern democracies practising some variation of mixed-member proportional representation to impose an electoral floor when awarding 'party' seats, so as to deter 'fringe' extremist parties from taking root in Parliament.[37]

introduced, which provides that a constitutional amendment can only be passed in Taiwan now if it receives the support of at least three-fourths of the Legislative Yuan members present at a meeting attended by at least three-fourths of the total members of the Legislative Yuan, and approved by voters at a referendum wherein 'the number of valid votes in favour exceeds one-half of the total number of electors' in Taiwan.

35 JY Interpretation No. 721, 6 June 2014 (Constitutional Court, Taiwan) <www.judicial.gov.tw/constitutionalcourt/en/p03_01.asp?expno=721> accessed 1 February 2017.

36 *Ibid.*

37 For example, in New Zealand, there are two types of seats in Parliament: (1) 'constituency seats' – those filled by independents or party-affiliated candidates who win the most votes in each constituency/electorate and (2) 'list seats' – those filled by political parties only. There are usually 120 Parliamentary seats in total, comprising of 71 'constituency seats' and 49 'list seats'. In a general election, voters cast two votes: one 'electorate vote' for a candidate in his or her constituency, and one 'party vote' for the political party of his or her choice. But a political party will only get a share of the seats in Parliament that reflects its share of the 'party vote' if it wins (1) at least one 'constituency seat', or (2) at least 5% of the 'party vote': see section 191 (4) of the Electoral Act 1993.

Interestingly, in a concurring opinion, Justice Dennis Tang argued that the Court could not impose substantive constraints on constitutional amendments passed after April 2000.[38] In response to Interpretation No. 499, the Constitution was amended in 2000 whereby the National Assembly was reduced to an ad-hoc institution, with its delegates only elected and called into session when there was a constitutional amendment to be voted on. More importantly, each delegate was legally bound to vote in an open ballot and in accordance with his or her party's position on the constitutional amendment; and the party's position would be reflected on the ballot paper when the electorate voted for their delegates. Therefore, according to Justice Tang, such amendments reflected the democratic will and could not be invalidated by the Court on substantive grounds.

More troubling, however, is the seat allocation for district elections. With each county or city allocated one seat, regardless of its population size, the disparity of voting power of individuals living in differently populated counties becomes very stark. For example, the electoral district of Hsinchu County has a population of about 460,667 residents, while the electoral district of Matsu has a population of about 10,130 residents.[39] Yet, both counties can return one legislator each. In particular, this electoral scheme favours the KMT, which has traditionally been popular in the sparsely populated districts (e.g., off-shore islands and aboriginal areas).

But, in Interpretation No. 721 (2014), the Constitutional Court avoided ruling on this issue. As the petitioner, the Taiwan Constitution Association, only participated in the party election and not in the district election, the Court held that it had no standing to challenge the constitutionality of the seat allocation for the district election.[40]

It is unclear why the Court exercised more restraint over this constitutional amendment. Perhaps the substance of this amendment was less objectionable than the previous ones invalidated back in 2000. Or, as Ming-Sung Kuo has argued, the Constitutional Court has consciously decided to retreat to the political side-lines and be less activist than before.[41] But this state of affairs is unlikely to persist for long. With DPP's

[38] JY Interpretation No. 721 (Concurring and dissenting opinions are only available in the Chinese language) <www.judicial.gov.tw/constitutionalcourt/p03_01.asp?expno=721> accessed 1 February 2017.

[39] Yeh (n 7), 105–106.

[40] A second petitioner – the Green Party – also had its constitutional petition refused as the Court held that it had not been a party to the original lawsuit in the lower court.

[41] Ming-Sung Kuo, 'Moving Towards a Nominal Constitutional Court: Critical Reflections on the Shift from Judicial Activism to Constitutional Irrelevance in Taiwan's Constitutional Politics' (2016) 25 (3) *Washington International Law Journal* 597.

Tsai Ing-wen elected as Taiwan's President in 2016, and a Legislative Yuan that is now dominated by the DPP – a first in Taiwan's history – it is very plausible that future justices nominated to the Court by a DPP President and confirmed by a DPP-controlled Legislative Yuan would be keen to review any systemic electoral practices that singularly skew in favour of the KMT.[42] It is noteworthy that President Tsai would have the opportunity to appoint at least 11 new justices to the Court in her first term alone,[43] and with a Legislative Yuan that is controlled by her own party, the ideological make-up of the bench is going to shift dramatically.

The Constitutional Court as Non-partisan Arbiter

Even as the Constitutional Court, operating within a dynamic democracy, has the political capital and capacity to amplify the competitiveness of elections and electoral institutions, it is vital to its success for the Court to display non-partisanship and exercise restraint when its ruling may potentially overturn key elections or remove top leaders.

In Taiwan, after President Chen Shui-bian (from the DPP) was re-elected with a razor-thin margin in the 2004 Presidential Election, the KMT insisted that he had staged an assassination attempt on his life on the eve of the election so as to gain sympathy votes for his re-election.[44]

[42] Currently, the DPP has control of the Presidency and the Legislative Yuan. But even if the DPP loses its majority in the legislature in the 2020 election, Constitutional Court judges confirmed and appointed in President Tsai's first term will remain on the bench. But for any future constitutional amendment to be passed, bipartisan support and endorsement by the people in a referendum are needed. To avoid a legislative lacuna from arising if the 'seat allocation' constitutional amendment is deemed unconstitutional, the Court would have to issue on its own a remedial interpretation of the constitutional clause or a 'soft' remedy in the vein of Interpretation No. 419.

[43] Since 2003, the Constitutional Court is composed of 15 justices and each of them – except for the President and Vice President – serves a non-renewable eight-year term. See Article 5 of the Additional Articles of the Constitution of the Republic of China (Taiwan) <http://english.president.gov.tw/Page/95> accessed 1 February 2017. See Jau-Yuan Hwang, 'Taiwan's Constitutional Court from 2003 to 2011: New Appointments and Different Performance' (2012) 53 *Seoul Law Journal* 41, 52. As at 1 January 2017, six new Constitutional Court judges have been confirmed by the DPP-controlled legislature in President Tsai's first term. In addition, Hsu Tzong-li was confirmed as the President of the Constitutional Court, even though he was first appointed as a Constitutional Court justice in 2003 by President Chen Shui-bian. See Alison Hsiao, 'Legislature Approves Judicial Nominees', *Taipei Times*, 26 October 2016 <http://www.taipeitimes.com/News/front/archives/2016/10/26/2003657934> accessed 1 February 2017.

[44] A gunman attempted to assassinate both President Chen Shui-bian and Vice President Annette Lu when they were campaigning on 19 March 2004, the eve of Taiwan's presidential

As the KMT retained a parliamentary majority in the Legislative Yuan, it statutorily created a special commission to investigate the foiled assassination attempt.[45] One may note that members on the special commission were primarily KMT affiliates and the deeply partisan commission was statutorily authorised to launch criminal prosecutions relating to the assassination attempt and overturn any factual findings in a court of law if they differed from the outcome of the investigation conducted by the commission.

In Interpretation No. 585 (2004), the Constitutional Court accepted that the Legislative Yuan was empowered to create a special commission to investigate the assassination attempt, but it decisively invalidated the statutory provisions that authorised the commission to launch criminal prosecutions and revoke judicial findings.[46] The Court's decision rendered on 15 December 2004, in essence, prevented the special commission from overturning a High Court's ruling on 4 November 2004, which decided that the assassination attempt was neither staged by President Chen nor did the gunshot incident illegally interfere with the conduct of the election.[47]

It is noteworthy that the judges on the Court – appointed by both KMT[48] and DPP Presidents (after being confirmed by a KMT-dominated Legislative Yuan) – were unanimous in disallowing the KMT from using a partisan special commission to overturn the election of a DPP President, especially when he had already been vindicated in the lower court. Thwarted by the Court, the KMT-controlled Legislative Yuan retaliated by removing bonuses from the salaries of the Constitutional

election; but both of them suffered only minor injuries. This event has been termed the '319 Shooting' in Taiwan.

45 See Yeh (n 13), 932.

46 JY Interpretation No. 585, 15 December 2004 (Constitutional Court, Taiwan) <www.judicial.gov.tw/constitutionalcourt/en/p03_01.asp?expno=585> accessed 1 February 2017.

47 Gaodeng Fayuan [High Court], Civil Division, 93 Hsuan 2 (2004); For a discussion of the High Court's decision, see Wen-Chen Chang and Yi-Li Lee, 'Judicial Strategies to Resolving Presidential Election Disputes: the Case of Taiwan', in Po Jen Yap (ed.), *Judicial Review of Elections in Asia* (London: Routledge, 2016), 154–157. The High Court's decision was upheld by the Supreme Court on 17 June 2015.

48 In 2003, President Chen Shui-bian reappointed four Constitutional Court justices who were originally appointed by KMT's Lee Teng-hui <http://www.judicial.gov.tw/constitutionalcourt/p08.asp> accessed 1 February 2017. Now, each Constitutional Court judge, with the exception of the President and the Vice President, can only serve a non-renewable eight-year term. See Article 5 of the Additional Articles of the Constitution of the Republic of China (Taiwan) <http://english.president.gov.tw/Page/95> accessed 1 February 2017.

Court judges,[49] but the Court swiftly deemed this budgetary change unconstitutional and restored its own pay.[50]

Nevertheless, President Chen soon faced more legal woes. In 2006, allegations surfaced that the President and his wife had misappropriated public funds. As the President was immune from all criminal prosecutions (save for rebellion or treason) during his term in office,[51] the prosecution only charged his wife with embezzlement, though the President was expressly named as her accomplice in the charges. Inevitably, the Constitutional Court was tasked to adjudicate over the scope of the President's immunity and the legality of the prosecution's actions.

In Interpretation No. 627 (2007), the Constitutional Court unanimously rebuffed President Chen's argument that his immunity against prosecution also extended to the First Lady. Furthermore, although the President was immune from prosecution while he remained in office, the Court held that the immunity did not foreclose any investigation which sought to collect evidence that might be used against him after his term in office ended. But the Court was also judicious about imposing additional safeguards on the President's behalf against potential prosecutorial abuse. The President himself, his residence, and his office could not be searched, nor could the 'ordinary exercise of the presidential authorities be impeded'.[52]

In essence, the Constitutional Court was even-handed and non-partisan in its treatment of a beleaguered sitting President.[53] Insofar as the Court did not gang up against the President and remove him prematurely from office, the Court also safeguarded the rule of law by allowing the ordinary judicial process to take its course.[54]

[49] J. Chuang, 'Judiciary "disappointed"', *Taipei Times*, 22 January 2005 <www.taipeitimes.com/News/taiwan/archives/2005/01/22/2003220461> accessed 1 February 2017.

[50] JY Interpretation No. 601, 22 July 2005 (Constitutional Court, Taiwan) <www.judicial.gov.tw/constitutionalcourt/en/p03_01.asp?expno=601> accessed 1 February 2017.

[51] Article 52 of the Republic of China (ROC) Constitution reads: 'The President shall not, without having been recalled, or having been relieved of his functions, be liable to criminal prosecution unless he is charged with having committed an act of rebellion or treason.'

[52] JY Interpretation No. 627, 15 June 2007 (Constitutional Court, Taiwan) <www.judicial.gov.tw/constitutionalcourt/en/p03_01.asp?expno=627> accessed 1 February 2017.

[53] See Wen-Chen Chang, 'Strategic Judicial Responses in Politically Charged Cases: East Asian Experiences' (2010) 8(4) *International Journal of Constitutional Law* 885.

[54] Chen Shui-bian was arrested after his term in office ended in 2008. He was convicted by the Taipei District Court for corruption and money laundering in 2009 and received a life sentence. The life sentence was reduced by the High Court to a 20-year prison term in 2010. See Jon ST Quah, 'Taiwan's Anti-corruption Strategy: Suggestions for Reform' (2010) 2 *Maryland Series in Contemporary Asian Studies* 1, 49–51.

Conclusion

While Taiwan remained a dominant-party democracy, a constrained Constitutional Court was unable to rule against the reigning KMT interests with impunity. But this does not mean that the Court was politically irrelevant during this period. In 1990, the Constitutional Court had seized the opportunity to ally itself with the ascending faction within the KMT, led by President Lee Teng-hui, and forced out the geriatric delegates on the National Assembly, thereby ushering in elections for those vacated seats. Even where the Court felt unable to rule directly against mainstream KMT interests, it nevertheless engaged in 'soft' review by nudging the political branches towards an outcome that would be more compatible with constitutional mandates. Interpretation No. 419 (1996) is the best illustration of this. Whilst the Court did not outright invalidate President Lee's decision to retain his Vice-President as Premier concurrently, the Court nevertheless suggested that this dual appointment would not be in complete conformity with the Constitution. Even though the Court did not impose a deadline on Vice-President Lien to relinquish his concurrent Premiership, he did so in 1997, nine months after the judicial ruling.

With President Chen's victory in 2000, the KMT lost its stranglehold over Taiwan. Operating within a dynamic democracy whereby opposing political parties are able to take turn in office, the 'tolerance zones of institutions that might discipline the courts expand'.[55] In turn, a recalibrated Constitutional Court gains 'policy' ground to make systemic changes to the electoral scene, even if such changes are contrary to the interests of the establishment. In Interpretation No. 499 (2000), the Constitutional Court decisively invalidated constitutional amendments that attempted to extend the existing term of the National Assembly delegates and allow elected legislators to appoint delegates to the said Assembly. This ruling eventually led to the abolition of the anachronistic National Assembly in 2005. While the Constitutional Court may have the power and capacity to make systemic electoral reforms, this does not mean that it would always live up to its full potential. Its decision to duck the constitutional issue raised by the seat allocation for district elections – the disparity of voting power for individuals living in differently populated counties – is one such example. But with the Presidency and Legislative Yuan now under the control of the DPP for the first time in Taiwan's history, it is very plausible that the future justices appointed in President Tsai Ing-wen's

[55] Ginsburg (n 1), 252.

first term – at least 11 judges, to be exact – would be keen to review any systemic electoral practices that singularly skew in favour of the KMT.

But, to remain successful, the Constitutional Court of Taiwan must exercise restraint and remain non-partisan when its ruling may potentially overturn key elections or remove top leaders. In Interpretations Nos. 585 (2004) and 627 (2007), the Court was even-handed in its treatment of a beleaguered President Chen. By permitting the ordinary adjudicative process to take its course and not prematurely removing President Chen from office, the Court played a pivotal role in safeguarding the rule of law in Taiwan and sustaining the nation's democratic development.

Courts in dynamic democracies have the political capital and capability to introduce major systemic electoral reforms successfully. Where power is diffused and fragmented across rivalling political factions, courts are less likely to face legislative retaliation when they 'exercise independent input into politically salient decisions'.[56] Consequently, these dynamic courts can open up pathways for democratisation that would ordinarily be resisted by self-serving political incumbents.

[56] *Ibid.*

7

The Constitutional Court of Korea and Systemic Electoral Barriers

The Constitutional Court of Korea was conceived as an independent safeguard against authoritarian political rule when the current Constitution was passed in 1987. The establishment of the Sixth Republic[1] in 1988 was the culmination of the democratisation movement that had demanded for political change since South Korea's last military regime – headed by Chun Doo-hwan – took power in a coup in 1979.[2]

With direct elections for the Presidency introduced in 1987, Roh Tae-woo, a former general and close associate of Chun Doo-hwan, was elected as the Sixth Republic's first President. However, it is noteworthy that unlike the other two dynamic democracies, i.e., India and Taiwan as discussed earlier, South Korea never experienced a phase with a dominant party or coalition in control of its legislature after democratisation. Roh's Democratic Justice Party (DJP) only took 125 out of the 299 seats in the Sixth Republic's first National Assembly election in 1988.[3] Even when Roh merged the DJP with the parties of two political enemies – Kim Young-sam and Kim Jong-pil – to form the Democratic Liberal Party (DLP), the DLP was only able to win 149 of the 299 seats in the 1992 election.[4]

[1] Korea has had six Republics since its independence in 1945. Only the Second Republic, which existed for less than one year between 1960 and 1961, and the current Sixth Republic have been democracies. See Tom Ginsburg, *Judicial Review in New Democracies: Constitutional Courts in Asian Cases* (Cambridge: Cambridge University Press, 2003), 208–209.

[2] Tom Ginsburg, 'Constitutional Courts in East Asia: Understanding Variation' (2008) 3 *Journal of Comparative Law* 80, 85. See also James M. West and Dae-Kyu Yoon, 'The Constitutional Court of the Republic of Korea: Transforming the Jurisprudence of the Vortex?' (1992) 40 *American Journal of Comparative Law* 73.

[3] Aurel Croissant, 'Electoral Politics in South Korea' in Aurel Croissant, Gabriele Bruns and Marei John (eds), *Electoral Politics in Southeast and East Asia* (Singapore: Friedrich Ebert Stiftung, 2002), 269.

[4] *Ibid.*

In fact, weak political parties have been a cardinal feature of South Korea's modern electoral scene. Political parties are largely instruments of their powerful leaders with strong regional appeal and these parties continuously split, merge, or reconfigure as their party bosses leave the political stage.[5] The DJP became the New Korea Party in 1995, the Grand National Party (GNP) in 1997, and finally the current Saenuri Party in 2012.[6] This cycle of party mergers and breakups is not unique to the DJP and its successors. In the same vein, the DJP's main opposition, the Democratic Party, fragmented and reconfigured multiple times before it took on its current incarnation as the Minjoo Party in 2014. Equally significantly, Kim Dae-jung from one of the incarnations of the Democratic Party finally won the Presidency in 1998, a first for any opposition candidate; and Roh Moo-hyun from Kim Dae-jung's party succeeded him in 2003, though the GNP/Saenuri Party wrested back control of the Presidency in 2008. At the time of writing, Hwang Kyo-ahn, the former Premier of Saenuri Party's Park Geun-hye is the Acting President[7] – but the opposition, the Minjoo Party, has the largest number of seats in the National Assembly.[8]

The Constitutional Court – created only in 1987[9] and unhampered by past institutional and bureaucratic baggage – benefitted from Korea's weak party system as it expanded its judicial power without facing legislative retaliation or reprisals. Therefore, unlike India and Taiwan, which democratised under a dominant party, the Constitutional Court of Korea was able to exercise high-equilibrium review[10] from its inception and make *systemic* changes to the political system.

[5] Byung-Kook Kim, 'Party Politics in South Korea's Democracy: The Crisis of Success', in Larry Diamond and Byung-Kook Kim (eds), *Consolidating Democracy in South Korea* (Boulder, CO: Lynne Rienner Publishers, 2000), 53–60.

[6] Jiyoon Kim, 'The Party System in Korea and Identity Politics', in Larry Diamond and Gi-Wook Shin (eds), *New Challenges for Maturing Democracies in Korea and Taiwan* (Stanford: Stanford University Press, 2014), 76.

[7] President Park Geun-hye was removed from office in March 2017 by the Constitutional Court of Korea.

[8] In the 2016 legislative election, the Minjoo Party won 123 of the 300 seats in the National Assembly, one more seat than the Saenuri Party. See Giancarlo Elia Valori, 'Legislative Elections in South Korea', *Modern Diplomacy*, 21 April 2016 <http://moderndiplomacy.eu/index.php?option=com_k2&view=item&id=1363:legislative-elections-in-south-korea&Itemid=645> accessed 1 February 2017.

[9] A Constitutional Committee existed formally in the Fourth and Fifth Republic, but it was never called upon by the Supreme Court to exercise its constitutional powers during this period. See Ginsburg (n 1), 212–213.

[10] Ginsburg (n 1), 244.

The Constitutional Court and Systemic Electoral Redress

Practically from the get-go, the Constitutional Court began to tear down systemic barriers of entry that stifled political competition. In 1989, the Court declared that a statutory provision which required independent candidates in a National Assembly election to pay a deposit of 20 million Korean won – a quantum that was twice that of a party candidate – was 'non-conforming to the Constitution'[11] as the law unjustifiably placed independents at 'substantial competitive disadvantages and suppress[ed] their candidacy'.[12] This ruling of non-conformity allowed the impugned law to remain in place until the legislature passed appropriate remedial legislation. But when no remedial law was forthcoming, the Court decisively struck down the law in 2001. As observed by the Court:

> *People of ordinary means cannot easily raise 20 million won ... and this state of affairs has not changed since the Court's decision in 1989. And deposit requirement of 20 million won would make most people give up their political aspiration to become a member of the National Assembly. It is in itself a large sum of money for people in low-income groups and people in their twenties or thirties. Moreover, it could be said that such deposit requirement may be a financial burden even for members of the middle class (The average monthly real income of all industries of Korea in 2000 was 1.422 million won ...) ... The problem goes beyond the infringement on the rights of individual political aspirants, and it becomes a problem of social classes and generations. Excessive deposit requirements would make it difficult for people of ordinary means and members of younger generations from running for the National Assembly, and this means that representatives reflecting their voices would be absent in the National Assembly.*[13]

Similarly, in 2008, the Court declared that a deposit of 500 million Korean won for Presidential candidates was excessively prohibitive and was thus incompatible with the Constitution.[14] Even as the Constitutional Court

[11] 1 KCCR 199, 88 Hun-Ka 6 (8 September 1989) (Official English Translation of Case Summary). *Ibid.*

[12] *Ibid.*

[13] 13-2 KCCR 77, 2000 Hun-Ma 91, 2000 Hun-Ma 112, 2000 Hun-Ma 134 (consolidated) (19 July 2001) (Official English Translation). The deposit required for a National Assembly candidate has been reduced to 15 million Korean won. See Article 56(1) of the Public Official Election Act. <http://www.nec.go.kr/engvote_2013/05_resourcecenter/02_01.jsp> accessed 1 February 2017.

[14] 20-2(B) KCCR 477, 2007 Hun-Ma 1024 (27 November 2008). The election deposit for Presidential candidates has now been reduced to 300 million Korean won. See Article 56(1) of the Public Official Election Act <http://www.nec.go.kr/engvote_2013/05_resourcecenter/02_01.jsp> accessed 1 February 2017.

extended the right of ordinary citizens to stand for public office, it also concurrently expanded ballot access for voters. In 2007, a blanket ban prohibiting all Korean nationals residing overseas from voting was deemed not in conformity with the Constitution, and the National Assembly was given 18 months to enact a more reasonable legislative response.[15] Similarly in 2014, a complete prohibition on prisoner voting – including those serving suspended sentences – was deemed disproportionate. As the Court observed:

> *Considering the importance of the principle of popular suffrage and the right to vote, the right to vote should be restricted to the minimum extent only when it is necessary. Even though it is necessary to restrict [a] criminal's right to vote, blanket restriction on ... prisoners ... without considering the gravity of illegality of crimes committed by each of them, is contrary to the least restrictive requirement.*[16]

Accordingly, the National Assembly was given two years to pass a more nuanced law.[17]

More remarkably, the Constitutional Court has been able to reconfigure the process by which legislators are voted into the National Assembly. Like Taiwan, South Korea has adopted a mixed-member proportional representation system with single-member electoral districts and 'party' seats. Party seats in the National Assembly used to be allocated to political parties in proportion to the votes their candidates won in the district elections. But in 2001, the Constitutional Court held that this allocation of seats for the 'party' legislators – known as proportional representatives – was unconstitutional as it distorted democratic will:

> *Under the present election system, allowing one vote per person, a voter's support for a particular political party is assumed through one's vote for the candidate in the electoral district. This means that an elector has no option but to express one's choice of a candidate as well as one's support for a particular political party in a single vote. This poses a serious problem when the candidate of one's choice is not from the political party that he or she supports. In this case, the voter is in a dilemma. The elector has to choose whether to cast a vote for a candidate or for the political party, or has to find the best way*

[15] 19-1 KCCR 859, 2004 Hun-Ma 644 et al. (consolidated) (28 June 2007) (Official English Translation). Articles 218-4 and 218-5 of the Public Official Election Act now authorise absentee voting for Koreans residing overseas.

[16] 26-1(A) KCCR 136, 2012 Hun-Ma 409·510, 2013 Hun-Ma 167 (consolidated) (28 January 2014) (Official English Translation).

[17] Article 18 of the Public Official Election Act was amended and now permits prisoners serving suspended sentences to vote.

> *to maximize the value of his or her vote. In another case when the voter's favourite party does not nominate a candidate in the electoral district, it is impossible for the voter to express his or her support for that party. In sum, the present election system deprives the voter of the freedom to choose either the candidate or the party.*[18]

Furthermore, insofar as a voter has only a single ballot to determine both the district representative and the proportional representative, he or she would be less likely to vote for candidates from newly formed political parties that are less organised and have fewer resources. Therefore, the impugned electoral system also perpetuated the 'oligopoly of political parties, and hinder[ed] a new party from making its appearance in the National Assembly'.[19] Consequently, the Court unanimously required the National Assembly to introduce electoral reform and allow each voter to have two votes – one for his or her preferred district representative and the other for his or her preferred political party. This change was introduced in time for the subsequent 2004 National Assembly election, and currently 47 of the 300 National Assembly seats are reserved for these proportional representatives.[20]

This judicially imposed two-ballot electoral scheme has led to the rise of small political parties in the National Assembly as voters can now 'split' their support when choosing their lawmakers.[21] In the same vein, the Constitutional Court in 2014 invalidated a statutory law that automatically de-registered political parties that did not win at least 2% of the total number of electoral votes cast in the National Assembly election.[22] While the Court acknowledged that the legislature was pursuing a legitimate purpose in fostering the growth and 'development of party democracy'[23] by excluding fringe political parties that are not sufficiently electable, the Court held that the law was overbroad as 'less restrictive means' could be used to pursue the same goals. To illustrate its point, the Court offered the following observation:

18 13-2 KCCR 77, 2000 Hun-Ma 91, 2000 Hun-Ma 112, 2000 Hun-Ma 134 (n 13).

19 *Ibid.*

20 Valori (n 8).

21 See Jongcheol Kim, 'Upgrading Constitutionalism; The Ups and Downs of Constitutional Developments in South Korea since 2000', in Albert Chen (ed.), *Constitutionalism in Asia in the Early Twenty-First Century* (Cambridge: Cambridge University Press, 2014), 83; Yeonho Lee and Yoo-Jin Lim, 'The Rise of the Labour Party in South Korea: Causes and Limits' (2006) 19(3) *The Pacific Review* 305.

22 26-1(A) KCCR 155, 2012 Hun-Ma 431, 2012 Hun-Ka 19 (consolidated) (28 January 2014) (Official English Translation).

23 *Ibid.*

> *For example, the cancellation of registration, not based on the result of a single National Assembly election, can be decided depending on the result of election[s] after providing such a political party with several chances to participate in elections for a certain period of time. Also, since it is hard for newly established political parties to attain high level[s] of political support from the beginning, the cancellation of registration may be decided in combination of the number and distribution of constituencies from which candidates were recommended and the rate of votes earned in the constituencies.*[24]

Similarly, the Constitutional Court has ameliorated the systemic problem of gerrymandering by political incumbents who manipulate the legislative reapportionment process for partisan gain.[25] Unchecked, political incumbents can always carve up or redistribute electoral constituencies such that political opposition is always 'sliced and diced' into electoral irrelevance. As such systemic problems are unlikely to be corrected by self-serving legislators themselves, the Court has taken upon itself the role of supervising this apportionment process. Therefore, in 1995, the Court held that the population ratio of the smallest electoral constituency to the largest constituency must not exceed 1:4.[26] In 2001, the Court further reduced this population ratio to 1:3.[27] Finally, in 2014, the Court imposed a 1:2 population ratio.[28] As the Court recognised in its 2014 decision, any significant deviance in population between electoral constituencies is undemocratic as it perpetuates the disparity of voting power between electorates living in different constituencies. Furthermore, this move toward equinumerosity – that all electoral districts must have equal populations – is also important as this requirement prevents political incumbents from creating additional small electoral seats that favour them while enlarging the size of individual electoral constituencies that support the opposition, such that political insiders can gain more seats in the legislature with fewer votes.

Nevertheless, this principle of equinumerosity would be insufficient without a concurrent contiguity constraint.[29] The concept of contiguity basically requires electoral seats to be made up of counties/districts that

[24] *Ibid.*

[25] Samuel Issacharoff, 'Judging Politics: The Elusive Quest for Judicial Review of Political Fairness' (1992) 71 *Texas Law Review* 1643, 1661.

[26] 7-2 KCCR 760, 95 Hun-Ma 224 (27 December 1995).

[27] 13-2 KCCR 502, 2000 Hun-Ma 92, 2000 Hun-Ma 240 (consolidated) (25 October 2001).

[28] 2013 Hun-Ma 781, 2014 Hun-Ma 53 (consolidated) (30 October 2014).

[29] Daniel D. Polsby and Robert D. Popper, 'The Third Criterion: Compactness as a Procedural Safeguard against Partisan Gerrymandering' (1991) 9(2) *Yale Law and Policy Review* 301, 330.

are geographically connected to each other. Without this constraint, the principle of equinumerosity would be meaningless as political incumbents can still engineer victories by combining to their advantage equal-size electoral seats composed of counties/districts that are all over the electoral map. The principle of contiguity exponentially shrinks the number of available electoral districting options,[30] thereby making it more difficult for political insiders to gerrymander away votes for the opposition or cobble together disparate voting blocs for themselves. To this end, the Constitutional Court has invalidated redistricting plans where electoral seats are composed of districts/counties that are not geographically contiguous.[31]

Constitutional Anomaly of Campaign Regulations

In sharp contrast to the systemic electoral reforms that the Constitutional Court has spearheaded in South Korea, the judges have been uncharacteristically tolerant of the highly restrictive rules on election campaigns in the country.

While the Constitutional Court in 1994 had invalidated a law that only permitted election candidates and their staff to participate in electoral campaigns,[32] deemed unconstitutional a complete ban on political parties receiving any donations from the public[33] in 2015, and in 2016 struck down a blanket prohibition on the participation of journalists in electoral campaigns,[34] the Court has practically upheld every other campaign regulation in force, the most egregious of which is Article 93(1) of the Public Official Election Act.

This infamous law prohibits anyone from distributing any material or running any advertisement in favour of or against any political candidate six months before an election,[35] save limited campaign work undertaken by the registered election candidates (known as preliminary candidates)

30 *Ibid.*

31 7-2 KCCR 760, 95 Hun-Ma 224·239·285·373 (consolidated) (27 December 1995); 10–2 KCCR 742, 96 Hun-Ma 54 (26 November 1998).

32 6-2 KCCR 15, 93 Hun-Ka 4 (29 July 1994). But note that the impugned law was repealed by the National Assembly during the deliberation of the case. See Article 58(2) of the Public Official Election Act.

33 27-2(B) KCCR 511, 2013 Hun-Ba 168 (23 December 2015). The National Assembly was given until 30 June 2017 to pass remedial legislation.

34 2013 Hun-Ka 1, Gongbo Vol. 237, 1011 (30 June 2016).

35 Article 93(1) of the Public Official Election Act <http://www.nec.go.kr/engvote_2013/05_resourcecenter/02_01.jsp> accessed 1 February 2017.

and their staff[36] during the authorised campaign period – which is 120 days for National Assembly elections.[37] Notwithstanding the sweeping nature of this electoral restriction, this law has been regularly upheld by the Constitutional Court.[38]

It is also noteworthy that this campaign restriction favours political incumbents, as a statutory exemption has been carved out to allow incumbent lawmakers to report on their parliamentary activities and 'achievements' to the electorate.[39] Consequently, incumbents are given a pretext and head-start over political outsiders to campaign unofficially. But this tactical advantage conferred solely on incumbents has also been upheld by the Constitutional Court on the basis that it is 'an essential part of the job of a legislator'[40] and his or her 'political duty'[41] to brief the electorate.

All of these restrictive campaign laws were legacies of Korea's authoritarian past and they were conveniently retained by the political establishment to entrench their incumbency.[42] But with the advent of the internet age, the political class was also swift to extend these restrictions into cyberspace. In 2004, the National Assembly passed a law that required all political candidates, parties, and internet news sites hosting online forum boards to implement technical measures that could determine the actual identities of persons that post any material on the websites they manage.[43] Notwithstanding the chilling effect that this restriction would pose on the free circulation of electoral speech, the Constitutional Court in 2010 validated its legality:

[36] See Article 60–3 of the Public Official Election Act <http://www.nec.go.kr/engvote_2013/05_resourcecenter/02_01.jsp> accessed 1 February 2017.

[37] Article 60–2 of the Public Official Election Act <http://www.nec.go.kr/engvote_2013/05_resourcecenter/02_01.jsp> accessed 1 February 2017.

[38] 13-2 KCCR 174, 99 Hun-Ba 92, 2000 Hun-Ba 39, 2000 Hun-Ma 167·168· 199·205·280 (consolidated) (30 August 2001); 17-2 KCCR 160, 2004 Hun-Ba 52 (29 September 2005); 2014 Hun-Ba 253, Gongbo Vol. 237, 1049 (30 June 2016).

[39] Article 111 of the Public Official Election Act <http://www.nec.go.kr/engvote_2013/05_resourcecenter/02_01.jsp> accessed 1 February 2017.

[40] 13-2 KCCR 263, 2000 Hun-Ma 121 (consolidated) (30 August 2001) (Official English Translation of Case Summary).

[41] *Ibid.*

[42] Woo-Young Rhee, 'The Electoral Process and the Judicial Review of Elections in the Republic of Korea', in Po Jen Yap (ed.), *Judicial Review of Elections in Asia* (London: Routledge, 2016), 142–143.

[43] Article 82–6 of the Public Official Election Act <http://www.nec.go.kr/engvote_2013/05_resourcecenter/02_01.jsp> accessed 1 February 2017. This law was once again upheld by the Constitutional Court in 2015. See 27-2(A) KCCR 308, 2012 Hun-Ma 734, 2013 Hun-Ba 338 (consolidated) (30 July 2015).

> *The principle of the least restrictive means is also satisfied on the grounds that the fast circulation of malicious propaganda or false facts may distort information due to the nature of the Internet, that the distorted information may not be rectified during the short election campaign period.*[44]

But the dissenting judges were right to cast doubt on whether the impugned law was the least restrictive means of safeguarding the dissemination of political falsehood:

> *[T]here are existing sanctions such as defamation or slander against candidates; and the person posting messages can be identified ex post. Further, it cannot be found that the balance between legal interests would be achieved, because the disadvantages from the restriction of freedom of anonymous expression would weigh over the public interest of the fairness of the election, considering that election campaign period is important for the freedom of expression on politics and guaranteeing the freedom of expression is the significant constitutional value founding democracy.*[45]

In the same vein, the Constitutional Court in 2010[46] upheld an electoral law that imposed a ban on all online election campaigns before the commencement of the designated campaign period, with a very narrow exception carved out for internet homepages hosted by political candidates themselves.[47] Once again, the Court endorsed a prophylactic approach to campaign management:

> *If election campaigns using Internet homepages are allowed to everybody before the designated election period, it is likely to result in overheated and unfair election campaigns, which would then affect the result of the elections. Therefore, considering the need to prevent such unintended effects, as well as the practical difficulties of election management, there seems no other effective means to harmonise the freedom of election campaign and the fairness in elections than prohibiting Internet-based election campaigns, like any other types of election campaigns.*[48]

Fortunately, the Constitutional Court has recently begun to mitigate its past sympathies for these intrusive campaign regulations. In 2011, the

[44] 22-1(A) KCCR 347, 2008 Hun-Ma 324, 2009 Hun-Ba 31(consolidated) (25 February 2010) (Official English Translation of Case Summary).

[45] *Ibid.*

[46] 22-1(B) KCCR 497, 2008 Hun-Ba 169 (24 June 2010) (Official English Translation of Case Summary).

[47] The law has since been 'liberalised' to also allow for campaign staff to engage in online campaign work. See Article 59(3) of the Public Official Election Act <http://www.nec.go.kr/engvote_2013/05_resourcecenter/02_01.jsp> accessed 1 February 2017.

[48] 22-1(B) KCCR 497, 2008 Hun-Ba 169 (24 June 2010) (n 46).

Court held that the statutory ban on the distribution of any material in favour of or against any political candidate six months before an election would no longer apply to the Internet. As reasoned by the Court, a complete ban on the political expression in cyberspace for 180 days is no longer defensible, 'considering the reality that communication through the Internet has become common'[49] and 'the excessively long [period] for a fundamental right to be restricted'.[50]

But the Court has remained intransigent about preserving the law insofar as it is applied to the real world. As recent as 2014, the Constitutional Court repelled a constitutional challenge against Article 93(1) of Public Official Election Act and affirmed unequivocally that this law was necessary to prevent the dissemination of false political information, which 'cannot be effectively prevented or regulated solely by regulating the candidate's election expenses'.[51] But the crux of the dissenting judges' rebuttal was left unanswered:

> *[T]he damage to [a] fair election caused by malicious propaganda can be prevented by punishing dissemination of false information and slander. Additionally, the person who receives [campaign materials] can accept written information only when he or she actively reads them, and it is also possible to engage in rebuttal, discussion, and correction of information.*[52]

It is unclear why the Constitutional Court has been so indulgent on the restrictive campaign rules that hark back to Korea's autocratic past. While the judges have been rigorous in examining whether the legislature has adopted the 'least restrictive means' when imposing election deposits on candidates[53] and restrictions on ballot access,[54] and have even intervened aggressively in how National Assembly legislators are elected[55] and the redistricting of electoral constituencies,[56] the Court has been shockingly blasé about the authoritarian campaign regulations that – like other partisan self-dealing rules – equally exclude political

[49] 23-2(B) KCCR 739, 2007 Hun-Ma 1001, 2010 Hun-Ba 88, 2010 Hun-Ma 173·191 (consolidated) (29 December 2011) (Official English Translation of Case Summary).

[50] *Ibid.*

[51] 26-1(A) KCCR 628, 2011 Hun-Ba17, 2012 Hun-Ba 391(consolidated) (24 April 2014).

[52] *Ibid.*

[53] See 13-2 KCCR 77, 2000 Hun-Ma 91, 2000 Hun-Ma 112, 2000 Hun-Ma 134 (n 13) and 20–2(B) KCCR 477, 2007 Hun-Ma 1024 (n 14).

[54] See 19-1 KCCR 859, 2004 Hun-Ma 644 et al. (n 15) and 26-1(A) KCCR 136, 2012 Hun-Ma 409·510, 2013 Hun-Ma 167 (n 16).

[55] See 13-2 KCCR 77, 2000 Hun-Ma 91, 2000 Hun-Ma 112, 2000 Hun-Ma 134 (n 13).

[56] See 2013 Hun-Ma 781, 2014 Hun-Ma 53 (n 28) and 7-2 KCCR 760, 95 Hun-Ma 224·239·285·373 (n 31).

outsiders from public office. This contradiction and inconsistency is inexplicable, and should hopefully be addressed and resolved by a future bench.

Constitutional Court as Strategic Arbiter

Even as the Constitutional Court – operating within a diffused electoral system – removes political barriers of entry, consolidates Korea's democratic development, and enhances the competitiveness of elections, it has been strategic in preserving its political capital by exercising restraint when its ruling may potentially remove top leaders.

In March 2004, the National Assembly brought impeachment proceedings against President Roh Moo-hyun and the Constitutional Court was expressly authorised to adjudicate over his removal.[57] Since his inauguration in 2003, President Roh had faced a hostile National Assembly, with the opposition GNP – the then largest political party in the legislature – in control of 39% of the elected seats. His political fortunes took a turn for the worse when his own Millennium Democratic Party (MDP) splintered and pro-Roh forces within the MDP had to leave and form a new Uri Party in September 2003.[58] As the hearings proceeded and President Roh was suspended from office pending judicial resolution, the tide of public opinion turned against the impeachment and his Uri Party swept into office on this popular wave – with 152 out of the 299 electoral seats – after the April 2004 National Assembly election. Plausibly yielding to public will, the Constitutional Court reinstated Roh a month later in May 2004.

It is noteworthy that the Court actually agreed that Roh had violated the law in three instances.[59] First, President Roh had violated a statutory mandate on public officials to remain politically neutral[60] when he publicly expressed support for the Uri Party at a press conference. Second, the

[57] See Article 111 of the Constitution of the Republic of Korea.

[58] Youngjae Lee, 'Law, Politics, and Impeachment: The Impeachment of Roh Moo-hyun from a Comparative Constitutional Perspective' (2005) 53 *American Journal of Comparative Law* 403, 409–410.

[59] 16-1 KCCR 609, 2004 Hun-Na 1 (14 May 2004) (Official English Translation).

[60] Article 9(1) of the Public Official Election Act reads: 'A public official or a person who is required to maintain political neutrality (including an agency and organisation) shall not exercise any unreasonable influence over the election or perform any act likely to have an effect of the election result.' <http://www.nec.go.kr/engvote_2013/05_resourcecenter/02_01.jsp> accessed 1 February 2017.

President had violated his duty to abide by and protect the Constitution[61] when he criticised the National Election Commission for chastising him for his abovementioned partisan act. Finally, the Court concluded that the President had abused his authority by suggesting that a national referendum[62] be called to assess the public's opinion of his job performance as this constitutional mechanism could not be used for political grand-standing.

Notwithstanding the violations, the Constitutional Court stated that it should not remove a President simply when there is a valid ground[63] for impeachment. Instead, the Court declared that an implied limitation must be read into the law: 'the principle of proportionality'[64] would require the judges to give due regard to the 'gravity of [the] illegality'.[65] Extrapolating from this *implied* proportionality constraint, the Court opined that a President could only be removed from office if he had committed an act that 'threatened the basic order of free democracy'[66] or had betrayed the trust of the people. Examples of the latter would include corruption and treason. Therefore, the Court concluded that President Roh's misconduct, whilst illegal, was not sufficiently grave to constitute 'a threat to the basic order of free democracy'[67] that justified his removal from office.

The Constitutional Court's opinion on Roh's impeachment was a masterful act of judicial statecraft. By acknowledging that the *outgoing* faction in the National Assembly had valid grounds to bring the impeachment proceedings, while restoring a President whose party had just been validated at the polls, the Court produced a win-win situation that benefited even the outgoing party.[68] Furthermore, if the Court had intervened and

[61] Article 66(2) of the Constitution of the Republic of Korea reads: 'The President shall have the responsibility and duty to safeguard the independence, territorial integrity and continuity of the State and the Constitution.'

[62] Article 72 of the Constitution of the Republic of Korea reads: 'The President may submit important policies relating to diplomacy, national defence, unification and other matters relating to the national destiny to a national referendum if he deems it necessary.'

[63] Article 53(1) of the Constitutional Court Act reads: 'Where a request for an impeachment is well-grounded, the Constitutional Court shall pronounce a decision that the respondent shall be removed from the relevant public office.'

[64] See 16-1 KCCR 609, 2004 Hun-Na 1 (n 59).

[65] *Ibid.*

[66] *Ibid.*

[67] *Ibid.*

[68] Wen-Chen Chang, 'Strategic Judicial Responses in Politically Charged Cases: East Asian Experiences' (2010) 8 (4) *International Journal of Constitutional Law* 885, 899. See also Jiunn-rong Yeh, 'Presidential Politics and the Judicial Facilitation of Dialogue between Political Actors in New Asian Democracies: Comparing the South Korean and Taiwanese Experiences' (2010) 8 (4) *International Journal of Constitutional Law* 911.

removed the incumbent President for these trivial violations – conduct that would be absolutely legal in any other liberal democracy – it would have lost significant goodwill with the public and drastically changed the course of Korean politics. Instead, by reflecting public opinion and restoring the President, the Court asserted its institutional supremacy in constitutional adjudication whilst safeguarding its political capital to resolve more conflicts in the future.

In contrast, when the Constitutional Court removed President Park Geun-hye from office in 2017 for colluding with Choi Soon-sil, a close confidante, to pressure big corporations into making huge donations to non-profit foundations that support presidential initiatives, her approval ratings were in single digits – the lowest for any sitting President in South Korea[69] – and the Court was merely reflecting public opinion when it chose to remove a deeply unpopular President for serious misconduct and abuse of power.[70]

Conclusion

The Constitutional Court of Korea was established by the 1987 Constitution, which expressly repudiated autocratic politics and introduced into Korea a system of open elections and accountable leadership. The Court has taken advantage of the country's weak-party politics, asserted its authority swiftly, and gone beyond the expectations of sceptics by ushering into Korea an even more liberal model of democratic diversity.

The political diffusion in the legislature, coupled with a President who is constitutionally limited to one five-year term,[71] provided the Court with the 'policy' space to extend ballot access to the disenfranchised and remove political barriers of entry that were erected by incumbents to consolidate their rule. While the Court's record may be inconsistent – authoritarian campaign regulations remain in force and effect – it is indisputable

[69] Reuters, 'Choi-gate: South Korean President's Approval Rating Tanks at 4%', *Guardian*, 25 November 2016 <https://www.theguardian.com/world/2016/nov/25/choi-gate-south-korean-presidents-approval-rating-tanks-at-4> accessed 1 February 2017.

[70] Since the influence-peddling scandal broke in October 2016, hundreds of thousands of South Koreans have marched through the streets of Seoul – in weekly protests – demanding for President Park's resignation. See also '"Santa protest" against South Korea President Park Geun-hye', *BBC* <http://www.bbc.com/news/world-asia-38427931> accessed 1 February 2017.

[71] Article 70 of the Constitution of the Republic of Korea reads: 'The term of office of the President shall be five years and the President shall not be re-elected.'

that the absence of long-standing parties and long-lasting Presidents have empowered the rise of South Korea's Constitutional Court. This Korean narrative confirms the symbiotic relationship that exists between a country's state of democratisation and the long-term sustainability of constitutional review. In short, democracy both fosters and is fostered by the exercise of judicial power.

PART III

Fragile Democracies

8

The Constitutional Court of Thailand and Partisan Judges

Since Thailand became a constitutional monarchy in 1932, the country has raced through 19 Constitutions, and its 20th Constitution was officially endorsed by King Maha Vajiralongkorn on 6 April 2017.

Thailand's most democratic and inclusive Constitution had been the 1997 'People's Constitution',[1] which also created – for the first time – a Constitutional Court that was vested with the exclusive authority to interpret the Constitution.[2] But with the rise of Thaksin Shinawatra in Thai politics and the political imbroglio that followed,[3] the Constitutional Court had contributed to the demise of the rule of law by acting hand-in-glove with anti-Thaksin forces to invalidate two general elections, remove three Prime Ministers, and dissolve six political parties affiliated with the beleaguered leader.[4] While the Court was not directly responsible for the two military coups staged in Thailand since Thaksin took office, insofar as the judges have been deeply partisan in eliminating him and his associates from the country's political life, the Court had facilitated the army's takeover by indicating that it was equally hostile to the democratic impulses that had recurrently validated Thaksin's clan and affiliates at the polls.

Thaksin Shinawatra and the Demise of the 1997 Constitution

Thaksin Shinawatra and his Thai Rak Thai (TRT) Party came into power in 2001 – on the back of the 1997 Asian financial crisis – by promising

[1] See Andrew Harding and Peter Leyland, *The Constitutional System of Thailand: A Contextual Analysis* (Oxford: Hart Publishing, 2011), 22–24.

[2] *Ibid.*, 160.

[3] See Björn Dressel, 'Thailand's Elusive Quest for a Workable Constitution, 1997–2007' (2009) 31(2) *Contemporary Southeast Asia* 296; See Federico Ferrara, 'Democracy in Thailand: Theory and Practice', in William Case (ed.), *Routledge Handbook of Southeast Asian Democratisation* (London: Routledge, 2015), 351–369.

[4] See Khemthong Tonsakulrungruang, 'Thailand: an Abuse of Judicial Review', in Po Jen Yap (ed.), *Judicial Review of Elections in Asia* (London: Routledge, 2016), 173–191.

to generate economic growth and overhaul a bureaucracy that had stymied innovation.[5] Relying on a swathe of populist socio-economic programmes, Thaksin appealed to the rural poor in Thailand and easily won re-election in 2005, with the TRT taking 377 of the 500 parliamentary seats in the legislature.[6]

But Thaksin's dominance in Thai politics posed a threat to the traditional centres of power – an oligarchy composed of the local business enterprises, the monarchy, and the military. The local business community was resentful that the spoils of Thaksin's rule only benefitted his small circle of family and friends. Thaksin's personal popularity and his appeal to the people's aspiration for greater equality also challenged the hierarchical social structure perpetuated by the nation's royalist order, and the 'network monarchy'[7] was equally concerned about having Thaksin preside over a royal succession when the ailing king passed.[8] Also, the military bristled at Thaksin's constant attempts to promote his own allies and friends within the ranks of the armed forces.[9]

Thaksin's political fortunes turned in early 2006 when his family sold shares in their company to Singapore for US$2 billion dollars, without incurring any tax liability in Thailand. This self-serving transaction infuriated Thaksin's political enemies and opposition coalesced in the form of the People's Alliance for Democracy (PAD), an anti-Thaksin coalition that organised mass demonstrations in the streets for weeks. Seeking to appease his critics, Thaksin called for a snap election in April 2006. Certain of defeat, but determined to deny Thaksin any validation at the polls, the opposition boycotted this election *en masse*,[10] and the TRT swept 460 electoral seats as a result. With no end to the street protests in sight, King Bhumibol Adulyadej intervened. In a rare public address, the Thai King told the courts that a one-party

[5] See Thitinan Pongsudhirak, 'Thailand's Uneasy Passage' (2012) 23(2) *Journal of Democracy* 47, 48.

[6] Pasuk Phongpaichit and Chris Baker, 'Populist Challenge to the Establishment: Thaksin Shinawatra and the Transformation of Thai Politics', in Richard Robison (ed.), *Routledge Handbook of Southeast Asian Politics* (London: Routledge, 2011), 88.

[7] Duncan McCargo, 'Network Monarchy and Legitimacy Crises in Thailand' (2005) 18(4) *Pacific Review* 499.

[8] Federico Ferrara, *The Political Development of Modern Thailand* (Cambridge: Cambridge University Press, 2015), 234. King Bhumibol Adulyadej eventually passed away on 13 October 2016.

[9] James Ockey, 'Thailand in 2006: Retreat to Military Rule' (2007) 47(1) *Asian Survey* 133, 136.

[10] Ferrara (n 8), 237.

democracy was abnormal and asked rhetorically whether the election should be nullified.[11]

The Constitutional Court hitherto had played a limited role in Thai politics, but from this point onward, the judiciary became an additional member of the anti-Thaksin alliance.[12] In response to the King's address, the Constitutional Court nullified the results of the snap election in May 2006. The electoral results were invalidated on two main grounds. First, the Court noted that the number of valid ballots cast in TRT's favour was dwarfed by the number of invalid ballots and votes that expressly abstained from endorsing any candidate. Therefore, the Court concluded that the 'election was not fair and not truly democratic since the candidates did not truly receive the votes of the people under the democratic system'.[13] Second, the Court argued that the arrangement of the voting booths potentially allowed onlookers to observe whom voters chose, thereby violating the secrecy of the vote.[14] On these grounds, the past election was deemed undemocratic and the results were quashed.

The nullification of the 2006 election took Thai commentators by surprise. It is noteworthy that the 1997 Constitution did not require elected candidates to win a majority of the votes cast. In fact, the law only required a re-election to be called in any constituency if the winner garnered less than 20% of the total votes cast.[15] The Court also overlooked the government's argument that the opposition had not acted in good faith when the latter refused to negotiate with the government on a suitable date for the snap election.[16] Furthermore, the Constitutional Court did not explore how the arrangement of the voting booths *actually impacted* the choices voters made; the mere fact that voters could be observed by onlookers sufficed for the entire election to be voided.

New elections were called for October 2006, but before that could transpire, the military intervened. A coup was executed on 19 September 2006 and the armed forces took over command of the government. The

[11] For an English translation of the King's address, see Björn Dressel, 'Judicialisation of Politics or Politicisation of the Judiciary? Considerations from Recent Events in Thailand' (2010) 23(5) *Pacific Review* 671, 680.

[12] Phongpaichit and Baker (n 6), 90.

[13] Summary of the Constitutional Court Ruling No. 9/2549 (8 May 2006), 32 [Official English Translation].

[14] *Ibid.*, 32–33.

[15] Section 74(2) of the Organic Act on Election of Members of the House of Representatives and Senators B.E. 2541 (1998).

[16] Khemthong Tonsakulrungruang, 'The Anti-Majoritarian Constitutional Court of Thailand' (2017) 26 *Washington International Law Journal* 247.

1997 Constitution was scrapped and an interim Charter, promulgated on 1 October 2006, replaced the Constitutional Court with a smaller Constitutional Tribunal – staffed with judges who were junta sympathisers – that retained its predecessor's jurisdiction to dissolve political parties.[17] This was an unfortunate portent of things to come.

True to form, the Constitutional Tribunal disbanded the TRT in May 2007 on the basis that the latter had financed two small political parties – Pattana Chart Thai (PCT) party and the Paen Din Thai (PDT) party – to run against it in the 2006 Election, so as to create a veneer of political competition.[18] The two complicit parties were also disbanded. While the Tribunal was authorised to disband political groups for electoral infractions, the Tribunal did not explain why it should not have imposed a less severe penalty, short of a complete dissolution. More significantly, *after* the coup, the juntas had issued a military order[19] that banned the executive committee members of any political party from public office for five years when their party committed electoral infractions. This military order was *retrospectively* applied to all of the executive members of the TRT, PCT, and PDT. As a consequence, 111 executives from Thaksin's TRT party were barred from politics for five years. One should further note that a dissolution order had also been brought against the Democrat Party – the leading anti-Thaksin political party – on the basis that it had colluded with Prachatipatai Gao Na (PGN) party to frame the TRT for electoral fraud back in 2006. While the PGN was found responsible and therefore disbanded, the Democrat Party was cleared of all wrongdoing and escaped unscathed.[20]

The Constitutional Court and the 2007 Constitution

Military rule ended in Thailand with the promulgation of a new Constitution in October 2007. The Constitutional Court was reinstated, and this time it was expressly conferred with the power to revoke the political rights of those who were found responsible for electoral infractions.[21]

17 Ferrara (n 8), 238.

18 Summary of the Constitutional Tribunal Ruling No. 3–5/2550 (30 May 2007), 9–15 (Official English Translation).

19 Announcement of the Council for Democratic Reform No. 27: 30 September B.E. 2549 (2006).

20 Summary of the Constitutional Tribunal Ruling No. 1–2/2550 (30 May 2007), 3–8 (Official English Translation).

21 Section 237 of the 2007 Thai Constitution.

As a safeguard against populist politics, the fully elected Senate under the 1997 Constitution was also replaced with a partially appointed one.[22]

But Thaksin and his surrogates proved to be more resilient than the military expected. His allies regrouped under the banner of a new People's Power Party (PPP); and, against all odds, the PPP won 233 of the 480 elected House of Representative seats in the December 2007 election and earned the right to form the next government, with Thaksin's proxy – Samak Sundaravej – installed as Prime Minister.

In protest, the anti-Thaksin PAD returned to the streets in May 2008. Tensions further escalated in August 2008 when the PAD demonstrators blockaded major roads in Bangkok, stormed and occupied the Government House, and temporarily disrupted air and rail services in Thailand. As violent clashes between the PAD and the anti-PAD camp continued amidst the Samak-led government's failure to reach a compromise with the opposition, the Constitutional Court decided to jump into the political fray.

On 9 September 2008, the Constitutional Court unanimously dismissed Samak as Prime Minister on the pretext that his guest appearances on a cooking show created a conflict of interest with his ministerial responsibilities. Section 267 of the 2007 Constitution had prohibited the Prime Minister from being an 'employee' of third parties. Consequently, the Court held that Samak's remunerated guest appearances on the cooking shows made him an employee of the show's organisers, and 'the conflict between [Samak's] personal interest and the exercise of official functions would result in the personal interests being obtained at the expense of the public interests'.[23] Without examining whether the Prime Minister's guest appearances in a cooking show was a malfeasance that justified his removal, the Constitutional Court unilaterally terminated Samak's term in office with immediate effect.

The PPP replaced Samak with another Thaksin surrogate – Somchai Wongsawat – his brother-in-law. Infuriated by another display of nepotism, the PAD continued its violent campaigns and eventually upped the ante by laying siege to two international airports in November 2008, including Bangkok's busy Suvarnabhumi International Airport. With no political solution in sight, the Constitutional Court decided to resolve the

[22] Section 111 and 113 of the 2007 Thai Constitution. The appointed Senators would be selected by a Committee composed of judges, the Chair of the Election Commission, and the Chair of the State Audit Commission.

[23] Summary of the Constitutional Court Ruling No. 12–13/2551 (9 September 2008), 70 (Official English Translation).

impasse on its own. In December 2008, the Constitutional Court – relying on an earlier Supreme Court conviction of the PPP's deputy leader for bribing voters ahead of the 2007 Election – dissolved the PPP and barred all the members on the executive committee from politics for five years.[24] It is noteworthy that a party dissolution and a five-year political ban was authorised under Section 237 of the Constitution if any member of the executive committee had 'connived at or allowed the commission' of the electoral fraud. However, where the culprit himself was a member of the executive committee – as the deputy leader of the PPP was – the Court held that it was unnecessary for any other party executive to be complicit; everyone in the executive committee would be punished as a consequence of that executive member's misconduct. In one fell swoop, the Constitutional Court also removed Somchai Wongsawat from his premiership. On the same day, the PPP's coalition partners – the Matchima Thippathai Party and the Chart Thai Party – were also dissolved on similar charges of electoral fraud, and the collapse of the PPP-led government paved the way for Thaksin's main opponent – the Democrat Party leader Abhisit Vejjajiva – to become Thailand's next Prime Minister.

Abhisit's term as Premier did not bring peace and stability to Thailand. Instead, it was the Thaksin supporters' turn to take to the streets. The pro-Thaksin United Front for Democracy against Dictatorship shut down Bangkok's financial district for months, and a subsequent military crackdown in May 2010 resulted in over 90 fatalities, the bloodiest in Thailand for decades. As violence unfolded in the streets, the Constitutional Court remained in the thick of the political drama. In April 2010, the Democrat Party was accused by the Election Commission of misusing 29 million Thai baht in electoral campaign funds back in 2005 and faced the prospect of dissolution as a consequence. But the Court swiftly dismissed the case in November that year on the basis that the suit was time-barred: the Election Commission had failed to file its petition within the 15-day time-limit imposed under the electoral law.[25] But this same deadline was also missed when a petition was brought to dissolve Thaksin's TRT in 2007, and the Court had completely ignored the procedural irregularity then.[26]

[24] Summary of the Constitutional Court Ruling No. 20/2551 (2 December 2008), 113–121 (Official English Translation).

[25] Royal Thai Embassy of Singapore, 'Thailand's Constitutional Court Dismisses Democrat Party Dissolution Case', 29 November 2010 <http://www.thaiembassy.sg/press_media/news-highlights/thailands-constitution-court-dismisses-democrat-party-dissolution-case> accessed 1 February 2017.

[26] Harding and Leyland (n 1), 183; Tonsakulrungruang (n 4), 182.

It was evident that the Constitutional Court was intent on keeping Abhisit and his Democrat Party in play for the upcoming 2011 election.

But once again the Thai electorate came out for Thaksin and rebuffed the Democrat Party at the polls. Thaksin's coalition, organised now under the banner of the Pheu Thai party and led by his sister Yingluck, won handily at the 2011 election and swept 265 of the 500 House of Representatives seats.

In 2012, the Yingluck-led government attempted to replace the procedure by which constitutional amendments were passed. Specifically, Section 291 of the 2007 Constitution vested the power of amendment with the House of Representatives and the Senate, but the government wanted to confer this power on a new Constitution Drafting Council. Yingluck's foes swiftly filed various petitions before the Constitutional Court, alleging in essence that the impugned amendment violated Section 68 of the 2007 Constitution, which prohibited 'the overthrow [of] the democratic regime of government with the King as Head of the State'. Although Section 68 of the Constitution explicitly required the Prosecutor General to endorse such complaints before they could be heard by the Constitutional Court, the judges decided to hear the individual petitions anyway.[27] Furthermore, while the Court conceded that the government could make piecemeal reforms to the 2007 Constitution, it decided that this particular amendment to Section 291 could only be passed if it was first endorsed by the people at a national referendum.[28] While the government's plan to amend the Constitution was thereby derailed, the Court exercised some restraint insofar as it decided that it was too speculative to determine whether the impugned amendment was an unconstitutional attempt to subvert democracy and the monarchy in Thailand, and consequently dismissed the constitutional petitions to remove the government.

But Yingluck's good fortune ran out when she tried to pass an amnesty bill in late 2013, which would have paved the way for her brother's return from exile. After the bill was passed in the Pheu Thai-controlled lower house, tens of thousands of protestors took to the streets in Bangkok. Caving in to public pressure, the Senate rejected the controversial bill on 12 November 2013. It was against this political backdrop that the Constitutional Court ruled a week later to invalidate a constitutional

[27] Constitutional Court Ruling No. 18–22/2555 (13 July 2012).

[28] Tonsakulrungruang (n 16). It is noteworthy that Section 291 of the 2007 Constitution did not expressly require a national referendum to be held before any provision of the Constitution was to be amended.

amendment that would have replaced the partially appointed Senate with one that was constituted fully by universal suffrage.[29] The defeat of the amnesty bill emboldened the protestors. Violence escalated in Bangkok as demonstrators stormed multiple government buildings and blockaded major roads in their bid to pressure Yingluck to resign. In a show of support for the protestors, the opposition Democrat Party resigned *en masse* from Parliament in December 2013, forcing Yingluck to dissolve Parliament and call for new elections in February 2014.

Fully aware that it would lose at the polls, the Democrat Party announced it would boycott the upcoming election. The People's Democratic Reform Committee (PDRC) – an anti-Thaksin protest coalition – also attempted to derail the election by blockading registration venues for prospective election candidates. Since many constituencies had no or only one registered candidate, and in view of potential violence breaking out on election day, the Election Commission petitioned the Constitutional Court to determine whether the general election could be postponed. While Section 108(2) of the 2007 Thai Constitution expressly provided that an election must be held within 60 days of the lower house's dissolution,[30] the Court decided that this constitutional mandate was not cast in stone. Specifically, the Court declared that when the nation faced any public calamity or in times of necessity, the election could be re-scheduled.[31] Notwithstanding the Court's decision, Yingluck insisted that the election should proceed as planned.

Unsurprisingly, the election turned out to be a complete mess. Protestors obstructed voters and election officials from entering the polling stations, ballot boxes were looted, and many Southern provinces – the Democrat Party's strongholds – held no voting at all.[32] For 28 electoral constituencies, the Election Commission was compelled to hold an election separately in

[29] Constitutional Court Ruling No. 15–18/2556 (20 November 2013). See also Michael H. Nelson, 'Delaying Constitutionalism to Protect Establishment Hegemony in Thailand: Designing the Election System and the Senate in the Constitution of 2007', in Marco Bünte and Björn Dressel (eds), *Politics and Constitutions in Southeast Asia* (London: Routledge, 2017), 63.

[30] Section 108(2) of the 2007 Thai Constitution read: 'The dissolution of the House of Representatives shall be made in the form of a Royal Decree in which the day for a new general election must be fixed within the period of not less than forty-five days but not more than sixty days as from the date of the dissolution of the House of Representatives and such election day must be the same throughout the Kingdom.'

[31] Constitutional Court Ruling No. 2/2557 (24 January 2014).

[32] Kitti Prasirtsuk, 'Thailand in 2014: Another Coup, a Different Coup?' (2015) 55 *Asian Survey* 200, 202.

March 2014. And on this ground alone, the Constitutional Court intervened on 21 March 2014 and annulled the entire election.[33] According to the Court, Section 108(2) of the Constitution expressly stipulated that the 'election day must be the same throughout the Kingdom', and hence the postponement of the election in 28 constituencies violated this mandate. But this very same constitutional clause also required the government to hold an election within 60 days of the lower house's dissolution, yet just two months ago, the Court had authorised for the postponement of the election on the basis that an implicit exception could be made when the country was in turmoil. Herein, when the postponement of the election in the 28 constituencies would have benefitted the Yingluck-led government, the Court refused to entertain any exception and strictly enforced the constitutional rule.

New elections were re-scheduled for July 2014. But on 7 May 2014, the Constitutional Court removed Yingluck from office for violating Section 268 (read with Section 266 of the Thai Constitution) when she appointed Priewpan Damapong – a relative of hers – as the new police chief after she took office in 2011.[34] While Section 266 of the Thai Constitution prohibited the appointment or removal of a public official for a politician's private gain or for the 'benefits … of a political party, whether directly or indirectly', such partisan considerations had influenced countless appointments under the Thaksin and Abhisit administrations.[35] Once again – as it did with Samak and Somchai Wongsawat – the Constitutional Court dismissed another sitting Prime Minister unilaterally.

By vitiating the election and forcing out another Prime Minister at this juncture of political uncertainty, the Court created a power vacuum where the State had neither a legislature nor a leader. Within two weeks of Yingluck's dismissal, the military moved in. Martial law was declared on 20 May 2014 and the army officially seized power two days later.[36]

Conclusion

Since the establishment of a constitutional monarchy in 1932, Thailand has experienced recurring cycles of coups and constitutions. With the public

[33] Constitutional Court Ruling No. 5/2557 (21 March 2014).

[34] Constitutional Court Ruling No. 34/2557 (7 May 2014).

[35] See Duncan McCargo, 'Competing Notions of Judicialisation in Thailand,' (2014) 36 *Contemporary Southeast Asia* 417, 433.

[36] International Crisis Group, 'Thailand's Lengthening Roadmap to Elections', *Asian Report* N°274, 10 December 2015 < https://www.crisisgroup.org/asia/south-east-asia/thailand/thailand-s-lengthening-roadmap-elections> accessed 1 February 2017.

voting in favour of the new Charter at the August 2016 plebiscite, elections are set to return to Thailand after a three-year hiatus. But the 2017 Constitution is set to entrench a form of 'guided democracy' in Thailand, with the junta empowered to appoint all the members of the Senate, which in turn would have a new role in selecting the Prime Minister, a prerogative that was previously solely conferred on the lower house.

The demise of the 1997 and 2007 Thai Constitutions is obviously not solely attributable to the Constitutional Court. But the fact is, since 2006, the Court has vitiated two general elections, removed three Prime Ministers, dissolved six political parties, and banned hundreds of party executives from politics – all of which were only directed against Thaksin and his affiliates. The partisan Constitutional Court has frustrated elected governments, fostered political gridlock, and facilitated hostile take-overs by the military. Under the new Constitution, the powers of the Constitutional Court will be even enhanced. The Court shall be expressly tasked to adjudicate over all exercises of power by the House of Representative, the Senate, and the Council of Ministers.[37]

By acting hand-in-glove with the royalist/military elites to keep majoritarian impulses in check and elected governments at bay, the Constitutional Court has actively perpetuated Thailand's 'democratic rollback'[38] by rendering constitutional safeguards ineffectual and ephemeral.[39] If the Constitutional Court persists in this partisan role when democracy – albeit a custodial one – returns to Thailand, the country will inexorably head towards more turmoil.[40]

[37] Section 210(2) of the Draft 2016 Constitution of the Kingdom of Thailand (Unofficial English Translation) <http://www.un.or.th/wp-content/uploads/2016/06/2016_Thailand-Draft-Constitution_EnglishTranslation_Full_Formatted_vFina…pdf> accessed 1 February 2017.

[38] Larry Diamond, 'The Democratic Rollback: The Resurgence of the Predatory State', (2008) 87(2) *Foreign Affairs* 36.

[39] Tom Ginsburg, 'Constitutional Afterlife: The Continuing Impact of Thailand's Postpolitical Constitution', (2009) 7(1) *International Journal of Constitutional Law* 83, 105.

[40] Thitinan Pongsudhirak, 'Thailand's Democracy in Military Custody', Straits Times, 14 May 2016 <http://www.straitstimes.com/politics/thailands-democracy-in-military-custody> accessed 1 February 2017.

9

The Supreme Court of Pakistan: Accommodation and Defiance of Military Authority

Since the Partition of India, and the concomitant establishment of Pakistan in 1947, the country has been governed under three finalised Constitutions,[1] all of which were aborted or held in abeyance by the military at some point. In fact, martial law has been imposed by the military throughout the country five times, though martial law was not officially declared on the fourth and fifth occasions as General Pervez Musharraf had instead declared a State of Emergency throughout Pakistan on 14 October 1999 and 3 November 2007, respectively, and held the 1973 Constitution to be in abeyance both times.

Martial Law and the Courts

In *State* v. *Dosso*,[2] the Supreme Court of Pakistan had its first brush with martial law. On 7 October 1958, President Iskander Mirza, in collusion with the military, annulled the 1956 Constitution (Pakistan's first Constitution), dissolved the National and Provincial Assemblies, and declared martial law throughout the country. Six days after the coup, the Court was confronted with a set of consolidated criminal appeals. The lower courts, prior to the coup, had declared various provisions in the Frontier Crimes Regulation, under which the accused were detained, inconsistent with the 1956 Constitution. The issue before the Supreme Court was whether the appeals should be decided on the basis of the annulled Constitution or the operative Martial Law Regulation – Law (Continuance in Force) Order (LCFO) – which retained the validity of all laws in force immediately before the Proclamation other than the Constitution.

[1] These are the Constitutions of 1956, 1962, and 1973.

[2] PLD 1958 SC 533.

Chief Justice Muhammad Munir, who wrote the leading opinion in *Dosso*, was quick to legitimise the military coup:

> *[T]he essential condition to determine whether a Constitution has been annulled is the efficacy of the change ... a victorious revolution or a successful coup d'état is an internationally recognised legal method of changing a Constitution.*[3]

Therefore, the regime imposed by LCFO constituted 'a new legal order'[4] and all laws had to be judged against that military Order, and not the defunct Constitution.[5] The *Dosso* judgment has since been termed 'a carte blanche for treasonable conduct';[6] and indeed right after the judgment was handed down, in an ironic twist of fate, the military exiled President Mirza from Pakistan the next day, and General Ayub Khan took over as his successor.

Ayub Khan's regime fashioned a new Constitution for Pakistan, which provided for a strong executive President and a unicameral federal National Assembly; the President and members of the National Assembly would be elected by an electoral college composed of 80,000 Basic Democrats.[7] With the promulgation of the Constitution in 1962, martial law was lifted; but prolonged civil unrest and mass demonstrations eventually led to Ayub's resignation as President and General Yahya Khan's declaration of martial law throughout the country on 25 March 1969. The 1962 Constitution was also abrogated. Nevertheless, with the country's humiliating defeat to India and loss of East Pakistan in 1971, unity within the military ranks was deeply fractured;[8] and the military regime decided to relinquish power in favour of Zulfikar Ali Bhutto's Pakistan Peoples Party (PPP), which had won a majority of seats in the 1970 National Assembly election in West Pakistan, the part of Pakistan that remained.

[3] *Ibid.*, 539.

[4] *Ibid.*, 540.

[5] But one must note that the LCFO did not expressly state that it had retrospective effect. Therefore, as argued by Cornelius J, the sole dissenting judge in *Dosso*, judgments issued by the lower courts, prior to the military coup, should still be enforced.

[6] Farooq Hasan, 'A Juridical Critique of Successful Treason: A Jurisprudential Analysis of the Constitutionality of a Coup d'état in Common Law' (1984) 20 *Stanford Journal of International Law* 191, 217.

[7] The Basic Democrats were directly elected by the people to manage local government affairs. See Tayyab Mahmud, 'Praetorianism and Common Law in Post-Colonial Settings: Judicial Responses to Constitutional Breakdowns in Pakistan' (1993) *Utah Law Review* 1225, 1252.

[8] Aqil Shah, *The Army and Democracy: Military Politics in Pakistan* (Cambridge, MA: Harvard University Press, 2014), 113.

Bhutto remained Chief Martial Law Administrator and he only lifted martial law on 21 April 1972, upon the promulgation of the Interim Constitution of 1972. On the day before martial law was officially lifted by Bhutto, the Supreme Court handed down its decision in *Asma Jilani* v. *Government of Punjab*, which concerned the appeals of two persons detained under the military orders/regulations issued by Yahya Khan.[9] The Supreme Court decisively overruled its previous decision in *Dosso* and deemed Yahya Khan's actions 'illegal and illegitimate'.[10] Interestingly, the Chief Justice, who wrote the leading opinion, held that the Court could 'condone'[11] illegal acts that fell within one of the following categories:

(1) *All transactions which are past and closed, for no useful purpose can be served by reopening them,*
(2) *All acts and legislative measure which are in accordance with, or could have been made under the abrogated Constitution or the previous legal order,*
(3) *All acts which tend to advance or promote the good of the people,*
(4) *All acts required to be done for the ordinary orderly running of the State.*[12]

On the facts, the Court held that the impugned military regulation could not be justified on any of the abovementioned grounds of necessity and the detention orders of the applicants were thus quashed.

One may note that while the decision in *Asma Jilani* was groundbreaking, it was handed down after the Yahya Khan's regime had collapsed and martial law in Pakistan was coming to a close. In fact, the Chief Justice was quick to emphasise that this decision had 'nothing whatsoever to do with the validity of the present regime',[13] thereby insulating the Court from any potential attacks from the Bhutto administration.

The 1973 Constitution came into force on 14 August 1973 and Bhutto was sworn in as Prime Minister. But civilian rule did not last long as the political crisis that ensued from the 1977 parliamentary elections paved the way for the military to reassert itself over the civilian government.

9 The Jurisdiction of Courts (Removal of Doubts) Order, President's Order No. 3 of 1969, had ousted the jurisdiction of all civilian courts over affairs of the Martial Law Authority; and Martial Law Regulation No. 78 of 1971 authorised the indefinite detention of persons without trial.

10 *Asma Jilani* v. *The Government of the Punjab and Another*, PLD 1972 SC 139.

11 *Ibid.*, 207.

12 *Ibid.*, 205–207.

13 *Ibid.*, 208.

Bhutto's PPP won 155 out of the 200 seats in the National Assembly. The opposition, the Pakistan National Alliance (PNA), was quick to reject the results and demanded new elections under the supervision of the army.[14] Mass protests and violent demonstrations started in Karachi and swiftly spread to Lahore; martial law was subsequently declared in these cities in April 1977. Apprehensive that a military coup would occur if the political impasse persisted, Bhutto agreed on 4 July 1977 to a series of demands from the PNA, which included the conducting of a new round of elections in October that year. The agreement was scheduled to be signed the next day, but the military, under the command of General Zia-ul Haq, intervened shortly after midnight on 5 July, arrested Bhutto, overthrew the PPP government, and imposed martial law across the country.[15]

Unlike the previous two occasions, the Constitution was not formally abrogated this time but was held to be in abeyance; nevertheless, all enshrined fundamental rights were suspended.[16] The legality of Bhutto's detention soon came up before the Supreme Court in *Begum Nusrat Bhutto* v. *Chief of Army Staff*.[17] Interestingly, the Supreme Court in *Bhutto* was reluctant to resurrect *Dosso* and deem the effectiveness of the political change the sole criterion of the coup's legality; but neither was it ready to take on the military and deem the coup an illegal usurpation as the Court in *Jilani* did. Instead, the Court held that the 'true character of the new Legal Order' can only be determined by examining the following:

> *the objective political situation prevailing at the time, its historical imperatives and compulsions, the motivation of those responsible for the change, and the extent to which the old Legal Order is sought to be preserved or suppressed.*[18]

According to Chief Justice Anwar-ul Haq, who wrote the leading opinion, the country was at the 'brink of disaster',[19] and Zia-ul Haq had merely acted to 'save the country from further chaos and bloodshed';[20] therefore the military had merely taken an 'extra-constitutional step'[21] that was 'justified

[14] Shah (n 8), 134.

[15] Hamid Khan, *Constitutional and Political History of Pakistan*, 2nd edn (Karachi: Oxford University Press, 2009), 217.

[16] Article 2(3) of The Laws (Continuance in Force) Order 1977, C.M.L.A. Order No. 1 of 1977.

[17] PLD 1977 SC 657.

[18] *Ibid.*, 692–693.

[19] *Ibid.*, 693.

[20] *Ibid.*, 703.

[21] *Ibid.*

by State necessity and welfare [sic] of the people'.[22] Consequently, the Court held that the military was entitled to take all acts or legislative measures which could have been made under the 1973 Constitution, including the power to amend it; and any of these changes could even be carried out by means of Presidential Orders or Martial Law Regulations.[23] But it is notable that the Court did not capitulate to all of the military's substantive demands. Judicial review had in fact been completely ousted by a military Order issued by Zia-ul Haq after the coup;[24] but the Court held that the doctrine of necessity that justified the declaration of martial law could not abolish judicial review, as the courts were in no way culpable for the governmental failures that necessitated the military take-over.[25] Notwithstanding this laudable pronouncement, the Court quickly took the wind out of this decision by stating that the military was entitled to suspend all constitutional rights as the conditions prevailing in the country were 'obviously of such a nature as to amount to an Emergency'[26] and as the occurrence of an Emergency was a valid ground for suspending fundamental rights even under the 1973 Constitution, the military herein was entitled to do the same. It is noteworthy that the Supreme Court also refused to impose a time-table on the military for the calling of new elections and the end to martial law, but merely expressed its hope that 'the period of constitutional deviation shall be of as short a duration as possible'.[27] Accordingly, Bhutto's petition for release was rejected by the Supreme Court.

Soon after, in *Zulfikar Ali Bhutto* v. *State*,[28] the Supreme Court further watered down the doctrine of necessity by stating that the judiciary would only examine whether an impugned action reasonably fell within one of the enumerated objectives for the imposition of martial law,[29] but it

[22] *Ibid.*

[23] *Ibid.*, 716.

[24] Article 4(1) of the Laws (Continuance in Force) Order 1977 provided: 'No Court, tribunal … shall call or permit to be called in question the proclamation of the fifth day of July 1977, or any Order or Ordinance made in pursuance thereof or any Martial Law Regulation or Martial Law Order.'

[25] *Begum Nusrat Bhutto* (n 17), 716–717.

[26] *Ibid.*, 723.

[27] *Ibid.*

[28] PLD 1978 SC 40.

[29] In *Begum Nusrat Bhutto* (n 17) at p. 716, the Supreme Court held that the doctrine of necessity would authorise 'all such measures that would establish or lead to the establishment of the declared objectives of the proclamation of Martial Law, namely, restoration of law and order, and normalcy in the country, and the earliest possible holding of free and fair elections for the purpose of restoration of democratic institutions under the 1973 Constitution'.

would not further question whether the specific measures introduced by the military were necessary.[30]

This 'period of constitutional deviation'[31] lasted for over eight years; and it was only on 30 December 1985 that martial law was finally lifted and the 1973 Constitution restored. In return, Zia-ul Haq secured passage of the 8th Amendment to the Constitution, which *inter alia* validated all acts made in pursuance of the military regulations and orders that had been operative during the martial law period and immunised all persons from any liability in their discharge of those regulations and orders.[32] Equally significant was the inclusion of a new constitutional provision – Article 58(2)(b) – that authorised the President to 'dissolve the National Assembly in his discretion where, in his opinion, a situation had arisen in which the Government of the Federation could not be carried on in accordance with the provisions of the Constitution and an appeal to the electorate was necessary'.[33]

Civilian Rule in Pakistan

With the end of martial law, the Supreme Court gradually returned from its extended hiatus. In *Benazir Bhutto* v. *Federation of Pakistan*,[34] the Court invalidated a statutory provision that barred an unregistered political party from taking part in the general elections and authorised the Election Commission to determine the political party's eligibility for registration.[35] The restriction was deemed unreasonable as it did not provide for any safeguards or remedy against the Commission's discretion to end a party's political existence. Several months later, in another constitutional petition brought by Benazir Bhutto, daughter of Zulfikar Ali Bhutto,[36] the Supreme Court invalidated a statutory prohibition on the use of party symbols in elections as their use was necessary for political parties to reach out to illiterates, a significant proportion of

[30] *Zulfikar Ali Bhutto* (n 28), 57–59. On the facts, a Post-Proclamation Military Order that allowed for a sitting Lahore High Judge to be concurrently appointed as the Chief Election Commissioner – a measure that was inconsistent with the 1973 Constitution – was challenged *inter alia* on the ground that the change was unnecessary.

[31] *Begum Nusrat Bhutto* (n 17), 723.

[32] For an extended discussion of the 8th Amendment, see Khan (n 15), 369–376.

[33] The revised Article 58(2)(b) of the 1973 Constitution, as amended by the 8th Amendment.

[34] PLD 1988 SC 416.

[35] Section 3B of the Political Parties Act, enacted on 30 August 1979.

[36] Zulfikar Ali Bhutto was sentenced to death in 1978 and was hung in 1979.

the Pakistan population.[37] Both decisions handed down in 1988 paved the way for the PPP, headed by Benazir Bhutto, to emerge as the largest winner in the elections held that year; and the PPP went on to form the next government.

Unfortunately, political instability did not abate with the return of civilian rule. Between 1988 and 1997, the National Assembly was dissolved four times by the President, at the behest of or in collusion with the military,[38] but with new elections called soon after each time. Interestingly, when the dissolutions were challenged before the Supreme Court, the judges were inconsistent about the standard of review they would apply vis-à-vis the President's exercise of this discretion.[39]

In *Federation of Pakistan* v. *Haji Muhammad Saifullah Khan*,[40] the first dissolution decision, the Court held that the President could only dissolve the National Assembly 'when the machinery of the Government has broken down completely, its authority eroded and the Government cannot be carried on in accordance with the provisions of the Constitution',[41] and these conditions were not satisfied on the facts. But as new elections were already scheduled for the next month (November 1988), the Court held that it would not vitiate the illegal dissolution as it was in the 'national interest'[42] for the elections to continue.

However, when the National Assembly was next dissolved in August 1990, and Benazir Bhutto removed from power, the Supreme Court in *Ahmad Tariq* v. *Federation of Pakistan*[43] modified the touchstone test and held that dissolution was permissible when there was 'extensive, continued and pervasive failure to observe not one but numerous provisions of the Constitution'.[44] Furthermore, Shafi ur Rahman J, who wrote the leading opinion, upheld the President's order after a very cursory review of the evidence and grounds for justifying the dissolution.[45] After the elections held in October that year, Nawaz Sharif formed the next government with his coalition winning the largest number of seats in the National Assembly.

[37] *Benazir Bhutto* v. *Federation of Pakistan*, PLD 1989 SC 66.

[38] Shah (n 8), 168–174.

[39] See also Osama Siddique, 'The Jurisprudence of Dissolutions: Presidential Power to dissolve Assemblies under the Pakistani Constitution and its Discontents' (2006) 23 *Arizona Journal of International and Comparative Law* 615.

[40] PLD 1989 SC 166.

[41] *Ibid.*, 188.

[42] *Ibid.*, 194–195.

[43] PLD 1992 SC 646.

[44] *Ibid.*, 664–665.

[45] *Ibid.*, 665–667.

In a starker departure from past practice, when the National Assembly was dissolved for the third time in 1993, the Supreme Court did not wait for the dispute to come up before it on appeal but instead for the first time exercised its original jurisdiction to hear the dissolution case directly. More surprisingly, in *Nawaz Sharif* v. *President of Pakistan*,[46] Shafi ur Rahman J, who wrote the leading opinion again, chose to ignore the previous two dissolution decisions completely, and went on to objectively and exhaustively review all the evidence for dissolution. And after determining that the President's order for the dissolution was illegal and unjustified, the Court restored Prime Minister Nawaz Sharif and the members of the National Assembly to office. This decision to restore the Assembly proved to be inconsequential as, within months of the decision, the military forced both the Prime Minister and the President to resign and new elections were held in 1993.[47]

The 1993 elections returned Benazir Bhutto and the PPP to power. But a rift soon grew between President Leghari and Prime Minister Bhutto, and the latter's government was once again dissolved in 1996. The President's dissolution order was challenged before the Supreme Court. But this time, in a separate challenge, the 8th Amendment, which inserted Article 58(2)(b) into the Constitution, was also challenged on the ground that the amendment violated the basic structure of the 1973 Constitution and was thus unconstitutional.

The Supreme Court in *Mahmood Khan Achakzai* v. *Federation of Pakistan*[48] unanimously held that there was no basic structure in the 1973 Constitution. Nevertheless, the Court noted that all of Pakistan's past and present Constitutions shared the same Preamble, which was based on the Objectives Resolution adopted by the Constituent Assembly of Pakistan on 12 March 1949. Therefore, the Court reasoned that Parliament was free to amend any part of the Constitution so long as the 'salient features and basic characteristics of the Objectives Resolution'[49] were left untouched. Notwithstanding this caveat, the constitutionality of the 8th Amendment was upheld as the Court held that the change did not violate any of the basic characteristics that include 'federalism, parliamentary democracy and Islamic provisions including independence of judiciary'.[50] This strategic move had two-fold benefits: the Court upheld the 8th Amendment, a

[46] PLD 1993 SC 473.
[47] Shah (n 8), 173–174.
[48] PLD 1997 SC 426.
[49] *Ibid.* [56].
[50] *Ibid.* [58].

central concern of the military; but henceforth, the Court had also carved out a role for the judiciary to examine whether any future constitutional amendments violated the salient features of the Objectives Resolution.

But in addressing the legality of the President's dissolution order, the Supreme Court in *Benazir Bhutto* v. *President of Pakistan*[51] – the fourth dissolution case – flagrantly deviated from its previous practice in *Nawaz Sharif*, the third dissolution decision. This time, it reaffirmed *Ahmad Tariq* and stated that the President could dissolve the National Assembly when there were 'extensive, continued and pervasive failure to observe not one but numerous provisions of the Constitution';[52] and instead of objectively reviewing the evidence of dissolution, as it did in *Nawaz Sharif*, the Court held that it would suffice 'if there is material having nexus with the order of dissolution'[53] and 'newspaper cuttings can be relied upon as material in support of the grounds'[54] for dissolution. It was widely believed that the deep animosity between the judges and Prime Minister Bhutto[55] doomed her restoration to office and this decision paved the way for new elections in 1997 in which the Pakistan Muslim League (N), led by Nawaz Sharif, won decisively.

Sweeping into office with over two-thirds control of both the National Assembly and the Senate, Nawaz Sharif passed the 14th Amendment with ease, which sought to end party defections by legislators. In essence, the Amendment inserted Article 63A(6) which empowered the Head of the Political Party to discipline a party member if he or she does the following:

(a) *commits a breach of party discipline which means a violation of the party's constitution, code of conduct and declared policies, or*
(b) *votes contrary to any direction issued by the Parliamentary Party to which he belongs, or*
(c) *abstains from voting in the House against party policy in relation to any Bill.*[56]

[51] PLD 1998 SC 388.
[52] *Ibid.* [8] (Short Order).
[53] *Ibid.*
[54] *Ibid.*
[55] Bad blood developed between Bhutto and the judiciary when the former began to pack the courts, including the Supreme Court, with ad-hoc judges. When this practice was challenged before the Supreme Court, it was widely believed that the government raided the home of the Chief Justice's daughter to apply pressure on the Chief Justice to rule in Bhutto's favour. The Supreme Court eventually invalidated the appointment of these ad-hoc judges, but a furious Bhutto deliberately delayed the implementation of the verdict. See Khan (n 15), 436–438.
[56] Clauses (a), (b), and (c) of the Explanation to Section 63A(1) of the Constitution, as inserted by the 14th Amendment.

Furthermore, an ouster clause was also added to bar judicial review over any legal proceedings in relation to this Amendment.[57]

The legality of the 14th Amendment was soon challenged before the Supreme Court on the basis that it violated the basic structure of the Pakistan Constitution. In *Wukala Mahaz Barai* v. *Federation of Pakistan*,[58] the Supreme Court reaffirmed *Mahmood Khan Achakzai* and unanimously declared that constitutional amendments could not violate salient features and basic characteristics of the Objectives Resolution. More importantly, six out of the seven judges on the panel[59] read down the effect of the ouster clause and held that Article 63A(6) did not bar the Court from examining whether any acts were 'performed without jurisdiction, *coram non judice* and *mala fide*'.[60] Furthermore, four judges on the panel, a bare majority, went on to read down the effect of Clause (a) of the Explanation to Article 63A(1) and held that Clause (a) did not apply to the legislators' conduct or breach of discipline outside of Parliament and should also be read in a way that preserves 'the right of freedom of speech of a member in the House subject to reasonable restrictions',[61] thereby neutralising the sting of this Amendment, which had sought to muzzle lawmakers inside and outside Parliament.[62]

Return of Military Rule

The decade of civilian rule in Pakistan came to a close in 1999 when General Pervez Musharraf deposed Prime Minster Sharif, suspended the National Assembly, and imposed emergency rule throughout the country on 14 October 1999. Sharif had attempted to remove Musharraf as Army Chief when the latter was out of Pakistan on 12 October 1999, but the military counter-attacked and took over the country instead.

[57] Article 63A(6), as inserted by the 14th Amendment, reads: 'Notwithstanding anything contained in the Constitution, no Court including the Supreme Court and a High Court shall entertain any legal proceedings, exercise any jurisdiction, or make any order in relation to the action under this Article.'

[58] PLD 1998 SC 1263.

[59] One dissenting judge would invalidate the ouster clause for violating the basic structure of the Constitution.

[60] *Wukala Mahaz Barai* (n 58) [15] (Ajmal Mian CJ).

[61] *Ibid.* [18].

[62] Two judges upheld Clause (a) on the basis that lawmakers could be disciplined for their conduct inside and outside of Parliament. One dissenting judge would invalidate Clause (a) on the basis that it violated the basic structure of the Constitution.

Musharraf assumed the position of Chief Executive of Pakistan; the Constitution was held to be in abeyance and judicial review against the military regime was ousted.[63] Notwithstanding the ouster clause, and to Musharraf's displeasure, the Supreme Court agreed to hear the constitutional petitions lodged against the coup. Musharraf retaliated by compelling all the superior court judges to take an oath of allegiance to the military regime and those judges who refused were removed from office. Six judges on the Supreme Court were removed this way, including the Chief Justice.

More interestingly, a re-constituted Supreme Court continued to hear the consolidated disputes and handed down its decision in *Zafar Ali Shah* v. *Pervez Musharraf*.[64] The coup was justified on the ground of necessity and military rule was explained away as merely 'a case of Constitutional deviation for a transitional period so as to enable the Chief Executive to achieve his declared objectives'[65] of restoring law and order to Pakistan. But one must note that the Supreme Court did not give Musharraf carte blanche to do as he pleased. First, the Court held that the military was not authorised to amend the Constitution to remove its 'salient features … i.e. independence of judiciary [sic], federalism, parliamentary form of Government blended with Islamic provisions'.[66] Second, notwithstanding the ouster clause, the superior courts would 'continue to have the power of judicial review to judge the validity of any act or action of the Armed Forces'.[67] Third, while the Court would not reopen the cases of those judges who were removed for refusing to take the oath, it held that, going forward, superior court judges could only be removed in accordance with the provisions of the 1973 Constitution.[68] Most importantly, the Court actually imposed a sunset clause on Musharraf's military rule: he had to call for elections within three years.[69]

But Musharraf was in no way deterred. On 20 June 2001, he removed the incumbent President and authorised himself to take up that position.

[63] Section 4 of the Provisional Constitution Order No 1. of 1999 read: '(1) No Court, tribunal or other authority shall call or permit to be called in question the Proclamation of Emergency of 14th day of October, 1999 or any Order made in pursuance thereof. (2) No judgment, decree, writ, order or process whatsoever shall be made or issued by any Court or tribunal against the Chief Executive or any authority designated by the Chief Executive.'

[64] 2000 SCMR 1137 (Short Order).

[65] *Ibid.* [13].

[66] *Ibid.* [6(iii)].

[67] *Ibid.* [6(vi)].

[68] PLD 2000 SC 869, [284].

[69] 2000 SCMR 1137 [17].

To lend legitimacy to his rule, Musharraf issued a military Order for a referendum to be held on 30 April 2002, ostensibly for the people to decide whether he should serve for five years as President; but the referendum was rigged and Musharraf was 'endorsed' by 97.5% of the voters.[70] The validity of the referendum was challenged before the Supreme Court; but in *Qazi Hussain Ahmad* v. *General Pervez Musharraf*,[71] the judges capitulated completely to the military regime:

> *In a time of Constitutional abeyance, therefore, the validity of the Orders issued by the Chief Executive … cannot be questioned on the basis of being at variance with the Constitutional provisions and while examining such acts or measures this Court would not sit in appeal on the political wisdom of such acts and measures.*[72]

After securing his Presidency, Musharraf was ready to re-introduce elections to the National Assembly, albeit on his terms. The Pakistan Muslim League (Q) was created to be the civilian face of his military regime and an alliance of six Islamist parties, Muttahida Majlis-e-Amal (MMA, United Action Front), was also co-opted. To disqualify several PML(N) and PPP members from elected office, Musharraf issued an Election Order that required candidates to possess a bachelor's degree;[73] but he also extended equivalence on madrassa degrees, which primarily benefitted the MMA. The Supreme Court meekly went along in *Pakistan Muslim League (Q)* v. *Chief Executive of Islamic Republic of Pakistan* by swiftly upholding these electoral restrictions in a subsequent constitutional challenge:

> *We are convinced that the educational qualification prescribed for membership of Assemblies will not only raise [the Members'] level of competence and change the political culture but will also be an incentive to education.*[74]

After the 2002 National Assembly Election, which was stage-managed by Musharraf to ensure his allies' electoral victory, the military regime finally agreed to restore the 1973 Constitution, subject to the passage of the 17th Constitutional Amendment. In essence, the 17th Amendment granted

70 Shah (n 8), 191.
71 PLD 2002 SC 853.
72 *Ibid.* [81].
73 Section 8A of the Conduct of General Elections Order, 2002 read: '[A] person shall not be qualified to be elected or chosen as a member of Majlis-e-Shoora (Parliament) or a Provincial Assembly unless he is at least a graduate possessing a bachelor degree in any discipline or any degree recognised as equivalent by the University Grants Commission.'
74 *Pakistan Muslim League (Q)* v. *Chief Executive of Islamic Republic of Pakistan*, PLD 2002 SC 994 [21].

indemnity to the military for all actions they had taken since the 1999 coup, validated all the laws and orders issued during the State of Emergency, and authorised Musharraf to remain as President until 2007. In return, the MMA extracted a promise from Musharraf that he would resign as army chief by 31 December 2004.[75] But in 2004, Musharraf decided to renege on the promise and the President to Hold Another Office Act (PHAOA) was passed by his loyalists in the ruling PML(Q) government to allow him to remain as army chief until the end of his Presidency in 2007.

The Supreme Court was equally not prepared to stand in Musharraf's way. In *Pakistan Lawyers Forum* v. *Federation of Pakistan*,[76] the Court, in a clear departure from its dictum in *Zafar Ali Shah* and *Mahmood Khan*, upheld the 17th Amendment on the basis that 'no constitutional amendment could be struck down by the superior judiciary as being violative of those [salient] features'[77] in the Constitution and any 'remedy lay in the political and not the judicial process.'[78] The PHAOA was also upheld on the basis that Article 63(1)(d) of the 1973 Constitution expressly authorised Parliament to make exceptions for concurrent appointments by law.[79]

Chief Justice Chaudhry and Musharraf

In a surprising turn of events, the Supreme Court became activist and anti-establishment when Iftikhar Muhammad Chaudhry was appointed Chief Justice on 7 May 2005. As a junior justice on the Supreme Court, Chaudhry had been Musharraf's loyal footsoldier on the bench, and he had consistently voted to validate Musharraf's reign in all the constitutional challenges brought against the regime since the 1999 military coup.[80] But within a year of Chaudhry's appointment as Chief Justice,

[75] Article 61(1)(d) of the 1973 Constitution provided that a Member of Parliament (including the President) shall not hold an office of profit in the service of Pakistan other than an office declared by law not to disqualify its holder; but the 17th Amendment inserted a proviso that Article 63(1)(d) would only become operative on and from 31 December 2014.

[76] PLD 2005 SC 719.

[77] *Ibid.* [57].

[78] *Ibid.*

[79] Article 63(1)(d) of the 1973 Constitution reads: 'A person shall be disqualified from being elected or chosen as, and from being, a member of the Majlis-e-Shoora (Parliament), if:– he holds an office of profit in the service of Pakistan other than an office declared by law not to disqualify its holder.'

[80] See Taiyyaba Ahmed Qureshi, 'State of Emergency: General Pervez Musharraf's Executive Assault on Judicial Independence in Pakistan' (2010) 35 *North Carolina Journal of International Law and Commercial Regulation* 485.

and in a remarkable about-turn, the Supreme Court expanded its use of *suo motu* powers to investigate the disappearances of hundreds of persons secretly detained for alleged terrorism links and even invalidated Musharraf's privatisation of state-owned enterprises,[81] a central plank of the regime's economic agenda. It should therefore come as no surprise that Musharraf was unnerved by Chaudhry and the latter was eventually suspended for alleged misconduct in March 2007. But the Supreme Court stood its ground and reinstated Chaudhry in July 2007.

Musharraf's second term as President was set to expire in November 2007; and he was eager for a third. He was re-elected on 6 October 2007, in a Presidential election that was largely boycotted by the opposition parties. Nevertheless, the Supreme Court ordered the Election Commission not to certify the results until the former reached a decision on whether Musharraf could serve a third term as President.[82] Fearing an adverse outcome, Musharraf declared a State of Emergency on 3 November 2007 and held the Constitution to be in abeyance once again. Judges who refused to swear allegiance to the Provisional Constitutional Order were removed from office; and over 60 superior court judges, including Chief Justice Chaudhry, were so dismissed.

Unsurprisingly, a new panel of Supreme Court judges, staffed with only those who swore allegiance to the military regime, upheld Musharraf's eligibility to serve a third term as President. The express constitutional prohibition against the President serving more than two terms was dismissed by Chaudhry's replacement, Chief Justice Abdul Hameed Dogar, in the following farcical terms:

> *[Musharraf's] first term is to be excluded from the tally having not been enjoyed as a result of election and being traceable to an extra-constitutional step which had made itself manifest through Proclamation of Emergency (Amendment) Order, 2001 … and President's Succession Order, 2001.*[83]

In other words, since Musharraf had taken office illegally in the first instance, his first term in office did not count to the term limit. Musharraf's military coup on 3 November 2007 was subsequently upheld by the Dogar

81 *Watan Party* v. *Federation of Pakistan*, PLD 2006 SC 697. For an overview of Chaudhry's expansive use of the Court's *suo motu* powers, see Moeen H. Cheema and Ijaz S. Gilani (eds), *The Politics and Jurisprudence of the Chaudhry Court: 2005–2013* (Karachi: Oxford University Press, 2015).

82 Article 44(2) of the Constitution reads: 'Subject to the Constitution, a person holding office as President shall be eligible for re-election to that office, but no person shall hold that office for more than two consecutive terms.'

83 *Wajihuddin Ahmed* v. *Chief Election Commissioner, Islamabad*, PLD 2008 SC 13 [4].

Court in *Tika Iqbal* v. *General Pervez Musharraf*[84] on the basis that the 'constitutional deviation'[85] was necessary and inevitable so as to 'save the country from chaos and anarchy'[86] inflicted by the Supreme Court. The Court also refused to review the dismissal of Chaudhry and the other superior court judges as those cases were deemed to be 'hit by the doctrine of past and closed transaction'.[87]

The Supreme Court might have validated Musharraf's second coup, but civil society and the public at large were outraged by the imposition of *de facto* martial law again. This time, the military was also less enthused about Musharraf's military presidency as the officer corps were disillusioned in part by what they saw as America's War on Terror being fought on their own soil.[88] Without the backing of his military commanders, and faced with domestic and international pressures, Musharraf relinquished command over the army on 28 November 2007 before assuming the Presidency as a civilian the next day. He also ended the Emergency and revived the 1973 Constitution in December 2007; and elections were scheduled for early 2008.

The anti-Musharraf parties, PPP and PML(N), won the most number of seats in the National Assembly elections in February 2008; and Yousuf Raza Gilani from the PPP was elected Prime Minister. With the formation of the new PPP-led government, the new army chief, General Kayani, decided to reduce the role of the military in domestic politics; officers were prohibited from meeting politicians and officers assigned to Musharraf's Presidential office were recalled.[89] With military support for Musharraf waning, and a civilian government opposed to Musharraf being in power, the Supreme Court also began taking swipes at him. In *Nasir Mahmood* v. *Federation of Pakistan*,[90] the Court overruled its earlier decision in *Pakistan Muslim League (Q)* v. *Chief Executive of Islamic Republic of Pakistan*,[91] and invalidated the Musharraf-sanctioned law that permitted only tertiary graduates to run for political office. As Dogar CJ opined:

> *The classification based on educational qualification for contesting election is unreasonable inasmuch as at the most 2.6% of the population and 6.9%*

[84] PLD 2008 SC 178.
[85] *Ibid.* [72].
[86] *Ibid.* [57].
[87] *Ibid.* [72].
[88] Shah (n 8), 219.
[89] *Ibid.*, 221.
[90] PLD 2009 SC 107.
[91] *Pakistan Muslim League* (n 74).

> *of the registered voters were allowed to contest the election while more than 93% of the registered voters were disenfranchised, which is against the spirit of democracy.*[92]

This decision was naturally warmly welcomed by the PPP and PML(N) as their candidates were the original victims of the law. As pressure mounted for Musharraf to resign or be impeached, the military eventually prevailed upon Musharraf to resign from his Presidency on 18 August 2008 and Asif Ali Zardari, co-chairman of the PPP and Benazir Bhutto's widower,[93] was elected President in September 2008.

Originally, the PPP and PML(N) had agreed in 2007 to the restoration of Chaudhry as Chief Justice. But it is widely believed that the PPP was never fully committed to this outcome. Chaudhry was renowned for his opposition to the National Reconciliation Ordinance (NRO), an amnesty law passed by Musharraf in October 2007 to absolve Zardari and senior PPP leaders of criminal charges, but which had also deliberately excluded PML(N) leaders from its coverage.[94] Zardari, leader of the PPP, was concerned that a restored Chaudhry Court might invalidate this amnesty and thus dragged his feet on the issue. While several ousted Supreme Court judges were reappointed in 2008, the PPP stalled on Chaudhry. In fury, the PML(N) left the coalition government in August 2008. It was only with the escalation of protests by the opposition parties and pressure from the military that the PPP government relented and finally reinstated Chaudhry as Chief Justice in March 2009.

One of the first acts Chaudhry performed upon his reinstatement was to overrule the Dogar Court's earlier decision in *Tikka Iqbal* and declare Musharraf's Proclamation of Emergency in 2007 'unconstitutional, illegal, mala fide and void ab initio';[95] and the ouster of the superior court judges was also deemed null and void. (By then, Musharraf had already resigned from his Presidency and left Pakistan.) But the Court was quick to emphasise that the national election of 18 February 2008 was held to be in accordance with the Constitution, thereby not upsetting the post-election political status quo. As to be expected, the NRO, Musharraf's amnesty law, which benefitted only the PPP, soon came under Chaudhry's pruning

92 *Nasir Mahmood* (n 90) [47-A].

93 Benazir Bhutto was assassinated on 27 December 2007 while she was out on the campaign trail in the run-up to the 2008 election.

94 Anil Kalhan, '"Gray Zone" Constitutionalism and the Dilemma of Judicial Independence in Pakistan' (2013) 46 *Vanderbilt Journal of Transnational Law* 1, 49–50.

95 *Sindh High Court Bar Association* v. *Federation of Pakistan*, PLD 2009 SC 879 [85].

knife. In *Mubashir Hassan* v. *Federation of Pakistan*,[96] the Chaudhry Court unanimously invalidated the NRO. This result, in itself, was not a shocker as the federal and all the provincial governments too had conceded before the Supreme Court that the NRO was unconstitutional.[97] What arguably took the government by surprise was that the Court also demanded the government to reinstate all investigations and prosecutions that were withdrawn as a consequence of the NRO, and even ordered the government to make requests for mutual legal assistance from foreign governments, in particular Switzerland, about information on illegal proceeds that were allegedly deposited in overseas bank accounts.[98] (The Court's explicit mention of Switzerland was an oblique reference to President Zardari's corruption charges that were halted by the NRO.)

The Chaudhry Court next went after corrupt politicians amongst the rank-and-file. In 2010, the Supreme Court ordered the Election Commission to initiate action against all politicians who were suspected of making fraudulent representations that they possessed tertiary qualifications.[99] While the tertiary requirement had earlier been invalidated by the Court, Chaudhry took the view that the false declaration of one's electoral eligibility nonetheless amounted to a corrupt practice. Displeased with the pace of investigation undertaken by the Election Commission, the Supreme Court subsequently held that any person would have standing to lodge a complaint of this nature against an elected official for the Court's determination.[100] By early 2013, the Election Commission had uncovered 54 Parliamentarians with fake degrees and the Supreme Court had ordered for their elections to be nullified.[101]

It is noteworthy that the Supreme Court decided to up the ante in 2012 and target Prime Minister Gilani too. Since the invalidation of the NRO in *Mubashir Hassan*, the PPP had been dragging its feet on implementing the decision; in particular, Gilani had refused to write to the Swiss authorities concerning money laundering charges that implicated its party co-leader, President Zardari. The government had asked for the NRO decision to be implemented after Zardari's term in office concluded in 2013, as the President possessed immunity against all criminal prosecutions while he was in office. But the Court rather incredulously held that this 'bench has

[96] PLD 2010 SC 265.
[97] *Ibid.* [34].
[98] *Ibid.* [178].
[99] *Muhammad Rizwan Gill* v. *Nadia Aziz*, PLD 2010 SC 828.
[100] *Mian Najibuddin Oawaisi* v. *Aamir Yar*, PLD 2011 SC 1.
[101] *Mian Najeebuddin Owasi* v. *Amir Yar*, PLD 2013 SC 482 [14].

no power to modify the judgments and delay implementation'.[102] Gilani was convicted of contempt and was sentenced to imprisonment 'till the rising of the Court today'.[103] After securing Gilani's conviction for contempt, the Court went on to remove him from office on the basis that his conviction disqualified him under Article 63(1)(g)[104] of the Constitution.[105] In essence, the Court decided that Gilani's flagrant refusal to write to the Swiss authorities brought the judiciary into ridicule; and this disobedience of a court order justified the removal of a sitting Prime Minister.

One must note that the Chaudhry Court was only able to get away with this hyper-activism because of the chasm that had opened up between the PPP civilian government and the military. In late 2011, it was revealed that Pakistan's Ambassador to the United States and an ally of President Zardari, Hussain Haqqani, had written a memorandum to the United States government in May 2011 and had requested for American intervention on behalf of the PPP government against a potential military coup in Pakistan in exchange for a reconfiguration of Pakistan's national security protocols that would favour American interests. A scandal, dubbed 'Memogate', ensued; and upon the request of opposition politicians and the military, the judiciary readily obliged by constituting a commission to inquire into the authenticity of the memo, notwithstanding protestations by the PPP government that this dispute concerned a non-justiciable political question.[106] The Commission submitted its findings to the Supreme Court on 11 June 2012, confirming that Haqqani was the author of the controversial memo; and, interestingly, the Supreme Court removed Gilani on 19 June 2012, a week after the report's release.[107]

102 Suo Motu Case No. 4 of 2010 [Contempt Proceedings against Syed Yousaf Gilani regarding non-compliance of this Court's Order dated 16-12-2009], PLD 2012 SC 553 [41].

103 *Ibid.* [72].

104 Article 63(1)(g) of the Constitution reads: 'A person shall be disqualified from being elected or chosen as, and from being, a member of the Majlis-e-Shoora (Parliament), if:– he is propagating any opinion, or acting in any manner, prejudicial to the Ideology of Pakistan, or the sovereignty, integrity or security of Pakistan, or morality, or the maintenance of public order, or the integrity or independence of the judiciary of Pakistan, or which defames or brings into ridicule the judiciary or the Armed Forces of Pakistan.'

105 *Muhammad Azhar Siddique* v. *Federation of Pakistan*, PLD 2012 SC 660.

106 *Watan Party* v. *Federation of Pakistan*, PLD 2012 SC 292.

107 Tensions had been simmering since July 2008, when Prime Minister Gilani attempted to place the military's Inter-Services Intelligence under the control of the Ministry of Interior, but this move was rejected by the military. As the *Memogate* controversy was unfolding, there were rumours that the military was plotting to remove the PPP civilian government and there were also media reports that the civilian government was planning to sack the army and ISI chiefs. See Salman Masood, 'Pakistani Premier Warns of Plotting

This is not to say that the Supreme Court acted hand-in-glove with the military. The reinstated Chaudhry Court in post-Musharraf Pakistan continued to investigate the whereabouts of the missing persons and illegally detained terror suspects, but the judges pulled their punches in their investigations. Arrest orders against senior military officials were halted by the Court and the judges did nothing when persons they demanded the military to produce in Court turned up dead by the roadsides.[108] Even when the Supreme Court dug into an old case, pending for over 16 years, concerning allegations that the military establishment had stolen the 1990 National Assembly elections, the Court only found two retired generals culpable, and left the top brass still serving in the military alone.[109] Furthermore, the Federal Government was only directed to take 'necessary steps under the Constitution and law'[110] against the retired Generals while the Court gave specific orders for politicians who had allegedly received bribes from the military to be investigated by the Federal Investigation Agency and face charges in court.

Therefore, it was due to the ongoing tensions between the military and the civilian government, and the Chaudhry Court's (relative) indulgence on the military, that the judiciary was able to carve out 'policy' space[111] and assert its autonomy vis-à-vis the civilian government.[112] In 2012, the Supreme Court in *Workers' Party* v. *Federation of Pakistan*,[113] in preparation for the upcoming 2013 National Assembly, handed down a series of directions for the Election Commission to comply with, which included the following: monitor candidates' electoral expenses; update the electoral

by Military', *The New York Times*, 22 December 2011 <http://www.nytimes.com/2011/12/23/world/asia/pakistani-premier-yousaf-raza-gilani-lashes-out-at-his-military.html> accessed 1 February 2017; Saeed Shah, 'Pakistan Army Steps Up Confrontation with Government', *Guardian*, 11 January 2012 <http://www.theguardian.com/world/2012/jan/11/pakistan-army-confrontation-government> accessed 1 February 2017.

108 Shah (n 8), 231.

109 *Asghar Khan* v. *Mirza Aslam Baig*, PLD 2013 SC 1.

110 *Ibid.* [102(13)].

111 Tom Ginsburg, *Judicial Review in New Democracies: Constitutional Courts in Asian Cases*, (Cambridge: Cambridge University Press, 2003), 81.

112 In *Munir Hussain Bhatti* v. *Federation of Pakistan*, PLD 2011 SC 407, the Supreme Court held that the Parliamentary Committee had no discretion to reject the appointment of judicial nominees put forward by the Judicial Commission as this would encroach upon judicial independence. This decision, in substance though not in form, essentially overturned the 19th Amendment which provided inter alia that 'The Committee on receipt of a nomination from the Commission may confirm the nominee by majority of its total membership within fourteen days, failing which the nomination shall be deemed to have been confirmed.'

113 PLD 2012 SC 681.

roll; increase the number of polling stations; and prohibit candidates' staff and supporters from camping in the vicinity of the polling stations during the election period.[114] The May 2013 National Assembly Elections saw the defeat of the PPP and the return of Nawaz Sharif's PML(N) to power. There were reports of electoral irregularities in several constituencies and all the major political parties, other than the PML(N), alleged that large-scale organised rigging of the elections occurred.[115] Nevertheless, with the retirement of Chief Justice Chaudhry in December 2013, the Supreme Court retreated from its activist stance; and to date, all the constitutional petitions alleging electoral fraud in the 2013 general election and seeking judicial intervention remain pending before the Supreme Court. It is highly plausible that with the departure of Chaudhry from the Court and the return to power of Nawaz Sharif, who had vigorously fought for the restoration of all the senior judges removed by Musharraf, the Supreme Court decided to withdraw as an active player in electoral politics and allow the Sharif government to finish its term.

Conclusion

This chapter on Pakistan illuminates a common theme in fragile democracies: where the military imposes an independent constraint on civilian governments, and martial law regularly emerges as a recurring alternative to democratic rule, judicial hyper-activism will often facilitate or precipitate a coup.

Operating within a political system that is in a state of dysfunctional 'institutional disequilibrium',[116] it is unsurprising that the Supreme Court of Pakistan, for most of its history, has acquiesced to the military's use of brute force to take over the State's political apparatus. This was so when martial law was imposed in 1958 and 1977, and when Musharraf imposed his nation-wide emergency rule in 1999 and 2007. It is noteworthy that where the Supreme Court had de-legitimised the military coups, it had only done so after the dictators had been ousted: *Asma Jilani* (1972) and *Sindh High Court Bar Association* (2009).

Where the judiciary lacks the financial and coercive resources of the military, its high-stakes political duels with the generals have often been

[114] *Ibid.* [81].

[115] Moeen H. Cheema, '"Election Disputes" or Disputed Elections? Judicial (Non-)Review of the Electoral Process in Pakistan', in Po Jen Yap (ed.), *Judicial Review of Elections in Asia* (London: Routledge, 2016), 76–77.

[116] Kalhan (n 94), 10.

short-lived or futile. In 1993, when the Supreme Court restored Prime Minister Nawaz Sharif to office after he was sacked by the President, the military rendered the decision inconsequential by forcing both parties to resign several months later. When the Chaudhry Court challenged Musharraf's fiscal and national security policies, the Chief Justice was suspended in 2007; and when Musharraf's third term as President came under threat by the Supreme Court, he went on to remove over 60 superior court judges and replaced Chaudhry with the more pliant Dogar.

Therefore, so far as the restored Chaudhry Court had been able to weaken the PPP government in post-Musharraf Pakistan, it had only succeeded in doing so with the acquiescence of the military's high command. Even as Chaudhry doggedly pursued the PPP leadership, he exercised restraint over the military's constant defiance of court orders over the missing persons' cases and even acted at the military's behest by weighing in on the *Memogate* controversy. In essence, active judicial review in Pakistan has only succeeded insofar as the judges pragmatically accommodated military demands and were able to exploit the cleavage between the weak civilian government and the armed forces.

But this is not to say that democracy is a lost cause in Pakistan. The fact remains that in 2013, Pakistan experienced its first democratic transfer of power from one elected civilian government to another. While it is unlikely that the military has retreated permanently to the barracks, or is willing to accept complete political subordination,[117] Pakistan may have nevertheless taken its first step toward a future where constitutional norms can be observed in both rhetoric and practice.[118]

If so, the Supreme Court's enduring legacy in Pakistan may be those instances where it stood up to the government and drew a line in the sand to defend its institutional independence: judicial review cannot be ousted by martial law or emergency rule[119] nor can the political branches of government cobble together constitutional amendments to violate 'basic characteristics'[120] of the Constitution that violate parliament democracy and the independence of the judiciary. While these declarations might

[117] In recent years, the Pakistani civilian government has attempted to keep the military happy by increasing the defence budget by about 11% each year, and it is noteworthy that the country's defence budget is even larger than its development budget. See Baqir Sajjad, 'Defence Budget Hiked by Usual 11pc', *DAWN*, 4 June 2016 <http://www.dawn.com/news/1262657> accessed 1 February 2017.

[118] Shah (n 8), 285.

[119] *Begum Nusrat Bhutto* (n 17); *Zafar Ali Shah* (n 64).

[120] *Mahmood Khan Achakzai* (n 48).

seem like empty or meaningless rhetoric that have been ignored with impunity by dictators governing under military law, these judicial declarations may one day serve as real constraints on political power when the country transitions into a stable democracy where martial law is no longer a viable political option for all actors operating within the constitutional system.

10

The Supreme Court of Bangladesh and Defensive Judicial Review

East Pakistan seceded from Pakistan in 1971 after a civil war, and Bangladesh emerged as an independent nation governed under the 1972 Constitution. Since then, the country has been governed twice under martial law – from 1975 to 1979 and from 1982 to 1986; and Emergency rule has been imposed four times, the most recent of which was between 2007 and 2008,[1] with the enshrined constitutional rights suspended each time.

Bangladesh and Martial Law

Following the independence of Bangladesh, the Awami League (AL), the main political party in East Pakistan, led by Sheikh Mujibur Rahman (Mujib), won resoundingly in the country's first post-independence election in 1973 and dominated Parliament with an overwhelming majority.[2] Unfortunately, Mujib's administration was dogged by corruption, and as the economy deteriorated, public protests became increasingly violent.[3] Mujib responded by declaring a State of Emergency in 1974. He also passed the 4th Amendment to the Constitution in 1975, which abolished all political parties in Bangladesh and essentially introduced a one-party state.[4]

But Mujib's dictatorial regime did not last long. In August 1975, he was assassinated by pro-Pakistan elements in his army. A member of Mujib's cabinet, Khondaker Moshtaque Ahmed, quickly appointed himself as

[1] See Ridwanul Hoque, 'The Recent Emergency and the Politics of the Judiciary in Bangladesh' (2009) 2(2) *National University of Juridical Science Law Review* 183.

[2] The AL received 293 out of 300 seats. See Ali Riaz, 'Political Parties, Elections, and the Party System', in Ali Riaz and Mohammad Sajjadur Rahman (eds), *Routledge Handbook of Contemporary Bangladesh* (London: Routledge, 2016), 67.

[3] Harry Blair, 'Party Overinstitutionalisation, Contestation, and Democratic Degradation in Bangladesh', in Paul R. Brass (ed.), *Routledge Handbook of South Asian Politics: India, Pakistan, Bangladesh, Sri Lanka and Nepal* (London: Routledge, 2010), 99–100.

[4] See Nizam Ahmed, 'The Parliament', in Ali Riaz and Mohammad Sajjadur Rahman (eds), *Routledge Handbook of Contemporary Bangladesh* (London: Routledge, 2016), 82.

President and imposed martial law throughout the country. But Khondaker too was ousted from power by the military a few months later and Chief Justice Sayem took over as the Chief Martial Law Administrator and President in 1976. Sayem also did not last long in office as General Ziaur Rahman (Zia), the Army Chief of Staff, grabbed the reins in 1977.

During the period of martial law first imposed by Khondaker in 1975 and continued by his successors, the Supreme Court of Bangladesh basically surrendered its role as guardian of the country's enshrined liberties. A military law regulation passed in 1977 permitted the military government to forcibly acquire the citizenry's property and ousted all judicial review over the acquisition. When it was challenged in *Halima Khatun* v. *Bangladesh* (1978),[5] the Supreme Court of Bangladesh (Appellate Division) was emphatic that the courts have no option but to give effect to the martial law regulations and proclamations, and ignore the Constitution:

> *If the laws which this court administers does, therefore, amount to what is known as harsh or unjust legislation the court will still have to administer it.*[6]

In the same vein, when the applicants challenged the legality of a Military Regulation that permitted the military government to transfer any case from the Criminal Court to the Martial Law Court, the Appellate Division in *State* v. *Haji Joynal Abedin* (1978)[7] held by a majority of three to one that the Constitution had been 'reduced to a position subordinate to the [1975 Martial Law] Proclamation'[8] and Clause (g) of the said Proclamation stated that no court could call into question any action taken by or under any Martial Law Regulation. But one should note that the accused applicants' offences were committed and their cases pending before the Criminal Court prior to the imposition of martial law; and the impugned Regulation did not expressly state that the provisions for transfer were to be applied retrospectively. This was the view of the lone dissenting judge, KM Subhan J, who argued that the Regulation, in the absence of clear language to the contrary, should be presumed not to apply retrospectively to the accused.[9]

Zia promised fresh national elections in 1978 and he intended to run for President. Although a pre-existing military regulation barred

[5] [1978] 7 CLC (AD) 2370.

[6] *Ibid.* [19].

[7] [1980] 9 CLC (AD) 1254.

[8] *Ibid.* [18].

[9] *Ibid.* [54].

a military officer from running for political office, Zia introduced an amendment that effectively removed this prohibition. Unsurprisingly, the Supreme Court of Bangladesh (High Court Division)[10] upheld this amendment as constitutional and found no 'act of mala fide'.[11] With his candidacy secured, Zia won the Presidential election in June 1978. The Parliamentary election was scheduled for February 1979 and Zia formed the Bangladesh Nationalist Party (BNP) to contest in the multi-party election. The BNP eventually won 207 of the 300 seats, and with the overpowering majority in Parliament, it successfully passed the 5th Amendment of the Bangladesh Constitution to legitimise Zia's martial law regime. After securing amnesty for the military for all past actions taken, martial law was lifted in April 1979.

In view of the fact that the 5th Constitutional Amendment had immunised all acts taken by the martial law government from judicial review, the Appellate Division in *Khandaker Ehtehshamuddin Ahmed* v. *Bangladesh* (1980)[12] refused to reopen past criminal cases that had been resolved by the Martial Law Court.

However, Zia was assassinated in 1981, and his successor was ousted in a bloodless coup in 1982 by the Army Chief of Staff, General Hussain Mohammad Ershad, who had justified military intervention on the basis that the civilian government was corrupt and incompetent. Martial law was once again imposed throughout the nation and the Constitution was suspended. The Martial Law Proclamation of 1982 expressly stated that 'all proceedings arising out of and in connection with writ petitions under … the suspended Constitution shall abate';[13] and the Appellate Division obliged by confirming that all appeals pending before the Court were abated, including the finalised judgments of the High Court Division under appeal.[14]

Taking a leaf from Zia's playbook, Ershad formed the Jatiya Party (JP) to contest the parliamentary election scheduled for 1986. With the elections rigged in Ershad's favour, the JP managed to win a bare majority of the Parliamentary seats;[15] Ershad then secured his election as President a few months later. With Ershad in control of Parliament, the 7th Constitutional Amendment was passed to legitimise his martial law regime from March 1982 and November 1986. Once all laws and decisions taken under

[10] *A.K. Mujibur Rahman* v. *Returning Officer* [1978] 7 CLC (HCD) 9253.
[11] *Ibid.* [6].
[12] [1980] 9 CLC (AD) 1551.
[13] Clause (g) of the Martial Law Proclamation was issued on 24 March 1982.
[14] *Bangladesh* v. *Md. Salimullah* [1981] 10 CLC (AD) 4960.
[15] The JP won 153 out of 300 seats in the parliamentary election in 1986. See Riaz (n 2), 67.

Ershad's martial law were immunised from judicial review, he lifted martial law and restored the 1972 Constitution in November 1986.

But democracy did not take root under Ershad's government even with the return of civilian rule. Ershad's JP won the general election again in 1988 when major opposition parties, including the BNP and AL, agreed to a joint boycott. Opposition and protests against Ershad's autocratic civilian rule intensified, and he was eventually forced to resign from his Presidency in 1990 when the military also withdrew their support.

The Post-Martial Law Judiciary

At the close of Ershad's autocratic reign, even the Appellate Division began to take swipes at his faltering administration. In *Anwar Hossain Chowdhury* v. *Bangladesh*,[16] the Court, by a majority of three to one, invalidated the 8th Amendment to the Constitution, which was passed by Ershad's supine Parliament in June 1988 to formally establish six additional permanent benches of the High Court Division in various parts of Bangladesh, to co-exist alongside the pre-existing bench in Dhaka. In essence, this constitutional arrangement enshrined into formal law a Martial Law Proclamation issued by Ershad in 1982 that split the High Court into seven separate benches, with each bench conferred with exclusive jurisdiction over a designated territory, thereby decentralising and diluting the power that the unitary High Court Division traditionally wielded.

Badrul Chowdhury J, who wrote the leading opinion, was emphatic that Parliament's power to amend the Constitution was not unlimited. As his Lordship argued, echoing the Indian Supreme Court in *Kesavananda Bharati* v. *State of Kerala*,[17] the power to frame a Constitution was a primary power while a power to amend a constitution was a derivative one.[18] Furthermore, a constitutional amendment was qualitatively different from its repeal or replacement[19]; therefore, no 'basic feature'[20] of the original Constitution could be 'dismantled by an authority created by the Constitution itself – namely the Parliament'.[21] Chowdhury J noted that the 8th Amendment did not provide for the transfer of any cases from one territorial Bench to another; therefore the 'absence of such provision of

[16] (1989) BLD (Special) (AD) 1.
[17] (1973) AIR (SC) 1461 (Supreme Court of India).
[18] *Anwar Hossain Chowdhury* (n 16) [161].
[19] *Ibid.* [294].
[20] *Ibid.* [220].
[21] *Ibid.*

transfer shows that territorial exclusive courts, independent of each other, have been created dismantling the High Court Division'.[22] In view of this ruling, the 8th Amendment was declared unconstitutional as 'the basic structural pillar, that is [the] judiciary, has been destroyed and plenary judicial power of the Republic vested in the High Court Division has been taken away'[23] by the impugned Amendment that purported to establish 'rival courts'[24] with the same powers as the original High Court such that it essentially 'ceases to exist except in name'.[25]

In the same vein, Shahabuddin Ahmed J, in a concurring opinion, observed as follows:

> *[T]he 'constituent power', that is power to make a Constitution, it belongs to the people alone. It is the original power. Even if the 'constituent power' is vested in Parliament the power is a derivative one and the mere fact that an amendment has been made in exercise of the derivative constituent power will not automatically make the amendment immune from challenge.*[26]

A fortiori, Ahmed J argued that any constitutional amendment was subject to the 'retention of the basic structures'[27] of the original Constitution and the Court was empowered to 'undo an amendment if it transgresses its limits and alters a basic structure of the Constitution'.[28] Given that the 8th Amendment had 'broken the "oneness" of the High Court Division and thereby damaged a basic structure of the Constitution',[29] it was deemed void by Ahmed J. In a concurring opinion, M.H. Rahman J invalidated the 8th Amendment on a different ground. By breaking up the High Court into seven territorial benches, Rahman J expressed concern that different benches might reach different outcomes on similar issues, and there were also uncertainties over which bench had jurisdiction in cross-border or inter-territorial disputes, such that the subordinate courts and potential litigants would be left in a legal quandary.[30] This state of legal uncertainty, he argued, violated the rule of law and thus justified the invalidation of the 8th Amendment.[31] Nevertheless, all three judges in the

22 *Ibid.* [297].
23 *Ibid.* [295].
24 *Ibid.* [297].
25 *Ibid.*
26 *Ibid.* [381].
27 *Ibid.* [417].
28 *Ibid.*
29 *Ibid.* [419].
30 *Ibid.* [518].
31 *Ibid.* [523].

majority accepted that the Chief Justice could provide for Sessions of the High Court to be held outside of its permanent seat in Dhaka from time to time so as to expedite the disposal of cases.[32]

Interestingly, the lone dissenting judge, A.T.M. Afzal J, agreed that no constitutional amendment could abrogate the Constitution or 'any of its "structural pillars"',[33] e.g., the complete removal of judicial review. On the facts, however, he upheld the constitutionality of the 8th Amendment by reading down its substantive effect: the Amendment did not expressly bar the Chief Justice of Bangladesh from introducing Rules of Court that permit Benches to transfer cases between one another; and each territorial Bench would be allowed to hear a dispute so long as the 'party, property, right, obligation, violation, etc.'[34] had a connection to the assigned territory of the bench.[35]

Soon after the restoration of a unitary High Court Division at Dhaka, an upsurge of mass protests against Ershad forced him to resign in December 1990. The Chief Justice, Shahabuddin Ahmed, was appointed President, and his administration served as a caretaker government until the February 1991 elections. The BNP, led by Khaleda Zia – General Zia's widow – was returned to power in what was perhaps the fairest election in Bangladesh since its independence. After the election, the 12th Constitutional Amendment was also passed in late 1991 to roll back the authoritarian changes Mujib had introduced in 1975 with the 4th Amendment.

But peace did not prevail for long. In a by-election held in 1994, the AL lost a seat to the BNP, but the opposition insisted that they had lost only because the ruling government had engaged in electoral fraud.[36] Opposition Members of Parliament demanded that the government introduce a constitutional amendment that would provide for a Non-party Caretaker Government (NCG) to manage the country right before a new election was held, as had been the case for the 1991 election. They

[32] *Ibid.* [297, 420, 527].

[33] *Ibid.* [600].

[34] *Ibid.* [623].

[35] One may note that Subsection (5) as introduced by the 8th Amendment read as follows: 'The President shall, in consultation with the Chief Justice, assign the area in relation to which each permanent Bench shall have jurisdictions, powers and function conferred or that may be conferred on the High Court Division.'

[36] M. Jashim Ali Chowdhury, 'Elections in "Democratic" Bangladesh', in Mark Tushnet and Madhav Khosla (eds), *Unstable Constitutionalism: Law and Politics in South Asia* (New York: Cambridge University Press, 2015), 208.

also sought to pressure the government into compliance by boycotting Parliamentary sittings until their demands were met.

As the boycott dragged on for months, the High Court Division in December 1994 finally decided to intervene in the dispute and ordered the opposition members to return to Parliament. Interestingly, Article 78(1) of the Constitution provides that 'the validity of the proceedings in Parliament shall not be questioned in any Court', but the Court held that this ouster of judicial review only applied to the internal proceedings of Parliament and was inapplicable vis-à-vis the controversy at issue:

> *It cannot be conceded that indulging in strike, hartal and street propaganda for realisation of the demand for a caretaker government shunning the Constitutional obligation in participating in parliamentary proceedings and destroying the fundamentals of the Parliament, in other words, affecting the constitution of the House cannot by any stretch of imagination be called internal proceedings to be barred under Article 78 of the Constitution. This abstention for realisation of the demand is not a matter which pertains neither to the regulation of the business or the maintenance of order in the National Assembly or affecting any of its privileges.*[37]

However, the High Court's decision was never enforced as an appeal was lodged before the Appellate Division and a stay of the High Court's decision was granted. (Interestingly, the Appellate Division dragged its feet on the case for over a decade and only handed down its decision in 2007, stating categorically that the judiciary could not compel Members of Parliament to attend parliamentary sittings.[38])

As the legality of the boycott remained in limbo, all of the opposition Members of Parliament decided to resign *en masse* in December 1994. Eventually, the President of Bangladesh sent a constitutional reference to the Appellate Division, asking the Court to decide whether the members' deliberate boycott of Parliamentary sittings – such that they would be absent from Parliament for ninety consecutive sitting days – would lead to their seats being deemed vacated under Article 67(1)(b).[39] The Appellate Division in *Special Reference No. of 1995*[40] decided that 'a distorted meaning'[41] could not be given to the word 'absent' so as to 'exclude

[37] *Anwar Hossain Khan* v. *Speaker of Bangladesh* (1995) 47 DLR (HCD) 42 [22].

[38] *Moudud Ahmed* v. *Anwar Hossain Khan* [2007] 36 CLC (AD) 3199 [32].

[39] Article 67(1)(b) reads: 'A member of Parliament shall vacate his seat if he is absent from Parliament without leave of Parliament for ninety consecutive sitting days.'

[40] [1995] 24 CLC (AD) 841.

[41] *Ibid.* [67].

walkout and boycott'[42] from its meaning. As observed by Chief Justice A.T.M. Afzal:

> *The scheme of the Constitution is that if a member or members of Parliament remain absent without the leave of the Parliament for ninety consecutive sitting days, he or they do it on pain of vacating his or their seats. The philosophy behind this is that his or their constituencies cannot be left unrepresented.*[43]

Nevertheless, the Court held that in computing this period of ninety consecutive sitting days, the time period when Parliament was adjourned or not in session had to be excluded.[44] Nevertheless, even by this count, all the opposition Members of Parliament lost their seats.

Under immense public and political pressure, the BNP government finally introduced the 13th Constitutional Amendment in 1996, which provided for all future parliamentary elections to be overseen by an unelected Non-party Caretaker Government (NCG), headed by a retired Chief Justice, and for the interim government to manage the country until the elected government takes office.[45] Pursuant to this new system, the AL defeated the incumbent party in the June 1996 election and its leader, Sheikh Hasina – Mujib's daughter – took over the government. Now in opposition, the BNP repeated the same tactics that AL had resorted to in the past and constantly staged *hartals* (violent strikes) and parliamentary boycotts.

As the 2001 elections drew near, the AL government stepped down and allowed an NCG to preside over the parliamentary elections. Interestingly, five weeks before the election, the Appellate Division[46] ruled that former military dictator and Bangladeshi President Hussain Mohammad Ershad's conviction on corruption charges and sentence of imprisonment exceeding three years[47] disqualified him from elected office.[48] But it is noteworthy that Article 66(4) of the Constitution provides that any dispute on a

[42] *Ibid.*

[43] *Ibid.*

[44] *Ibid.* [76].

[45] Section 6 of the 13th Amendment provided that a general election had to be held within 90 days after Parliament was dissolved.

[46] *Hussain Mohammad Ershad* v. *Zahedul Islam Khan* [2002] 31 CLC (AD) 1316.

[47] Ershad was convicted by the Sessions Court in 1993 for corruption and sentenced to seven years of imprisonment. His sentence was eventually reduced to three years and eight months by the Appellate Division in 2000.

[48] Article 66(2) of the Constitution reads: 'A person shall be disqualified for election as, or for being, a member of Parliament who– has been, on conviction for a criminal offence involving moral turpitude, sentenced to imprisonment for a term of not less than two years unless a period of five years has elapsed since his release.'

candidate's disqualification 'shall be referred to the Election Commission' for determination and its decision is final. In apparent disregard of Article 66(4), the Court held that once a candidate had been convicted of a crime involving moral turpitude – as corruption was – and his sentence of not less than two years imprisonment affirmed by the Appellate Division, 'there remains no dispute to be decided by the Election Commission'[49] and the politician would be disqualified automatically. With that, Ershad was swiftly barred from the parliamentary election that was scheduled for several weeks later, and the BNP (still led by Khaleda Zia) emerged victorious as the ruling party in Bangladesh once again.[50]

While the Supreme Court had affirmed the basic structure doctrine in *Anwar Hossain Chowdhury*, no other constitutional amendment was invalidated for over two decades after that landmark decision. In 2005, the Appellate Division in *Farida Akhter* v. *Bangladesh*[51] upheld the constitutionality of the 14th Constitutional Amendment, which allowed for 45 additional seats in Parliament to be reserved only for women. The seats would be allocated to political parties in proportion to their overall share of seats in Parliament. The Court emphasised that this Amendment did not violate any basic structure of the Constitution as Article 28(4) authorised affirmative action in favour of women. But this Amendment is not without controversy, as it has been criticised by women's rights groups on the ground that it merely provides a means for a minority government to gain majority control of the Parliament through the additional reserved unelected seats they control, and that the women representatives are only chosen by the party leaders and not elected by the people.[52]

Similarly, in response to a constitutional challenge brought by a private citizen, the High Court Division affirmed the constitutionality of the 13th Constitutional Amendment and the concomitant NCG system, and held that it was not a violation of the basic structure of the Constitution.[53] It is noteworthy that both the BNP and the AL had argued for the retention of the Amendment and the Court accepted their argument:

> *Fair, independent and impartial election was not possible for the reason that although the Prime Minister used to run the government during the*

[49] *Hussain Mohammad Ershad* (n 46) [10].

[50] With the fall of Ershad, his Jantiya Party became very much a regional enterprise, popular only in Rangpur (Ershad's district) and Sylhet. See Blair (n 3), 102.

[51] [2005] 34 CLC (AD) 1907.

[52] In 2011, the 15th Amendment was passed whereby the number of reserved seats for women was increased from 45 to 50.

[53] *M Saleem Ullah* v. *Bangladesh* [2004] 33 CLC (HCD) 7029.

> *interregnum and held the general election to the Parliament but the election was not free and fair as much as the government men and machinery were used by such government to influence the election result in favour of the political party to which the Prime Minister belonged. This was the major factor necessitating the passing of the impugned Act for engrafting the non-party caretaker system in the Constitution in 1996 by amending the Constitution.*[54]

But this is not to say that the Supreme Court has retreated to the political side-lines. Indeed, in post-martial law Bangladesh, the Supreme Court has chosen to facilitate democratic reforms in more modest ways, most of which were imposed on the Election Commission. In 2005, the High Court Division required the Election Commission to publicly disclose information relating to the election candidates' academic qualifications, criminal antecedents, occupation, assets and liabilities, and sources of income.[55] In 2006, the Appellate Division vetoed the Election Commission's plans to create a fresh electoral roll for the 2007 election by making house-to-house visits. Instead, the Court required the Commission to prepare the electoral register by 'taking into consideration … the existing Roll',[56] and adding new eligible voters and removing the deceased from the electoral roll where necessary. This judicial move was in response to the widespread allegation that the Election Commission, staffed with pro-BNP officers, had padded the latest 'fresh' electoral roll with millions of bogus voters.[57]

The AL-led opposition remained unconvinced that the upcoming 2007 election would be conducted fairly by the BNP-controlled Election Commission. Much of the controversy also centred around the passage and implications of the 14th Amendment to the Constitution, pushed through by the BNP government in 2004, which had raised the retirement age of judges by two years. It was believed that this move was designed by the incumbent BNP to allow for Chief Justice K.M. Hasan – a former BNP leader – to retire from his judicial office just in time to head the NCG government prior to the 2007 election. (The 13th Amendment, passed after the 1996 election, provided for the preceding retired Chief Justice to head the NCG.) As the BNP clashed with AL over the formation of the caretaker government in 2006, and violence and strikes escalated in the

[54] *Ibid.* [36].

[55] *Abdul Momen Chowdhury and Ors* v. *Election Commission* [2005] 34 CLC (HCD) 8941 [11].

[56] *Election Commission* v. *Alhaj Advocate Rahmat Ali MP* [2006] 35 CLC (AD) 1900 [129].

[57] See Blair (n 3), 107; Devin T. Hagerty, 'Bangladesh in 2007: Democracy Interrupted, Political and Environmental Challenges Ahead' (2008) 48 *Asian Survey* 177, 178.

streets, President Iajuddin Ahmed decided to assume the post of Chief Adviser to the NCG himself in October 2006 with elections scheduled for 22 January 2007.

The opposition was however not placated. In December 2006, the country was marred by mass rioting and killings between rival groups. Events took a dramatic turn when the military intervened and ordered President Ahmed to declare a State of Emergency and postpone the election indefinitely. After a State of Emergency was declared on 11 January 2007, President Ahmed resigned as head of the caretaker government and was replaced by Fakhruddin Ahmed – a former governor of Bangladesh's central bank who was backed by the military.

Emergency Rule in Bangladesh (2007–2008)

With Bangladesh under emergency rule and constitutional rights suspended, the NCG took the opportunity to arrest key BNP and AL political leaders on corruption charges and rounded up over 40,000 alleged criminals and thugs in January 2007 alone.[58] By September 2007, it was believed that more than 200,000 persons had been detained.[59] Interestingly, in August 2007, when emergency rule was well underway, the High Court Division in *Kazi Mamnur Rashid* v. *Government of Bangladesh*[60] handed down a carefully crafted judgment that imposed a legal obligation on the caretaker government to assist the Election Commission in the preparation of an updated electoral roll, voter identification cards, and the separation of the Election Commission Secretariat from the Prime Minister's Office. At the same time, however, the Court refused to impose a timeline on the Caretaker government for the calling of elections and in fact held that an election *could only be* conducted by the Election Commission with the assistance of the present caretaker Government *after* fulfilling the observations/directions given by the Court.[61] In other words, the Court in effect gave political space to the unelected government to postpone elections if it so chose.

[58] Freedom House, 'Bangladesh: Countries at the Crossroads 2007' <https://freedomhouse.org/report/countries-crossroads/2007/bangladesh> accessed 1 February 2017.

[59] Human Rights Watch, 'Bangladesh: Abuses Grow in Crackdown on Protests', 25 August 2007 <https://www.hrw.org/news/2007/08/25/bangladesh-abuses-grow-crackdown-protests> accessed 1 February 2017.

[60] Writ Petition No 713 of 2007 (27 August 2007).

[61] *Ibid.*

But the Supreme Court did not capitulate completely to the demands of the caretaker government during this period of emergency rule. Notwithstanding the deference displayed toward the political branches, the Court was willing to take on the government when the independence of the judiciary was at stake or under siege. Back in 1999 during civilian rule, the Appellate Division in *Secretary, Ministry of Finance* v. *Masdar Hossain* (1999)[62] had invalidated a law that included judicial officers within the civil service, and the Court further directed the government to establish a Judicial Service Commission for the recruitment of judges and a separate Judicial Pay Commission to review the terms of conditions of judges. But the BNP government dragged its feet on the issue and constantly asked for extensions to comply with the judicial order. Ironically, it was only when Bangladesh was under Emergency rule in 2007 that the unelected caretaker government took significant steps to comply with the *Masdar* judgment.[63] One such reform was the passage of the Supreme Judicial Commission Ordinance, which established a Supreme Judicial Commission chaired by the Chief Justice to recommend suitable candidates for appointment to the Supreme Court. But the High Court Division invalidated a statutory provision that authorised the President to reject the Commission's recommendation as that would render the independent appointment mechanism 'meaningless, futile, and ineffective'.[64] Therefore, even during the period of military rule, the courts would not stand by idly if the independence of the judiciary was perceived to be encroached upon by the government, especially in light of Bangladesh's chequered history of deeply partisan judicial appointments.[65]

But as the Emergency dragged on into its second year, the High Court Division grew impatient over Bangladesh's persisting rule under military law. In *Advocate Sultana Kamal* v. *Bangladesh* (2008),[66] the High Court invalidated various ouster clauses introduced by Emergency regulations

[62] [1999] 28 CLC (AD) 598.

[63] See Sara Hossain, 'Confronting Constitutional Curtailments: Attempts to Rebuild Independence of the Judiciary in Bangladesh', in Paul R. Brass (ed.), *Routledge Handbook of South Asian Politics: India, Pakistan, Bangladesh, Sri Lanka and Nepal* (London: Routledge, 2010), 196.

[64] *Idrisur Rahman* v. *Bangladesh* (2008) 60 DLR (HCD) 714. One may note that Abdur Rashid J would have invalidated the entire Ordinance as he argued that only Parliament, and not the President, was authorised to enact such changes.

[65] See Hossain (n 63), 194; Chowdhury (n 36), 223–224.

[66] (2009) 14 MLR (HCD) 105.

that barred judicial review, but the decision was swiftly stayed by the Appellate Division pending appeal.[67] The substantive merits of the latter decision were not argued before the Appellate Division as the military eventually kept their promise and lifted the Emergency on 17 December 2008. Elections that were widely perceived to be free and fair were held on 29 December 2008. The AL, still led by Sheikh Hasina, won 230 elected seats and thus formed the next government with a super-majority in Parliament.

Civilian Rule and the Demise of Unconstitutional Constitutional Amendments

Soon after civilian rule returned to Bangladesh, the Appellate Division was confronted with a series of challenges to constitutional amendments passed by martial law governments or civilian governments that sought to insulate past martial law regimes from legal liability.

In *Justice Syed Dastagir Hossain* v. *Idrisur Rahman* (2009),[68] the Appellate Division was faced with a challenge brought by several judges whose appointments to the Supreme Court had been rejected by the President, notwithstanding favourable recommendations by the Chief Justice. But it is noteworthy that Article 95(1) (as it stood then) merely provided that the 'Chief Justice and other Judges shall be appointed by the President'. Nevertheless, the Court held that a constitutional convention whereby the Chief Justice was consulted before any Supreme Court judge was appointed had 'hardened and matured into a rule of law'[69] and was 'binding on the executive';[70] and although the Chief Justice was consulted before the judicial candidates were rejected, they were rejected 'without any cogent reason'[71] and the President therefore had to reconsider them for appointment.

But what is even more significant about the *Idrisur* decision is that the judicial appointment clause at issue – Article 95(1) – was introduced by the 4th Amendment to the Constitution by Mujib in 1975 after he declared a State of Emergency across Bangladesh and imposed a one-party state.

[67] See Ridwanul Hoque, 'The Judicialisation of Politics in Bangladesh' in Mark Tushnet and Madhav Khosla (eds), *Unstable Constitutionalism: Law and Politics in South Asia* (New York: Cambridge University Press, 2015), 274.

[68] [2009] 38 CLC (AD) 3431.

[69] *Ibid.* [269].

[70] *Ibid.*

[71] *Ibid.*

Prior to the 4th Amendment, the original Article 95(1) actually imposed a constitutional duty on the President to consult with the Chief Justice,[72] but this requirement was repealed by the 4th Amendment. Therefore, in essence, the Appellate Division in *Idrisur* had restored the original Article 95(1) to the Constitution and implicitly invalidated this portion of the 4th Amendment. This judicial manoeuvre was justified by the Court on the basis that the independence of the judiciary was a basic structure of the Constitution[73] and 'consultation with the Chief Justice with primacy of his opinion in the matter of appointment of judges and the administration of judiciary is an essential part of independence of judiciary'.[74] What was particularly troubling to the Court was that since the 4th Amendment took effect, many otherwise qualified judges had been rejected by the President for purely political reasons. In particular, after taking office in 2001, the BNP government had rejected the re-appointment of 15 out of 31 judges who were first appointed by the previous AL government, notwithstanding a positive recommendation from the Chief Justice.[75]

Soon after *Idrisur*, in *Khondker Delwar Hossain* v. *Bangladesh Italian Marble Works* (2010),[76] the Appellate Division invalidated the entire 5th Amendment,[77] which was passed in 1979 by Zia's Parliament to legitimise his martial law rule in Bangladesh between 1975 and 1979. On the facts, the petitioner's property was forcibly acquired by the martial law

[72] Article 95(1) of the Constitution prior to the 4th Amendment read: 'The Chief Justice shall be appointed by the President, and the other Judges shall be appointed by the President after consultation with the Chief Justice.'

[73] *Justice Syed Dastagir Hossain* (n 68) [164].

[74] *Ibid.* [269].

[75] Chowdhury (n 36), 223. In June 2011, the AL government passed the 15th Amendment to the Constitution, and formally restored the original Article 95(1) to the Constitution.

[76] *Khondker Delwar Hossain* v. *Bangladesh Italian Marble Works* (Civil Petition for Leave to Appeals Nos 1044 & 1045 of 2009).

[77] The 5th Amendment added Paragraph 18 to the 4th Schedule of the Constitution, and it read: 'All Proclamations, Proclamation Orders, Martial Law Regulations, Martial Law orders and other laws made during the period between the 15th August 1975, and the 9th April 1979 (both days inclusive) all amendments additions, modifications, substitutions and omissions made in this Constitution during the said period by any such Proclamation, all orders made, acts and things done, and actions and proceedings taken, or purported to have been made, done or taken by any person or authority during the said period in exercise of the powers derived or purported to have been derived from any such Proclamation, Martial Law Regulation, Martial Law order or any other law, or in execution of or in compliance with any order made or sentence passed by any Court, tribunal or authority in the exercise or purported of such powers, are hereby ratified and confirmed and are declared to have been validly made, done or taken and shall not be called in question in or before any court, tribunal or authority on any whatsoever.'

government back in 1975 and a Martial Law Regulation passed in 1977 barred courts from granting the aggrieved applicants any remedy. The 5th Amendment further immunised all acts taken by the martial law government from judicial review. A past Appellate Division decision in *Khandaker Ehtehshamuddin Ahmed* (1980),[78] where the Court upheld all the Martial Law Regulations passed between 1975 and 1979 on the basis of the 5th Amendment, was distinguished on the ground that the constitutionality of that Amendment was not questioned therein. On the other hand, the Court in *Bangladesh Italian Marble Works* was faced with a direct challenge to its legality, a matter which it could decide afresh.

The Appellate Division went on to make the following empathic pronouncement against martial law:

> *Making … the Constitution subordinate and subservient to the Martial Law Proclamations, Regulations and Orders are absolutely illegal, void and non-est in the eye of law. So any attempt to legalise this illegality in any manner or method and by any Authority or Institution, how high so ever, is also void and non-est and remains so for ever.*[79]

As the Martial Law Regulations were illegal, they could not be ratified by the 5th Amendment. The impugned Amendment was thus unconstitutional as it 'not only violated the supremacy of the Constitution but also the rule of law and by preventing judicial review of the legislative and administrative actions, also violated two other more basic features of the Constitution, namely, independence of judiciary and its power of judicial review'.[80]

Lest one think that the Court appeared confrontational in this decision, one should note that the invalidation of the 5th Amendment was precisely what the Attorney General, on behalf of the AL government, argued for during the hearings. Now that the army had retreated back to the barracks and the AL government was back in power with supermajority control over Parliament, the Court was ready to lash out against military rule with the civilian government's unspoken blessing:

> *Let it be made clear that military rule was wrongly justified in the past and it ought not to be justified in future on any ground, principle, doctrine or theory whatsoever. Military rule is against the dignity, honour and glory of the nation that it achieved after great sacrifice; it is against the dignity and honour of the people of Bangladesh who are committed to uphold the sovereignty*

[78] *Khandaker Ehtehshamuddin Ahmed* (n 12).
[79] *Bangladesh Italian Marble Works* (n 76), 92.
[80] *Ibid.*, 156.

> *and integrity of the nation by all means; it is also against the honour of each and every soldier of the Armed Forces who are oath bound to bear true faith and allegiance to Bangladesh and uphold the constitution, which embodies the will of the people, honestly and faithfully serve Bangladesh in their respective services and also see that the Constitution is upheld, it is not kept in suspension or abrogated, it is not subverted, it is not mutilated, and to say the least it is not held in abeyance and it is not amended by an authority not competent to do so under the Constitution.*[81]

Notwithstanding its long tirade against the martial law regime, the Court accepted that it could not tear down the entire past martial law infrastructure or chaos might ensue; therefore certain 'measures taken during Martial Law period needs [sic] to be condoned/cured by the principles of doctrine of necessity'.[82] Accordingly, the Court condoned the following acts that were taken by Ershad's martial law regime: routine works which even a lawful government could have done and military law proclamations that had in fact enhanced the rule of law and the independence of the judiciary.[83]

In the concluding paragraph of the Appeal Division's judgment in *Bangladesh Italian Marble Works*, and in a parting shot directed at the military, the Court so pronounced:

> *[W]e are putting on record our total disapproval of Martial Law and suspension of the Constitution or any part thereof in any form. The perpetrators of such illegalities should also be suitably punished and condemned so that in future no adventurist, no usurper, would dare to defy the people, their Constitution, their Government, established by them with their consent. However, it is the Parliament which can make law in this regard. Let us bid farewell to all kinds of extra constitutional adventure for ever.*[84]

Relying on its supermajority in Parliament, the AL government passed the 15th Amendment a few months later in June 2011 to codify several

[81] *Ibid.*, 153.

[82] *Ibid.*, 157.

[83] The Second Proclamation (Seventh Amendment) Order 1976 and the Second Proclamation (Tenth Amendment Order) 1977 authorised the High Court Division to enforce constitutional rights; and the Second Proclamation (Tenth Amendment) Order 1977 provided that a Supreme Court judge could only be removed by the President upon a recommendation by a Supreme Judicial Council composed only of senior judges. The abovementioned military Proclamations were condoned by the Court *Bangladesh Italian Marble Works* as they advanced the rule of law and safeguarded the independence of the judiciary. After emergency rule ended in 2008, the AL government passed the 15th Amendment to the Constitution, which officially codified these changes in Article 44 and 96 of the Constitution respectively.

[84] *Bangladesh Italian Marble Works* (n 76), 184.

proposals and pronouncements of the Court into the Constitution explicitly. This included the criminalisation of military coups.[85] The principle of secularism – removed from the Constitution by martial law in 1977 (the repeal of which was later ratified by the 5th Amendment) – was restored. More fascinatingly, Article 7B was inserted into the Constitution, which now provides that Part I of the Constitution relating to the General Tenets of the Republic, provisions in Part II concerning Fundamental Principles of State Policy, and Part III relating to Fundamental Rights (save in an Emergency) may never be amended from the Constitution.[86]

In May 2011, the 7th Amendment, which immunised Ershad's martial law regime from liability, came under the pruning knife of the Appellate Division. In *Siddique Ahmed* v. *Bangladesh* (2011),[87] the petitioner was a fugitive who was convicted of murder in absentia under martial law in 1986. He was finally arrested in 2006 and was imprisoned pursuant to the sentence imposed by the martial law authorities back in 1986. He was also denied a retrial as Section 3 of the 7th Amendment provided that no judgment of the Martial Law Court passed between 1982 and 1986 could be reopened by the Supreme Court.

Ruling in favour of the petitioner, the Appellate Division in *Siddique Ahmed* affirmed unequivocally that the Constitution prevailed and would always prevail over all Martial Law Proclamations, Regulations, and Orders:

> *Let it be unquestionably declared that the supremacy of the constitution was unqualified, it is unqualified and it shall remain unqualified for all time to come ... No authority in Bangladesh can oust the jurisdiction, powers and functions of the Supreme Court granted under the Constitution.*[88]

But in a laudable departure from *Bangladesh Italian Marble Works*, the Appellate Division even went on to expressly overrule all past

[85] Article 7A (1) of the Constitution reads: 'If any person, by show of force or use of force or by any other un-constitutional means– (a) abrogates, repeals or suspends or attempts or conspires to abrogate, repeal or suspend this Constitution or any of its article; or (b) subverts or attempts or conspires to subvert the confidence, belief or reliance of the citizens to this Constitution or any of its article, his such act shall be sedition and such person shall be guilty of sedition.'

[86] Article 7B of the Constitution reads: 'Notwithstanding anything contained in article 142 of the Constitution, the preamble, all articles of Part I, all articles of Part II, subject to the provisions of Part IXA all articles of Part III, and the provisions of articles relating to the basic structures of the Constitution including article 150 of Part XI shall not be amendable by way of insertion, modification, substitution, repeal or by any other means.'

[87] *Siddique Ahmed* v. *Bangladesh* (Civil Appeal No. 48 of 2011) (15 May 2011).

[88] *Ibid.*, 54–55.

judicial decisions where the Court had authorised the subordination of the Constitution to martial law.

Section 3 of the 7th Amendment, which had attempted to ratify 'acts, actions, and proceedings … that subordinate the Constitution',[89] was accordingly deemed ultra vires the Constitution and thus void. But one must note that the invalidation of this constitutional amendment was again precisely what the Attorney General argued for on behalf of the AL government, and the Appellate Division was happy to oblige.

Siddique Ahmed is also noteworthy for another reason. In a concurring opinion in *Anwar Hossain Chowdhury*,[90] Shahabuddin Ahmed J had held that past constitutional amendments that were not challenged would form 'part of the Constitution by general acquiescence'[91] and could not be challenged subsequently. In *Siddique Ahmed*, the Appellate Division explicitly rejected this proposition:

> *If [the Constitution] is violated, the Court is bound to say so, no matter when it is raised. There is no period of limitation, no waiver, no acquiescence in this respect.*[92]

Therefore, even though the 7th Amendment was challenged over two decades after it was first passed in 1986, the Appellate Division held that the Court could still invalidate it.

Nevertheless, in recognition that it would be very disruptive if lawful and routine transactions performed by the martial law regime were also overturned, the Appellate Division acceded to the government's request and provisionally condoned previous actions taken by the martial law regime, and allowed past proceedings to be re-opened on a case-by-case basis.[93] With the invalidation of Section 3 of the 7th Amendment, the petitioner was thus granted a retrial in a criminal court.

A few days before the *Siddique Ahmed* decision was issued, the Appellate Division in *Abdul Mannan Khan* v. *Bangladesh*[94] invalidated the NCG system introduced by the 13th Amendment. In a Short Order issued on 10 May 2011, the Appellate Division held that the impugned Amendment

89 *Ibid.*, 105.

90 *Anwar Hossain Chowdhury* (n 16).

91 *Siddique Ahmed* (n 87), 65.

92 *Ibid.*

93 *Ibid.*, 114.

94 *Abdul Mannan Khan* v. Bangladesh (Civil Appeal No. 139 of 2005). See Adeeba Aziz Khan, 'The Politics of Constitutional Amendments in Bangladesh: The Case of the Non-political Caretaker Government' (2015) 9 *International Review of Law* <http://www.qscience.com/doi/pdf/10.5339/irl.2015.9> accessed 1 February 2017.

would be prospectively overruled; but the NCG system could nevertheless be retained for the next two Parliamentary elections. Interestingly, the full judgment was only handed down over a year later, in September 2012. By then, the AL government, with its supermajority control over Parliament, had already passed the 15th Amendment to repeal the NCG system, rendering the full judgment largely moot.

While the Short Order disclosed that the Appellate Division's decision was not unanimous, it was only revealed in the full judgment that the Court had split four to three, with the majority in favour of invalidating the 13th Amendment. According to the majority in the full judgment, the 13th Amendment was unconstitutional as it allowed for an unelected government to rule Bangladesh, thereby violating 'democracy', an unamendable basic feature of the Constitution. While the Amendment was introduced to facilitate free and fair elections, Bangladesh's recent encounter with a 'despotic government'[95] for nearly two years proved that the NCG had failed to achieve the 'desired goal and this is the right time to bury [sic] it up finally for the sake of democracy'.[96] The majority also emphasised that the NCG system had politicised appointments to the Supreme Court, as past incumbent governments had manipulated the retirement age of judges so that a Chief Justice sympathetic to their political cause could retire just in time to serve as the NCG's Chief Adviser. Such political manoeuvres had 'erode[d] the people's perception towards the independence of the judiciary',[97] another basic feature of the Constitution.

On behalf of Nazmun Ara Sultana J and himself, Abdul Wahhab Miah J, in dissent, argued that the NCG system did not subvert democracy as it was passed precisely to address the problem associated with 'elections held under the political government [that] were tainted with manipulation, rigging and hijacking',[98] and multiple free and fair general elections had been held under the system. Therefore, the NCG system 'in no way clashes with democracy rather it has strengthened democracy'.[99] Nevertheless, in light of the recent abuse of the NCG system and the suspension of elections for nearly two years, Miah J held that constitutional amendments should be passed so that the NCG government 'cannot extend/stretch its period beyond 90 days',[100] rather than have the entire

95 *Ibid.*, 447 (S.K. Sinha).

96 *Ibid.*

97 *Ibid.*, 515.

98 *Ibid.*, 620 (Abdul Wahhab Miah).

99 *Ibid.*, 641

100 *Ibid.*, 688.

system dismantled completely. In response to the argument that appointments to the Supreme Court had been politicised because of the NCG system, his Lordship however could only give a pithy reply:

> *[S]uch manipulation ... can very well be guarded against by the office being respected by the Executive on the one hand, and by those who are part of the judiciary when exercising their judicial powers strictly observing and maintaining strict neutrality, and not being susceptible to influence from any quarters.*[101]

On the other hand, in a separate dissenting opinion, Imman Ali J argued that the NCG system was constitutional. In his Lordship's view, the Emergency rule in Bangladesh was 'not a consequence of the legality or otherwise of the 13th Amendment',[102] but the result of the President's failure to comply with the Constitution. Nevertheless, in order to avoid such an 'unnatural and unconstitutional state of affairs'[103] from occurring again, he agreed that the method of setting up an interim government, prior to an election, should be replaced;[104] but this had to be done by Parliament and not by the courts.

But one must note that the abolition of the NCG system was precisely what the AL government wanted. And having received the blessing of the Court in May 2011, it immediately repealed the NCG system in the following month, without even waiting for the full judgment to be published. Furthermore, in proceeding swiftly with the repeal, the AL government also ignored the Appellate Division's suggestion that the NCG system, whilst unconstitutional, could be retained for the next two general elections.

Conclusion

Bangladesh is a transitional democracy that has oscillated regularly between military rule and civilian government. Since its independence in 1971, the country has experienced two martial law regimes and undergone four States of Emergency. Unsurprisingly, the Bangladesh Supreme Court (Appellate Division) has only questioned the legitimacy of these extraordinary governmental measures after the crises had abated.

[101] *Ibid.*, 665.
[102] *Ibid.*, 742 (Imman Ali).
[103] *Ibid.*, 746.
[104] *Ibid.*

The 8th Amendment, which split the High Court Division into seven separate permanent benches; the 5th and 7th Amendments, which ousted the Court's jurisdiction to review laws and orders passed when the country was governed during the two periods of martial law (1975–1979 and 1982–1986); and the 13th Amendment, which politicised appointments to the senior judiciary and allowed for an unelected caretaker government to run the country, were only all invalidated by the Appellate Division after martial law or emergency rule had formally ceased. Moreover, the invalidation of the 5th, 7th, and 13th Amendments was precisely what the incumbent civilian governments had wanted, and the Court therein could assert its judicial authority with minimal political backlash.

But this is not to say that the Bangladesh Supreme Court, as an institution, has merely been a handmaiden of the government. The Appellate Division's most confrontational decisions have been those whereby it drew a line in the sand when the government had encroached upon the independence of the judiciary. In 1999, the Appellate Division readily invalidated a law that included judicial officers within the civil service;[105] in 2009, the Appellate Division compelled the President to consult with the Chief Justice on every Supreme Court appointment and provide cogent reasons for rejecting the Chief Justice's recommendations.[106] In view of Bangladesh's chequered history with deeply partisan judicial appointments and executive interference with judicial functions,[107] the Appellate Division's ostensibly aggressive stance therein was necessary to prevent the fragile democracy from backsliding into a totalitarian state with no separation of powers in government.

While civilian rule has returned to Bangladesh since 2008, the political conflicts between the AL and the BNP have only intensified. In the lead-up to the 2014 general election, the country's first since the repeal of the NCG system, opposition groups declared a series of *hartals* (violent strikes) against the incumbent AL government, which escalated into political violence that took the lives of nearly 300 people.[108] With the BNP's boycott of the 2014 general election, over half of the elected seats in

[105] *Secretary, Ministry of Finance* (n 62).

[106] *Justice Syed Dastagir Hossain* (n 68).

[107] See Hossain (n 63); Chowdhury (n 36).

[108] Associated Press in Dhaka, 'Bangladesh Election Violence Throws Country Deeper into Turmoil', *Guardian*, 6 January 2014 <http://www.theguardian.com/world/2014/jan/06/bangladesh-election-violence-awami-league> accessed 1 February 2017.

Parliament were uncontested on polling day; and the AL won, amidst low voter turnout, 232 elected seats in Parliament.[109]

At the heart of much of the political drama in Bangladesh is the rivalry between two families. For over two decades, Bangladesh has been led by either one of the two battling Begums – AL's Sheikh Hasina (daughter of Bangladesh's founder, Mujib) and BNP's Khaleda Zia (widow of General Zia). If the two powerful women (and their parties) are unable to reach some form of political compromise on how the next election due by January 2019 should be conducted, and if political violence were to return to Bangladesh, it is not inconceivable that the Bangladesh military would intervene and arrest the country's democratic development once again.

Whilst the political violence that marred the 2014 general election was the worst in the nation's history, the armed forces had sat out that election and had merely observed from the sidelines. Observers have attributed the military's current self-restraint to the success of the AL government in cosying up to the generals by over-compensating them financially; the AL government believes that if the military's corporate interests are closely intertwined with the ruling party's fate, the latter would be less enthused about upsetting the status quo.[110] But such bribes may backfire if the present standoff between the BNP and the AL leads to a major economic crisis or some massive breakdown in law and order such that the generals perceive military intervention as necessary to safeguard their own growing business interests, as we have seen in Pakistan.

With neither purse nor sword, the Bangladesh Supreme Court never had nor will have a realistic chance of fending off the authoritarian inclinations of the military and/or the civilian government. But in pragmatically accommodating their core demands and interests, the Court has perhaps achieved moderate success in fencing off its own turf.

[109] Farid Ahmed, 'Bangladesh Ruling Party Wins Elections Marred by Boycott, Violence', *CNN*, 7 January 2014 <http://edition.cnn.com/2014/01/06/world/asia/bangladesh-elections/> accessed 1 February 2017. See also Shelley Feldman, 'Bangladesh in 2014: Illusive Democracy' (2015) 55(1) *Asian Survey* 67.

[110] International Crisis Group, 'Mapping Bangladesh's Political Crisis', *Asian Report* N°264, 9 February 2015 <http://www.crisisgroup.org/~/media/Files/asia/south-asia/bangladesh/264-mapping-bangladesh-s-political-crisis.pdf> accessed 1 February 2017. See also Al Masud Hasanuzzaman, 'Civil-military Relations' in Ali Riaz & Mohammad Sajjadur Rahman (eds), *Routledge Handbook of Contemporary Bangladesh* (London: Routledge, 2016), 115.

PART IV

Democratic Values and Courts in Comparative Perspectives

11

Democratic Values and the Conundrum of Unconstitutional Constitutional Amendments

In recent years, the doctrine of unconstitutional constitutional amendments has arisen and developed around the world.[1] Interestingly, in all nine Asian jurisdictions surveyed in this book, their courts of final resort have also recognised that there are implied substantive constraints on formal constitutional change; and many of them (Malaysia, India, Taiwan, Bangladesh, Pakistan, and Thailand) have, in practice, expressly or impliedly invalidated offending constitutional amendments that violate certain basic elements of their constitutions.

As I have explored in the earlier chapters, it is noteworthy that, in all of the jurisdictions discussed, the doctrine of unconstitutional constitutional amendments has been judicially conceived or applied as a safeguard against legislative worst-case scenarios where the political incumbents (or the military) abuse the amendment process to introduce constitutional amendments that erode democratic values.[2] In short, many of these impugned constitutional amendments relate directly to government restrictions on voting rights or constitute legislative attacks on judicial independence.

[1] See Yaniv Roznai, 'Unconstitutional Constitutional Amendments – The Migration and Success of a Constitutional Idea', (2013) 61 *American Journal of Comparative Law* 657; Gary Jacobsohn, 'An Unconstitutional Constitution? A Comparative Perspective' (2006) 4 (3) *International Journal of Constitutional Law* 460; David Gwynn Morgan, 'The Indian "Essential Features" Case' (1981) 30 *International and Comparative Law Quarterly* 307; Ridwanul Hoque, 'Constitutionalism and the Judiciary in Bangladesh', in Sunil Khilnani, Vikram Raghavan and Arun K. Thiruvengadam (eds), *Comparative Constitutionalism in South Asia* (New Delhi: Oxford University Press, 2013); Aileen Kavanagh, 'Unconstitutional Constitutional Amendments from Irish Free State to Irish Republic', in Eoin Carolan (ed.), *The Constitution of Ireland: Perspectives and Prospects* (Dublin: Bloomsbury Professional, 2012); William Parlett, 'Courts and Constitution Making' (2015) 50 *Wake Forest Law Review* 921.

[2] The most recent example was the extraordinary decision by the Federal Court of Malaysia in *Semenyih Jaya v Pentadbir Tanah Daerah Hulu Langat* (20 April 2017) to invalidate a constitutional amendment introduced in June 1988 to clip the wings of the judiciary. Prior to the amendment, Article 121 (1) of the Malaysia Constitution read as follows: 'The judicial power of the Federation shall be vested in a Supreme Court and such inferior courts as may be provided by federal law.' The 1988 constitutional amendment removed the term 'judicial power'.

Time and time again, as we have seen in the earlier chapters, courts have invoked this doctrine as a crucial weapon in their fight against partisan legislative self-dealing or in their defence against governmental encroachment on their institutional independence. Therefore, there is a close symbiotic relationship between the judicial recognition of this doctrine and its defence of a constitutional order that is committed to democracy.

But even as the notion of unconstitutional constitutional amendments gains currency, the more interesting question has been left unanswered, i.e., *should* constitutional amendments be invalidated by courts, an unelected branch of government? In other words, we know judges have shielded their constitutions from some constitutional changes. But *should* they have done so? Put differently, under what conditions is the doctrine of unconstitutional constitutional amendments most defensible, especially if it is deployed by judges against perceived legislative excesses when constitutions are amended?

As a preliminary note, I would emphasise that in this chapter, I only examine whether courts should impose implied constraints on the substantive content of constitutional amendments. This is a different question from whether courts should review the process by which the impugned constitutional amendment was enacted, an issue which I believe to be uncontroversial. If a constitution requires a constitutional amendment to be passed by a super-majoritarian vote in the legislature, then a judiciary, vested with the powers of constitutional review, surely must have the right to invalidate any amendment that does not satisfy this procedural requirement.

Part 1 of the chapter begins by exploring the normative or political considerations/conditions for recognising any implied substantive constraints on constitutional change. Part 2 continues by examining the normative arguments against this position. Finally, in Part 3, I argue that one must examine how a particular impugned constitutional amendment was passed in determining whether judges should render the substance of the amendment unconstitutional. For jurisdictions with malleable constitutions – where a constitutional amendment has been passed by a dominant party/coalition without bipartisan support and the public's approval – the courts may intervene, but only where the constitutional amendment in question is so manifestly unreasonable that such a revision is akin to a substantial destruction of the pre-existing constitution. But no constitutional amendment should ever be judicially invalidated for violating any implied basic features of the constitution when the amendment process is particularly cumbersome, i.e., where significant bi-partisan support and the general public's endorsement are required before the amendment takes legal effect.

Part 1: Justifications for Implied Substantive Limits on Constitutional Change

(1) Difference between Original Constituent Powers and Derivative Constituent Powers

A common justification for advocating that a constitutional amendment is inconsistent with certain implicit basic features of a constitution rests on a normative distinction drawn between a Constituent Assembly's power to create a constitution and the amending power vested in a constituted body that is derived from the constitution. Constitutional theorists, like Carl Schmitt and Emmanuel Sieyes, have argued that the power of creation is plenary and is free from any legal constraints, while the power of amendment is merely a *derivative* or *constituted* power and may not be exercised to alter any fundamental features of the constitution.[3] The decision to make fundamental changes to the constitution is a matter solely reserved for the Constituent Assembly. Ergo, judges may invalidate an exercise of the derivative amendment power that purports to violate the constitution's basic features.

This distinction between original and derivative constituent powers has also been endorsed by judges when they render constitutional amendments unconstitutional.

As I have examined more closely in Chapter 10, the Appellate Division of the Supreme Court of Bangladesh in *Anwar Hossain Chowdhury* v. *Bangladesh*,[4] by a majority of three to one, invalidated a constitutional amendment which sought to create six additional Permanent Benches in different regions of the country that would possess the same powers and functions as the original High Court Division of the Supreme Court. According to the majority, the judiciary was a 'basic structural pillar'[5] of Bangladesh's constitutional government and the creation of the new courts, parallel to the High Court Division, infringed upon the judicial powers vested in the High Court Division. Since 'the basic structural pillar, that is [the] judiciary, has been destroyed and plenary judicial power of the Republic vested in the High Court Division has been taken away',[6]

[3] Richard Stacey, 'Constituent Power and Carl Schmitt's Theory of Constitution in Kenya's Constitution-making Process' (2011) 9 *International Journal of Constitutional Law* 587, 601–602.

[4] (1989) BLD (Special) (AD) 1 (Supreme Court of Bangladesh).

[5] *Ibid.* [295] (Chowdhury J).

[6] *Ibid.*

the constitutional amendment that authorised such a fundamental change was invalidated.

In particular, Shahabuddin Ahmed J, in his concurring opinion, justified the invalidation of the constitutional amendment in the following terms:

> *As to the 'constituent power', that is power to make a Constitution, it belongs to the people alone. It is the original power ... Even if the 'constituent power' is vested in the Parliament, the power is a derivative one and the mere fact that an amendment has been made in exercise of the derivative constituent power will not automatically make the amendment immune from challenge.*[7]

The normative distinction drawn between the Constituent Assembly's plenary constituent power and the amending body's limited derivative power of revision is, however, not unproblematic as it is not plainly obvious why the amending body's power to revise the original constitution does not also comprise the right to change its fundamental features. Where the original Constituent Assembly has explicitly established the procedures by which the constitution may be amended, and it has not expressly imposed any substantive constraints on constitutional change, it is not self-evident why the original Constituent Assembly has not therein divested all of its amending powers to the future amending bodies. Scholars and jurists who defend an implied 'basic features' doctrine have merely asserted that the amending body's power of constitutional revision is *derivative*. But, in making this assertion, they still have not explained why the amending body has not inherited all powers of revision divested by the Constituent Assembly upon the completion of constitutional law-making process. Furthermore, as Carlos Bernal has asked rhetorically, 'if the foundation of a constitution is only a contingent social fact, namely, the result of a political decision, why should it be impossible to change the essential elements of the constitution by means of another contingent social fact, that is, a political decision made by means of a constitutional amendment'?[8]

(2) Prevent Amendments that Seek to Abolish Democracy and Fundamental Rights

More commonly, jurists and scholars argue that there must be implied substantive limits placed on constitutional changes or the constitution's

[7] *Ibid.* [381].

[8] Carlos Bernal, 'Unconstitutional Constitutional Amendments in the Case Study of Colombia: An Analysis of the Justification and Meaning of the Constitutional Replacement Doctrine' (2013) 11 *International Journal of Constitutional Law* 339, 349.

amending body would otherwise be legally authorised to abridge all fundamental freedoms or remove all vestiges of democracy within the state. In other words, the implied essential features doctrine is needed as a safeguard against abuse by the amending body, and to prevent a country from establishing totalitarianism, such that all its cherished democratic principles are rendered non-existent.

As observed by Walter Murphy:

> *Like democracy, constitutionalism rests on the notion of human worth ... Consent does not, however, function as a magic wand that can cast a benevolent spell over all political arrangements. A system that denies human worth cannot claim consent as the foundation of legitimacy, for what is worthless can confer nothing.*[9]

In the same vein, David Landau has discussed how the doctrine of unconstitutional constitutional amendments has been conceived as a response to the practice of 'abusive constitutionalism',[10] i.e., the politicians' use of *formal* mechanisms of constitutional change to make a state significantly less democratic.[11]

To this extent, it would be understandable if one is sympathetic towards the Supreme Court of Bangladesh (Appellate Division) for invalidating the 5th Amendment[12] and the 7th Amendment[13] to the Bangladesh Constitution, which had imposed martial law on the country over separate extended periods of time, as discussed in Chapter 10. Similarly, in Pakistan, as I have examined more closely in Chapter 9, when its Supreme Court first opined that certain basic characteristics of the Constitution could not be abrogated, it was in response to the 8th Amendment, which *inter alia*

[9] Walter Murphy, 'Merlin's Memory: The Past and Future Imperfect of the Once and Future Polity', in Sanford Levinson (ed.), *Responding to Imperfection: The Theory and Practice of Constitutional Amendment* (Princeton: Princeton University Press, 1995), 180.

[10] David Landau, 'Abusive Constitutionalism' (2013) 47 *UC Davis Law Review* 189, 196.

[11] *Ibid.*

[12] The 5th Amendment provided that all amendments or repeals made to the Bangladesh Constitution from 15 August 1975 to 9 April 1979 (inclusive) by any proclamation or Proclamation Order of the Martial Law Authorities were deemed to have been validly made, and could not be called into question before any court or tribunal or other authority. *See Khondker Delwar Hossain* v. *Bangladesh Italian Marble Works* (Civil Petition for Leave to Appeals Nos. 1044 & 1045 of 2009) (Supreme Court of Bangladesh).

[13] The 7th Amendment to Bangladesh Constitution provided that all proclamations, proclamation orders, Chief Martial Law Administrator's Orders, Martial Law Regulations, Martial Law Orders, Martial Law Instructions, ordinances, and other laws made from 24 March 1982 to 11 November 1986 (inclusive) had been validly made, and could not be called into question before any court or tribunal or other authority. See *Siddique Ahmed* v. *Government of Bangladesh* (Civil Appeal No. 48 of 2011) (Supreme Court of Bangladesh).

validated all acts made pursuant to the military orders that had been operative during the martial law period between 1977 and 1985. In the same vein, when the Constitutional Court of Korea suggested that the 'principle[s] of sovereignty and liberal democracy … are the fundamental principles of the [1987] Constitution'[14] and they 'should be the standard for construing the Constitution and laws, as well as setting forth the restriction in exercising legislative authority',[15] it did so in a constitutional challenge to the defunct Yushin Constitution, which had authorised emergency military rule in the Republic of Korea for close to a decade.[16] The Hong Kong Court of Final Appeal, too, in its *first* constitutional decision after China's resumption of sovereignty over Hong Kong, declared that it had the power to 'determine whether an act of the National People's Congress or its Standing Committee is inconsistent with the [Hong Kong] Basic Law',[17] only because it was seeking to ensure that communist China would not renege on its promise to preserve Hong Kong's way of life for 50 years.[18] Even in India, as explored more fully in Chapter 5, the constitutional amendment, invalidated by the Supreme Court of India in *Indira Nehru Gandhi* v. *Shri Raj Narain*,[19] was passed by its Parliament to insulate the Prime Minister's election from any judicial inquiry and render all pending proceedings against the Prime Minister in respect of such elections null and void; and it is noteworthy that the judicial decision was handed down *after* the government had declared a State of Emergency throughout the country.

Consequently, jurists who argue in favour of recognising implied substantive limits on constitutional change would point to past legislative abuses by politicians and suggest that the rule of law encapsulates a substantive ideal against which the propriety of all forms and varieties of legislation (including the Constitution) should be tested.[20]

[14] *Case on Presidential Emergency Decrees No. 1.2 and 9*; 25-1 KCCR 180, 2010 Hun-Ba70·132·170 (consolidated) (Constitutional Court, Korea) (21 March 2013) (Official English Translation).

[15] *Ibid.*

[16] Marie Seong-Hak Kim, 'Travails of Judges: Courts and Constitutional Authoritarianism in South Korea' (2015) 63 *American Journal of Comparative Law* 601.

[17] *Ng Ka Ling* v. *Director of Immigration* (1999) 2 HKCFAR 4, 26E-F (Hong Kong Court of Final Appeal).

[18] Article 5 of the Hong Kong Basic Law reads: 'The socialist system and policies shall not be practised in the Hong Kong Special Administrative Region, and the previous capitalist system and way of life shall remain unchanged for 50 years.'

[19] [1976] 2 SCR 347 (Supreme Court of India).

[20] John Laws, 'Law and Democracy' [1995] *Public Law* 72, 87; T.R.S. Allan, *Constitutional Justice: A Liberal Theory of the Rule of Law* (Oxford: Oxford University Press, 2001), 2.

Nevertheless, the trouble with this elusive rule of law ideal is not that people disagree with its normative force in the abstract but that this higher-order law, if enforceable, must be given substance, be interpreted, and be applied.[21] The appeal to a divine ideal may be irresistible but the devil is in the details. Judges do not uphold the rule of law in the abstract but have to apply sacrosanct constitutional rights to the specific and particularised facts that come before them.[22] Does the fundamental right to free speech exclude any attempts to use a constitutional amendment to ban hate speech inciting violence against racial or sexual minorities? Does the fundamental right to equality exclude all forms and varieties of race-based affirmative action programs that the amending body may want insulated from a constitutional challenge? The rule of law is a vague, contested ideal and is consistent with a variety of understandings and institutional arrangements.[23] As R. George Wright has argued, once a fundamental rights norm is sufficiently particularised to specific facts so as to be constitutionally useful, 'it is no longer clear why an amendment must be unconstitutional if, for example, it limits the protection or advancement of one conception of human dignity for the sake of some other equally plausible conception of human dignity'.[24]

Furthermore, there is evidence that this implied basic structure doctrine has tended to expand through time as courts deem more parts of the constitution to be basic features.[25] And as we have seen with Thailand in Chapter 8, this doctrine has been abused by the judiciary for partisan purposes. The Constitutional Court of Thailand, in its quest to drive former Premier Thaksin and his surrogates out of public office, invalidated a constitutional amendment that would allow the Thai Senate to be fully elected by the people, and restored the status quo that allowed for half the Senate to be composed of appointed members.[26] It is noteworthy that the

21 J.A.G. Griffith, 'The Brave New World of Sir John Laws' (2000) 63 *Modern Law Review* 159, 165.

22 Po Jen Yap, 'Defending Dialogue' (2012) *Public Law* 527, 538.

23 Jeffrey Goldsworthy, 'Homogenising Constitutions' (2003) 23 *Oxford Journal of Legal Studies* 505.

24 R. George Wright, 'Could a Constitutional Amendment be Unconstitutional?' (1991) 22 *Loyola University Law Journal* 741, 753.

25 Landau (n 10), 237.

26 See Constitutional Court of Thailand Ruling No. 15–18/2556 (20 November 2013). Arguably, the impugned Amendment could have been invalidated on procedural grounds. For example, there were significant substantive differences between the draft Amendment tabled for passage and the prior version distributed to individual Members of the Parliament; Members of Parliament were only given one day to propose changes to the proposed Amendment after it was formally approved at the First Reading; and when the

Thai Constitutional Court did so on the basis that the impugned amendment violated the rule of law, which overrode all written laws including the Constitution.[27]

Hence, if scholars are right that judges should recognise that certain implied basic features of the constitution are inviolable, such that fundamental rights may never be abrogated, they must then go on to demonstrate why the judges' perception of the rule of law or human rights in *every* concrete context would always be superior to the amending body's conception each time. Unfortunately, sympathisers of the implied basic features doctrine have never proceeded to make their case in support of the latter proposition.

Part 2: Justifications against the Judicial Imposition of Implied Substantive Limits on Constitutional Change

(1) Identifying Implied Basic Features is to Mull over Imponderables

On the other hand, scholars who are sceptical about the judicial identification of a constitution's implied essential features or basic structure would point to the sheer impossibility of determining these fundamental norms in an objective, value-neutral way. Given that the text of such constitutions are silent on what features are so basic or fundamental that they are beyond abrogation, any list of such norms are open to debate and 'cannot be objectively deduced or passively discerned in a viewpoint-free way'.[28]

Even in the Indian case of *Indira Gandhi*, which I discussed in Chapter 5, where the majority on the Supreme Court invalidated the constitutional amendment that ousted judicial review of the pending court proceedings over the Prime Minister's election, the judges could not agree on which part of the basic structure had been violated.[29] For Chandrachud J, the constitutional amendment had negated the right of equality as it

Amendment was voted on, several Members of Parliament, in contravention to the rules, voted on behalf of Members who were absent.

[27] *Ibid.*

[28] Lawrence Tribe, 'A Constitution We are Amending: In Defence of a Restrained Judicial Role' (1983) 97 *Harvard Law Review* 433, 440.

[29] See C.C. Aikman, 'The Debate on the Amendment of the Indian Constitution', (1978) 9 *Victoria University of Wellington Law Review* 357, 376. See also Sujit Choudhry, 'How to do Constitutional Law and Politics in South Asia', in Mark Tushnet & Madhav Khosla (eds), *Unstable Constitutionalism: Law and Politics in South Asia* (New York: Cambridge University Press, 2015), 26–27.

had discriminated in favour of the Prime Minister;[30] Khanna J held that the constitutional amendment infringed upon the 'principle of free and fair elections';[31] and Mathew J opined that the impugned amendment had attempted to undermine the 'exercise of judicial power [to] ascertaining the adjudicative facts'.[32]

The difficulty of identifying what exactly is the implied basic structure of a constitution was most astutely pointed out by Ray CJ in his concurring opinion in *Indira Gandhi*:

> *The theory of basic structure or basic features is an exercise in imponderables. Basic structures or basic features are indefinable.*[33]

Ray CJ's objection is fair and is premised on the argument that the court's exercise of judicial review must appeal to and draw support from the constitutional text it is interpreting. But one must concede that most, if not all, constitutional instruments enshrine abstract, open-textured rights that are often open to a multitude of interpretations in specific contexts, and that textualism alone cannot resolve this interpretive conundrum. In other words, even when courts invalidate *ordinary legislation* for violating open-textured constitutional rights, there may not be a specific textual mandate for a particular result. Therefore, the indeterminacy associated with 'judicial line-drawing'[34] is inherent in all forms of constitutional adjudication and is not unique to the judicial review of constitutional amendments.

(2) Judicial Invalidation of Constitutional Amendments Undermines the People's Will

Furthermore, sceptics would argue that the judicial invalidation of constitutional amendments would gravely 'threaten the notion of a government founded on the consent of the governed'.[35]

[30] *Indira Nehru Gandhi* (n 19) [680].
[31] *Ibid.* [222].
[32] *Ibid.* [309].
[33] *Ibid.* [140].
[34] Andrew Harding, 'The Death of a Doctrine? *Phang Chin Hock* v. *Public Prosecutor*' (1979) 21 *Malaya Law Review* 365, 373.
[35] John Vile, 'The Case against Implicit Limits on the Constitutional Amending Process', in Sanford Levison (ed.), *Responding to Imperfection: The Theory and Practice of Constitutional Amendment* (Princeton: Princeton University Press, 1995), 198.

Where the people's will has been expressed in the form of a constitutional amendment, the constraint on courts to give effect to this revision should be a very strong one. If the judiciary is allowed to independently pass judgment on the merits of constitutional amendments in such circumstances, it would ultimately be subordinating the amendment process to the constitutional status quo that the people had expressly intended to override. So far as a handful of unelected judges are empowered, under the guise of a nebulous essential features doctrine, to thwart constitutional changes authorised by the people, the integrity of a constitutional structure committed to democracy would be gravely threatened.[36]

However, one must note that whether a constitutional amendment is reflective of the people's will is dependent on the procedure by which the amendment is passed in that jurisdiction. For example, in Denmark[37] and Ireland,[38] a constitutional amendment takes effect only after it is passed in the legislature and approved by the people in a public referendum.

But in many national constitutions, constitutional amendments can be unilaterally achieved by the ruling government of the day. Inevitably, to appreciate this, one must take into account the constitutional politics and the institutional context of the state in question.

For instance, in India, amendments to most provisions in its Constitution, including enshrined fundamental rights, can be passed so long as they receive the support in 'each House [of Parliament] by a majority of the total membership of that House and by a majority of not less than two-thirds of the members of that House present and voting'.[39] In other words, so long as the ruling government in India has majority control over both Houses of Parliament, it can pass a constitutional

[36] Tribe (n 28).

[37] Section 88 of the Denmark Constitution reads: 'Should the Folketing pass a Bill for the purposes of a new constitutional provision, and the Government wish to proceed with the matter, writs shall be issued for the election of members of a new Folketing. If the Bill is passed unamended by the Folketing assembling after the election, the Bill shall, within six months after its final passage, be submitted to the electors for approval or rejection by direct voting. Rules for this voting shall be laid down by statute. If a majority of the persons taking part in the voting, and at least 40 per cent of the electorate, have voted in favour of the Bill as passed by the Folketing, and if the Bill receives the Royal Assent, it shall form an integral part of the Constitutional Act.'

[38] Article 46(2) of the Irish Constitution reads: 'Every proposal for an amendment of this Constitution shall be initiated in Dáil Éireann as a Bill, and shall upon having been passed or deemed to have been passed by both Houses of the Oireachtas, be submitted by Referendum to the decision of the people in accordance with the law for the time being in force relating to the Referendum.'

[39] Article 368(2) of the Indian Constitution.

amendment to abridge fundamental rights, even if the people do not support this measure. The basic structure doctrine was first conceived and developed as a judicial response to the legislative excesses of the Indira Gandhi government, which had relied on a supine Parliament to effect constitutional changes that the 'hyper-executive' government unilaterally wanted. Following a landslide victory at the 1971 polls, the Congress Party headed by Indira Gandhi was able to pass constitutional amendments with remarkable ease. The 25th Amendment was passed to insulate Gandhi's socialist policies from judicial review. In response to a lower court's finding that the Prime Minister had violated electoral laws and was disqualified from holding public office for six years, the 39th Amendment was enacted to insulate the Prime Minister's election from any judicial inquiry and render pending proceedings in respect of such elections null and void.[40] Furthermore, the 42nd Amendment made nearly 60 significant changes to the Indian Constitution, which included an express ouster of judicial review over constitutional amendments.[41] The Indian judges were convinced that, if they did not intervene, all vestiges of democracy in India would eventually be removed.[42]

Similarly, in Taiwan, prior to the 2005 reforms, constitutional amendments could only be initiated and passed by its National Assembly, a secondary and unpopular legislative branch of government.[43] Therefore, as we have examined in Chapter 6, when the Constitutional Court of Taiwan invalidated two constitutional amendments enacted by the said Assembly, which had sought to unilaterally extend the existing term of office of its delegates by over two years and allow political parties and independents with seats in the Legislative Yuan (Taiwan's primary legislative chamber) to appoint delegates to the said Assembly,[44] one cannot reasonably argue

[40] See *Indira Nehru Gandhi* (n 19). See Granville Austin, *Working a Democratic Constitution: The Indian Experience* (New Delhi: Oxford University Press, 1999), 318–324 for an insightful discussion on the history of the case.

[41] In *Minerva Mills* v. *Union of India* (1980) 3 SCC 625, the Supreme Court unanimously invalidated Article 368(4) of Indian Constitution, which ousted any judicial review over constitutional amendments.

[42] See O. Chinnappa Reddy, *The Court and the Constitution of India: Summits and Shallows* (New Delhi: Oxford University Press, 2008), 53–72.

[43] According to the now-defunct Article 174 of the Republic of China (Taiwan) Constitution: 'The Constitution may be amended upon the proposal of one fifth of the total number of Delegates to the National Assembly and by a resolution of three fourths of the Delegates present at a meeting with a quorum of two-thirds of all Delegates to the National Assembly.'

[44] JY Interpretation No 499, 24 March 2000 (Constitutional Court, Taiwan).

that such a judicial manoeuvre had undermined popular sovereignty. Of course, one may still query whether it would be right for the Court to invalidate any constitutional amendment it perceived to have violated these (judicially discerned) 'unchangeable provisions'[45] of the Republic of China (Taiwan) Constitution.

Part 3: Addressing the Constitutional Conundrum

In drawing a normative distinction between the Constitutional Assembly's *original* constituent power of constitution-making and the amending body's *derivative* power of revision, proponents that argue in favour of judges imposing implied substantive limits on constitutional change have never explained why the constitutional amending body could not have inherited all powers of revision divested by the Constituent Assembly upon the completion of the constitutional lawmaking process. Furthermore, while few would disagree that human dignity and democracy are fundamental features of a constitutional state, proponents of the implied inviolable essential features doctrine have never demonstrated why the judges' perception of the rule of law or human dignity in *every* concrete context would always be superior to the amending body's conception each time.

Ultimately, the best normative argument in favour of recognising implied substantive limits on constitutional change rests on the fact that this judicial innovation is necessary to prevent a temporary dominant authoritarian political party/coalition from harnessing the amending process to 'extend its own life [in Parliament] indefinitely'[46] or 'to debar any other (political) party from functioning, establish totalitarianism, enslave the people'.[47] As observed by Rosalind Dixon and David Landau, the doctrine of unconstitutional constitutional amendments is most defensible when it is deployed against constitutional changes that 'threaten to cut off future exercises of democratic decision-making'.[48] In other words, if courts are empowered to rein in any abuse of the amendment process, they can rescue the nation from legislative abuses and

[45] *Ibid.*

[46] *Kesavananda Bharati* v. *Kerala* (1973) 4 SCC 225; AIR 1973 (SC) 1461 [704] (Shelat and Grover JJ) (Supreme Court of India).

[47] *Ibid.* [309] (Sikri CJ).

[48] Rosalind Dixon and David Landau, 'Transnational Constitutionalism and a limited doctrine of unconstitutional constitutional amendment' (2015) 13 *International Journal of Constitutional Law* 606, 612.

perhaps 'save us from the abyss'.[49] Ergo, this judicial doctrine is needed as a safeguard against political worst-case scenarios.

On the other hand, one must also accept that the judicial development of an implied essential features doctrine is riddled with difficulties. For any judicial rule or standard to be workable in practice, it must be 'judicially manageable'. Richard Fallon has argued that for a doctrinal test devised by the courts to be judicially manageable, the legal doctrine must (i) be intelligible (rationally comprehensible); (ii) have 'analytical bite', i.e., the capacity to structure an analysis that could in principle lead to correct results; (iii) be able to generate predictable and consistent results; and (iv) be administrable without overstretching the court's empirical capabilities.[50] In view of the four criteria Fallon raised, one may indeed have concerns about how judges can objectively discern and defend what constitutes essential elements of a constitution.

My critics may reply that courts are institutionally well-placed to be the final adjudicator of the implied unwritten limits of a constitution, because unelected judges stand above the rancour of politics and are duty-bound to reach reasoned judgments, such that they are more likely to enforce a society's long-term principles.[51] This might be true but, as discussed by Adrian Vermeule, there is a trade-off in institutional design between freedom from bias and information.[52] Judges are insulated from the political winds and are arguably more impartial. But, comparatively, it is this insulation that limits their access to the requisite empirical evidence to make a fully informed constitutional judgment; and, due to their professional homogeneity, judges lack the necessary training to assess accurately the socio-economic consequences of their constitutional decisions.[53] (The reverse holds true for the political branches of government.) Therefore, judicial apologists tend to view the courts through rose-tinted glasses; they only see the institutional advantages that the judges enjoy in constitutional adjudication and fail to account for the institutional disadvantages inherent in the office.

49 Lon Fuller, *The Morality of Law* (New Haven: Yale University Press, 1964), 44.

50 Richard Fallon, 'Judicially Manageable Standards and Constitutional Meaning' (2006) 119 *Harvard Law Review* 1274, 1285–1292.

51 See T.R.S. Allan, *Constitutional Justice: A Liberal Theory of the Rule of Law* (Oxford: Oxford University Press, 2001); Ronald Dworkin, *Taking Rights Seriously* (Cambridge, MA: Harvard University Press, 1977); Ronald Dworkin, *Law's Empire* (Cambridge, MA: Harvard University Press, 1986).

52 Adrian Vermeule, *Law and the Limits of Reason* (Oxford: Oxford University Press, 2008), 86.

53 Yap (n 22), 534.

Furthermore, while the essential features doctrine was conceived as a safeguard against executive/legislative abuse, one must also admit that its introduction into any constitutional landscape would open up the possibility of judicial abuse. In other words, where the scope of the amending power is ultimately circumscribed by what a handful of judges might think constitutes its proper limits, every constitutional amendment approved by the people or their elected representatives may technically come under the pruning knife of the judges. Where the judiciary takes upon itself the power to void the substance of constitutional amendments that have been deliberated upon, debated, and popularly ratified, unelected judges may also be undermining the very essence of human dignity and the sanctity of democratic choice that they purport to protect.[54]

In resolving this constitutional conundrum on whether and how judges should enforce implied substantive limits on these changes, we should instead *weigh* the risks of any legislative abuse of the amendment process against the dangers of any judicial abuse that may follow from unelected judges enforcing a nebulous essential features doctrine that can frustrate legitimate constitutional revisions designed to meet changing times. To determine how this constitutional balance should be struck, one must inevitably examine how the constitutional change in question was achieved.

The existence of a 'hyper-executive' in government, where executive and legislative power is concentrated in the hands of one party/coalition, may allow for constitutional changes to be passed without the general public's approval or ratification. In such circumstances, the invalidation of the impugned constitutional amendments may seem less like a unilateral and indefensible arrogation of power by an unaccountable branch of government. Nevertheless, while such constitutional amendments may not necessarily have any popular mandate, the judicial power to invalidate constitutional amendments passed in these circumstances should still be exercised most sparingly. To allow judges to render the substance of a constitutional amendment unconstitutional merely on the basis that it is arguably inconsistent with, but falling short of a substantial destruction of, some essential features of the constitution would be to enthrone a handful of judges at the apex of the political system.

In light of the live dangers associated with the aggressive judicial enforcement of a nebulous and arguably limitless implied essential features doctrine, it is my view that for such *malleable* constitutions, judges

[54] Vile (n 35), 199.

may interfere with the substance of the amendment only when its passage would substantially destroy the pre-existing constitution, i.e., the constitutional change in question must be *manifestly unreasonable*.[55] With regard to *malleable* constitutions, I am referring herein to constitutions that are easily amended, taking into account any of the states' political realities where the dominant executive/legislature may have control over the amending process.[56]

Dixon and Landau have argued that, vis-à-vis constitutional amendments, courts should adopt a variation of Thayerian[57] review, and 'intervene only when they are quite confident that a given constitutional amendment, either alone or in conjunction with other changes, poses a substantial threat to core democratic values'.[58] Their argument echoes mine, save for one key distinction. Dixon and Landau do not distinguish between malleable constitutions and rigid ones; whilst for me, as I will explore later in this Chapter, this distinction is fundamental.

Furthermore, Dixon and Landau argue that courts should use transnational law as a 'second look or check'[59] against an initial judicial impulse that a value impacted by constitutional change actually is fundamental to democracy. I am in complete agreement with them, but I would like to sound a word of caution. In their insightful analysis, the learned scholars had only focussed on how transnational engagement can assist judges in assessing constitutional amendments, which, either alone or in conjunction with a package of reforms, attempt to 'instantiate constitutional principles or practices *not* found in any relevant constitutional order'.[60] The harder question, I believe, was left unaddressed. What if the constitutional amendment in question attempts to instantiate a constitutional practice which is *commonly* found in other constitutional orders, but in reality this would facilitate abusive and undemocratic political practices recurring in its own legal system that are absent elsewhere? For example, in Pakistan, the 19th Amendment to the Constitution was passed to allow for the Parliamentary Committee to confirm judicial nominees from the

[55] Po Jen Yap, 'The Conundrum of Unconstitutional Amendments' (2015) 4 *Global Constitutionalism* 114, 132.

[56] See David Landau, 'Political Institutions and Judicial Role in Comparative Constitutional Law' (2010) 51 *Harvard International Law Journal* 319.

[57] James Bradley Thayer, 'The Origin and Scope of the American Doctrine of Constitutional Law' (1893) 7 *Harvard Law Review* 129.

[58] Dixon and Landau (n 48), 608.

[59] *Ibid.*, 629.

[60] *Ibid.*, 634.

Judicial Commission by a majority vote. But, in *Munir Hussain Bhatti v. Federation of Pakistan*,[61] the Supreme Court, in substance but not in form, overturned the 19th Amendment by holding that the Parliamentary Committee had no discretion to reject the appointment of judicial nominees put forward by the Judicial Commission as this would encroach upon judicial independence. Giving elected politicians a role in confirming judicial nominees is not an uncommon practice in modern democracies. But in Pakistan, as we have seen in Chapter 9, the government, and especially military dictators, have routinely politicised the appointment and removal of senior judges, such that one could be more sanguine about its Supreme Court seeking to guard its own turf. Therefore, to this extent, comparative law may not shed light on Pakistan's peculiar political experiences that would make the 19th Amendment less defensible domestically, than if the same practice were implemented in established or dynamic democracies elsewhere.

On the other hand, my critics might ask whether this 'manifestly unreasonable' standard of review is sufficiently rigorous, especially since courts across the world are moving toward proportionality review.[62]

Proportionality review would require courts to balance various interests and substitute their judgment of what is *necessary* for that of the amending body's. This '*substitutionary* engagement'[63] with the merits of a constitutional amendment, as proportionality review essentially requires, would be tantamount to conferring upon judges the right to prune the Constitution as they deem fit.

So far as the judiciary does not interfere with the amending body's constitutional solution unless it is manifestly unreasonable, the courts would be under-enforcing the constitution against public officials. But we should not equate 'the scope of a constitutional norm as coterminous with the scope of its judicial enforcement'.[64] The most prominent rationale for the judicial under-enforcement of the constitution is premised on the belief that the political branches of government are better than judges in weighing costs and benefits in such circumstances.[65] Due to institutional

[61] PLD 2011 SC 407 (Supreme Court of Pakistan).

[62] Alec Stone Sweet and Jud Mathews, 'Proportionality Balancing and Global Constitutionalism' (2008) 47 *Columbia Journal of Transnational Law* 72.

[63] James Goodwin, 'The Last Defence of Wednesbury' (2012) *Public Law* 445, 454.

[64] Lawrence G. Sager, *Justice in Plain Clothes: A Theory of American Constitutional Practice* (New Haven: Yale University Press, 2004), 86.

[65] See Kermit Roosevelt III, 'Aspiration and Underenforcement' (2006) 119 *Harvard Law Review* 193.

constraints and the informational costs associated with the adjudication over the substantive content of constitutional amendments, judges may not want to exhaust the full content of these constitutional norms so that the political branches of the government can, on their own, flesh out the conceptual boundaries of these implicated rights. Judicial deference is generally justified in instances where the political branches of government usually have superior expertise and knowledge, vis-à-vis the judiciary, to assess the polycentric issues (often raised in constitutional amendments) that affect a large number of disparate interests, such that they are more likely than the courts to determine these constitutional questions correctly.[66] This is not to say that courts should always acquiesce to what the political branches deem to be legitimate constitutional change; for indeed where the amendment is perceived to be manifestly unreasonable, judicial intervention is warranted even if such an intrusion interferes with legislative or executive policy choices on these polycentric issues.[67] To this end, and on this basis, the courts were justified to have rendered the substance of constitutional amendments unconstitutional in the cases from Bangladesh, India (during the Indira Gandhi administration), and Taiwan discussed above. In all those instances, we witnessed authoritarian regimes harnessing the amending process with ease to achieve manifestly unreasonable and undemocratic goals.

But, with regard to India, even after the end of the controversial Indira Gandhi administration, and the country's transition to a dynamic democracy, the Supreme Court has continued to invoke the basic structure doctrine to *invalidate* constitutional amendments passed by its Parliament.[68]

66 See also Alison Young, 'In Defence of Due Deference' (2009) 72 *Modern Law Review* 554.

67 See Julian Rivers, 'Proportionality and Variable Intensity of Review' (2006) 65 *Cambridge Law Journal* 174.

68 In *L. Chandra Kumar v. Union of India* (1997) AIR (SC) 1125, the Supreme Court of India invalidated two constitutional amendments that empowered the federal and state legislatures to 'exclude the jurisdiction of all courts, except the jurisdiction of the Supreme Court' on matters that are exercisable by the Administrative Tribunals, while in *Sambamurthy v. State of Andhra* [1987] 1 SCR 879, the Supreme Court Of India invalidated Article 371D(5) of the Indian Constitution, which allowed for any state government in the Union, by special order made in writing, to modify or annul any order of the Administrative Tribunal. The latter decision is eminently sensible because it would be manifestly unreasonable for the government, a party involved in such litigation, to be given the unilateral power to override any decision of the Tribunal as it deems fit, as this would 'make a mockery of the entire adjudicative process'. But, in the former case, it is not self-evident why Parliament, in the interests of clearing the infamous backlog that was clogging up India's judicial process, could not, via a constitutional amendment, exclude the jurisdiction of the lower courts over decisions handed down by the Administrative Tribunals, especially since the Supreme Court of India retained jurisdiction to intervene in all such cases.

The most recent invocation was in 2015 when the Supreme Court voided a constitutional amendment that revamped appointments to the higher judiciary[69] – judges would be appointed by a six-member National Judicial Appointments Commission (chaired by the Chief Justice),[70] in lieu of the prior judge-led collegium where the judges themselves had near-complete control over the process. It is not self-evident why this constitutional amendment was a significant threat to democratic values, especially since this six-member Commission would have included three Supreme Court judges, including the Chief Justice.

The fact is, in framing doctrinal constitutional rules, courts often seek to 'minimise the sum of error costs and administrative costs',[71] i.e., they would seek to minimise both the costs of erroneous decisions, including their own, and the administrative costs of implementing a particular doctrinal rule. In jurisdictions with *malleable* constitutions, the judicial exercise of deferential review over any impugned constitutional amendments is an example of a doctrinal rule whereby courts take into account their institutional capabilities during constitutional adjudication, adopt a posture of deference toward the propriety of formal constitutional changes, and only invalidate constitutional amendments that are manifestly indefensible.

On the other hand, a constitutional amendment that has to 'travel a great distance from proposal to law'[72] should be treated differently. This is especially so for constitutional amendments to which the people have made 'significant temporal commitment'.[73] This precondition is satisfied when the amendment process is particularly cumbersome and requires significant bi-partisan support *and* the general public's endorsement for the amendment to pass.

Of the nine jurisdictions I have examined, the current Taiwan and Korea Constitutions are especially rigid. After the 2005 constitutional reforms, a constitutional amendment can only be passed now in Taiwan if it receives the support of at least three-fourths of the Legislative Yuan

[69] *Supreme Court Advocates-on-Record Association* v. *Union of India*, Writ Petition (Civil) No. 13 of 2015.

[70] The six members on the Commission would have been the Chief Justice, two most senior judges on the Supreme Court, the Law Minister, and two persons appointed by a Committee composed of the Chief Justice, the Prime Minister, and the Leader of the Opposition in the Lok Sabha.

[71] David Strauss, 'The Ubiquity of Prophylactic Rules' (1988) 55 *University of Chicago Law Review* 190, 193.

[72] Richard Albert, 'Nonconstitutional Amendments' (2009) 22(5) *Canadian Journal of Law and Jurisprudence* 5, 45.

[73] Jed Rubenfeld, *Freedom and Time: A Theory of Constitutional Self Government* (New Haven: Yale University Press, 2001), 175.

members present at a meeting attended by at least three-fourths of the total members of the Legislative Yuan, and approved by voters at a referendum wherein 'the number of valid votes in favour exceeds one-half of the total number of electors'.[74] In the same vein, in South Korea, under the current 1987 Constitution, a constitutional amendment is only passed if it receives the support of at least two-thirds of the legislators in the National Assembly and 'confirmed by more than one half of all votes cast by more than one half of voters eligible to vote'[75] at a national referendum.[76]

For these especially *rigid* constitutions, it is my considered view that any constitutional amendment passed should *never* be judicially invalidated for violating some implied substantive constraints against change.

My critics might respond by arguing that it is *possible* for manifestly unreasonable constitutional amendments to be passed in jurisdictions with *rigid* constitutions, such that there is no reason why judges should be barred from invalidating such constitutional amendments in those jurisdictions too. But one must note that precisely because these jurisdictions – South Korea and Taiwan – now have such *rigid* constitutions, the enactment of constitutional amendments of any kind would be rarer in practice. As I have discussed earlier, in deciding *ex ante* whether to recognise or reject any implied substantive limits on constitutional change, one should *weigh* the risks of any legislative abuse of the amendment process against the dangers of any judicial abuse that may follow from unelected judges enforcing a nebulous essential features doctrine that can frustrate legitimate constitutional changes intended to meet the

[74] Article 12 of the Additional Articles of the Constitution of the Republic of China reads: 'Amendment of the Constitution shall be initiated upon the proposal of one-fourth of the total members of the Legislative Yuan, passed by at least three-fourths of the members present at a meeting attended by at least three-fourths of the total members of the Legislative Yuan, and sanctioned by electors in the free area of the Republic of China at a referendum held upon expiration of a six-month period of public announcement of the proposal, wherein the number of valid votes in favour exceeds one-half of the total number of electors.'

[75] Article 130 of the 1987 Republic of Korea Constitution reads:

'(1) The National Assembly decides upon the proposed amendments within sixty days of the public announcement, and passage by the National Assembly requires the concurrent vote of two-thirds or more of the total members of the National Assembly.

(2) The proposed amendments to the Constitution are submitted to a national referendum not later than thirty days after passage by the National Assembly, and are confirmed by more than one half of all votes cast by more than one half of voters eligible to vote in elections for members of the National Assembly.

(3) When the proposed amendments to the Constitution receive the concurrence prescribed in Paragraph (2), the amendments to the Constitution is finalised, and the President promulgates it without delay.'

[76] See also Chaihark Hahm 'Beyond "Law vs. Politics" in Constitutional Adjudication: Lessons from South Korea' (2012) 10 *International Journal of Constitutional Law* 6, 32.

exigencies of a changing world. The risks of the legislature successfully abusing the amendment process are much lower in jurisdictions with *rigid* constitutions. If one were to allow the courts to have the exclusive and final say on the substantive propriety of constitutional amendments in these jurisdictions, one would ultimately be making a choice to place unelected judges at the apex of the constitutional system and to live with judicial errors over legislative ones.

Conclusion

The implied basic structure doctrine was judicially conceived to protect the 'core features of contested democratic governance'.[77] But precisely where the constitution does not *ex ante* determine what this core is, the parameters of the core can only be judicially determined *ex post*. In view of the counter-majoritarian danger of any such judicial exposition, this doctrine should therefore only be enforced in states with *malleable* constitutions, where the dominant party/coalition in power has unilaterally harnessed the amendment process to achieve manifestly unreasonable political outcomes.

On the other hand, the super-majoritarian support for an amendment (in a jurisdiction with a *rigid* constitution) lends legitimacy to the constitutional change not merely because of the sheer numbers in its favour, but because the process of revision requires the exhaustion of considerable political energy and time that ensures careful deliberation by the separate political branches of the government and the public's intention to make a temporal commitment to abide by it.[78] The people may not always be right, for popular sovereignty is not an absolute guarantee of substantive justice.[79] But neither are judges infallible in their moral deliberations. In these circumstances, the judiciary must cede to the expression of popular sovereignty, not merely because the amendment is an unmistakeable expression of public will, but because this convergence of interests is undisputable evidence of 'the triumph of the political process over the intervening institutional and electoral barriers erected by the separation of governmental powers'.[80]

[77] Samuel Issacharoff, 'Constitutional Courts and Democratic Hedging' (2011) 99(4) *Georgetown Law Journal* 961, 1002.

[78] Vile (n 35), 198, 211–212; Rubenfeld (n 73), 175.

[79] Vile (n 35), 211.

[80] Albert (n 72), 44.

12

Conclusion

In the foregoing chapters, I have explored how the type of democracy that the courts operate within affects the ability of their judges to address deficiencies in the electoral processes. At the heart of 'political jurisprudence'[1] is an open recognition that judges do not function in 'an institutional or ideological vacuum';[2] socio-political forces shape judicial behaviour just as the exercise of judicial power impacts positively or adversely on the governance of the polity.

In dominant-party democracies, courts can only take a narrow range of actions before their judges outrun the government's 'tolerance interval'[3] and the latter retaliates by punishing the courts.[4] On the other hand, in dynamic democracies, where political power regularly rotates between competing parties, the courts have more 'policy' space as active cooperation between rival factions in the legislature to overrule the judiciary occurs less frequently, especially since constitutional review by an independent branch of government provides a form of insurance for political parties when fortunes turn.[5] In such circumstances, the courts have more opportunities to innovate and make systemic changes to the electoral system. Finally, in fragile democracies, where the military is not under the firm control of the civilian government and the country regularly oscillates between martial law and civilian rule, high-octane judicial review by

[1] Martin Shapiro, 'Political Jurisprudence' (1963–1964) 52 *Kentucky Law Journal* 294.

[2] Ran Hirschl, 'The Judicialisation of Politics' in Keith Whittington, R. Daniel Keleman and Gregory Caldeira (eds), *The Oxford Handbook of Law and Politics* (Oxford: Oxford University Press, 2010), 119.

[3] Lee Epstein, Olga Shvetsova and Jack Knight, 'The Role of Constitutional Courts in the Establishment and Maintenance of Democratic Systems of Government' (2001) 35 *Law and Society Review* 117, 130.

[4] Po Jen Yap, *Constitutional Dialogue in Common Law Asia* (Oxford: Oxford University Press, 2015), 78.

[5] Tom Ginsburg, *Judicial Review of New Democracies: Constitutional Courts in Asian Cases* (Cambridge: Cambridge University Press, 2003).

partisan or imprudent judges can easily facilitate or precipitate a hostile take-over by the armed forces, and lead to the demise of the rule of law.

Genuine political competition is absent in dominant-party democracies. While their elections may generally be free of chicanery or coercion, the dominant incumbent has cemented its hold on power by controlling all facets of the State's electoral apparatus and its administration thereof. While their courts may be unable to dismantle the systemic cartel regulations imposed by the leviathan state, if judicial review is *not* to be denigrated as 'meaningless exercises in political theatre',[6] reform-minded judges must identify dialogic ways of applying 'subtle pressure for political reform at the margins'[7] or holding the ground against adverse change, even if they are unable to overturn the core interests of the regime.

With regard to Singapore, as I have examined in Chapter 2, its courts should enforce against its government constitutional conventions that the ruling party has practised for decades. By deterring the Singapore government from creating *bigger* multi-member electoral seats and redrawing electoral boundaries for constituencies won by the opposition in the preceding election, the judiciary would be merely crystallising as law political customs that the People's Action Party (PAP) has already observed for decades. Such 'soft' constitutional hand-cuffs on the government are not useless as they can prevent stealth electoral changes by mere executive fiat. Furthermore, with the rise of an electorate that is demanding for more political diversity, the PAP is unlikely to be willing to pay the political price of openly reversing such judicial decisions by legislation in Parliament. Therefore, insofar as the Singapore government acquiesces and stays the course, the judiciary would have prevented the country from backsliding politically and practising a more extreme variant of authoritarianism.

In Chapter 3, I explored the state of play in Malaysia. While its judges are also unable to countermand the formal electoral rules passed by the hegemonic Barisan Nasional (BN) to entrench its own incumbency, if the rule of law is to mean anything at all, the courts must ensure that the government – at the very least – abide by the very laws it passes and prevent elections from being stolen. Consequently, the judiciary must impose a set of legality principles that constrains the administrative practices of

[6] See Tom Ginsburg and Alberto Simpser (eds), *Constitutions in Authoritarian Regimes* (New York: Cambridge University Press, 2014).

[7] Tamir Moustafa and Tom Ginsburg, 'Introduction: The Function of Courts in Authoritarian Politics', in Tamir Moustafa and Tom Ginsburg (eds), *Rule By Law: The Politics of Courts in Authoritarian Regimes* (New York: Cambridge University Press, 2008), 15.

the Election Commission. If the Malaysian judges are reluctant to unseat elected officials *ex post*, the imposition of *ex ante* mandates on the Election Commission may be the most dialogic way for the courts to compel this beleaguered institution to deliver on clean elections in the country.

On the other hand, Hong Kong judges exercise more 'policy' discretion than their Singapore or Malaysia counterparts. As I have explained in Chapter 4, while China keeps Hong Kong on a tight leash vis-à-vis issues that directly impact Beijing's control over the city's executive and legislative branches, the fragile coalition between the Hong Kong executive government and the city's pro-Beijing lawmakers – on interests that are *non*-fundamental to China – has provided the courts with significant decisional space to rule against the Hong Kong government on a modest scale. Therefore, while major electoral systemic overhauls are out-of-bounds, the judiciary can and should dialogically question the disparity of voting power between individual Functional Constituency (FC) electors *inter se*, review how small companies are disadvantaged by large conglomerates that can cast more votes through their subsidiaries, and gently trim the regulatory scope of legislation that limits the citizenry's right to stand for elections.

Judiciaries in dynamic democracies have even more 'policy' space. Where competing political parties have the opportunity to take turns in office, this fragmentation of power reduces the ability and the incentives for the incumbent government to rein in the judges.[8] Correspondingly, the courts are more 'consequential'[9] and they are able to directly address systemic failures in the political system, including but not limited to the anti-competitive 'rules of engagement [enacted] to protect established powers from the risk of successful challenge'.[10]

As I explained in Chapter 5, the Supreme Court of India gained political space with the rise of minority governments in the 1990s and was able to directly address systemic material corruption and criminality in Indian politics. Accordingly, the Court was able to mandate election candidates to disclose the source of their political donations[11] and their criminal

[8] Hirschl (n 2), 136; Georg Vanberg, 'Constitutional Courts in Comparative Perspective: A Theoretical Assessment', (2015) 18 *Annual Review of Political Science* 167, 181; John Ferejohn, 'Judicialising Politics, Politicising Law', (2002) 65 *Law and Contemporary Problems* 41, 55.

[9] See Diana Kapiszewski, Gordon Silverstein and Robert A. Kagan (eds), *Consequential Courts: Judicial Roles in Global Perspective* (Cambridge: Cambridge University Press, 2013).

[10] Samuel Issacharoff and Richard H. Pildes, 'Politics as Markets: Partisan Lockups of the Democratic Process' (1997–1998) 50 *Stanford Law Review* 643, 646.

[11] *Common Cause* v. *Union of India* [1996] 3 SCR 1208 (Supreme Court of India).

antecedents;[12] and, soon after, even unseat convicted criminals from their elected office.[13] Similarly, as explored in Chapter 6, after Taiwan transitioned into a dynamic democracy, its Constitutional Court was even able to successfully invalidate two constitutional amendments that had attempted to extend the term of existing National Assembly delegates and allow elected lawmakers to appoint delegates to the said Assembly.[14] In the same vein, as I have examined in Chapter 7, the Constitutional Court of Korea has been able to ameliorate the effects of systemic political barriers of entry erected to preserve incumbency: excessively prohibitive deposits for National Assembly[15] and Presidential elections,[16] gerrymandering of electoral constituencies,[17] and the disenfranchisement of small political parties.[18]

Whilst these courts in dynamic democracies have achieved moderate success in ushering in *systemic* electoral reforms, their track records are not without blemish. For the Indian Supreme Court, its animus toward criminals in politics has hardened the judges against the plight of ordinary convicts who are disfranchised completely at the polls.[19] The Constitutional Court of Taiwan was also unmoved by the disparity of voting power for individuals living in differently populated counties,[20] whilst Korea's Constitutional Court has been shockingly tolerant of the highly restrictive rules on election campaigns that hark back to the country's authoritarian past.[21]

[12] *Union of India v Association for Democratic Reforms* [2002] 3 SCR 696 (Supreme Court of India).

[13] *BR Kapur* v. *State of Tamil* (2001) 7 SCC 231 (Supreme Court of India); *Lily Thomas* v. *Union of India* (2013) 7 SCC 653 (Supreme Court of India).

[14] JY Interpretation No. 499, 24 March 2000 (Constitutional Court, Taiwan) < http://www.judicial.gov.tw/constitutionalcourt/en/p03_01.asp?expno=499> accessed 1 February 2017.

[15] 13-2 KCCR 77, 2000 Hun-Ma 91, 2000 Hun-Ma 112 (consolidated) (19 July 2001) (Constitutional Court, Korea).

[16] 20–2(B) KCCR 477, 2007 Hun-Ma 1024 (27 November 2008) (Constitutional Court, Korea).

[17] 2013 Hun-Ma 781, 2014 Hun-Ma 53 (consolidated) (30 October 2014) (Constitutional Court, Korea).

[18] 26-1(A) KCCR 155, 2012 Hun-Ma 431, 2012 Hun-Ka 19 (consolidated) (28 January 2014) (Constitutional Court, Korea).

[19] *Chief Election Commissioner* v. *Jan Chaukidar (Peoples Watch)* [2013] 10 SCR 1163 (Supreme Court of India).

[20] JY Interpretation No. 721, 6 June 2014 (Constitutional Court, Taiwan); <www.judicial.gov.tw/constitutionalcourt/p03_01.asp?expno=721> accessed 1 February 2017.

[21] 13-2 KCCR 174, 99 Hun-Ba 92, 2000 Hun-Ba 39, 2000 Hun-Ma 167·168· 199·205·280 (consolidated) (30 August 2001) (Constitutional Court, Korea); 17-2 KCCR 160, 2004 Hun-Ba 52 (29 September 2005) (Constitutional Court, Korea); 2014 Hun-Ba 253, Gongbo Vol. 237, 1049 (30 June 2016) (Constitutional Court, Korea).

But in consolidating their nations' democratic development and amplifying the competitiveness of their elections, these dynamic courts have been strategic in exercising remarkable restraint when their rulings could potentially remove top leaders. The judges exercise such restraint not only when their courts operated within a dominant-party democracy – as we have seen with Prime Minister Indira Gandhi's election in India[22] – but even so *after* the nation transitioned into a dynamic democracy, as we observed in the impeachment trial of South Korean President Roh Moo-hyun[23] and the Constitutional Court of Taiwan's even-handed treatment of beleaguered President Chen Shui-bian.[24]

As we have observed in fragile democracies, courts that actively push their top leaders off the saddle would inevitably facilitate or foment a military coup. In fledgling democracies, the civilian government does not have control over its armed forces; aggressive judicial review herein is antithetical to the country's transition to a stable democracy as the generals often respond by aborting the constitution.

In Chapter 8, I examined how partisan judges in Thailand have facilitated hostile take-overs by the military by nullifying two general elections, removing three Prime Ministers, dissolving six political parties, and banning hundreds of party executives – all of which were directed against former Premier Thaksin Shinawatra and his surrogates. By stymying elected governments and fostering political gridlock, the Constitutional Court of Thailand created power vacuums that enticed the military to fill twice in a decade.

Where the judiciary lacks the financial and coercive resources of the military, it is unsurprising that the Supreme Court of Pakistan – for most of its history – has acquiesced to the army's use of brute force. As we have examined in Chapter 9, this was so when martial law was declared in 1958 and 1977, and when emergency rule was imposed nation-wide in 1999 and 2007. It is noteworthy that the judges had only denounced and delegitimised the military coups in Pakistan *after* the dictators were ousted.[25]

22 *Indira Gandhi* v. *Raj Narain* [1976] 2 SCR 347 (Supreme Court of India).

23 16-1 KCCR 609, 2004 Hun-Na 1 (14 May 2004) (Constitutional Court, Korea).

24 JY Interpretation No. 585, 15 December 2004 (Constitutional Court, Taiwan) <www.judicial.gov.tw/constitutionalcourt/en/p03_01.asp?expno=585> accessed 1 February 2017; JY Interpretation No. 627, 15 June 2007 (Constitutional Court, Taiwan) <www.judicial.gov.tw/constitutionalcourt/en/p03_01.asp?expno=627> accessed 1 February 2017.

25 *Asma Jilani* v. *The Government of the Punjab and Anor*, PLD 1972 SC 139 (Supreme Court of Pakistan); *Sindh High Court Bar Association* v. *Federation of Pakistan*, PLD 2009 SC 789 (Supreme Court of Pakistan).

In contrast, the Court's high-stakes political duels with the government (or the military) have always backfired or proved to be inconsequential. When the Supreme Court reinstated Prime Minister Nawaz Sharif in 1993 after he was fired by the President,[26] the military compelled both politicians to resign several months later. When Chief Justice Chaudhry challenged General Pervez Musharraf's national security and fiscal policies, the former was suspended in 2007. And when the Supreme Court came close to denying Musharraf a third term as President, over 60 superior court judges, including Chaudhry, were removed and replaced in the same year.

On the other hand, as I have examined in Chapter 10, the Supreme Court of Bangladesh (Appellate Division) has consciously avoided going on a collision course with the government. In a country that has experienced two martial law regimes and undergone four States of Emergency, the Appellate Division has only questioned the legitimacy of these extraordinary measures *after* the crises had ceased. The 8th Amendment that split the High Court Division into seven separate benches; the 5th and 7th Amendments that ousted judicial review during periods of martial law; and the 13th Amendment that allowed for an unelected caretaker government to govern the country were all invalidated by the Appellate Division after martial law or emergency rule had formally ceased. Furthermore, the invalidation of the 5th, 7th, and 13th Amendments was precisely what the incumbent civilian government had wanted, and the Court's assertion of judicial authority thus dovetailed with the interests of the administration. This is not to say that the Bangladesh superior courts have been mere handmaidens of the government of the day. The most confrontational decisions of the Appellate Division have been instances where it drew a line in the sand to defend its institutional independence,[27] which, as argued by Stephen Gardbaum, is the top priority for courts operating in fledgling or brittle democracies.[28]

Finally, in Chapter 11, I analysed the doctrine of unconstitutional constitutional amendments and the dilemma that its enforcement by these Asian courts might enhance or erode the spread of democratic values. Where the constitution does not *ex ante* determine the limits of this

[26] *Nawaz Sharif* v. *President of Pakistan*, PLD 1993 SC 473 (Supreme Court of Pakistan).

[27] *Secretary, Ministry of Finance* v. *Masdar Hossain* [1999] 28 CLC (AD) 598 (Supreme Court of Bangladesh); *Justice Syed Dastagir Hossain* v. *Idrisur Rahman* [2009] 38 CLC (AD) 3431 (Supreme Court of Bangladesh).

[28] Stephen Gardbaum, 'Are Strong Constitutional Courts Always a Good Thing for New Democracies?' (2015) 53 *Columbia Journal of Transnational Law* 285, 289.

doctrine, judicial exposition of its parameters *ex post* poses a counter-majoritarian danger that even exceeds that associated with the constitutional review of ordinary legislation. Therefore, its enforcement is most defensible in malleable constitutions where the dominant party or coalition has unilaterally harnessed the amendment process to achieve manifestly unreasonable political outcomes. In contrast, where the impugned constitutional amendment had passed with significant bi-partisan legislative support *and* was endorsed by the public at a national referendum, the judiciary must defer to this constitutional expression of popular sovereignty.

The democratisation of a country facilitates the rise of its judiciary; and the exercise of judicial power in turn can further enhance and upgrade the nation's electoral infrastructure. But the converse is also true. In failing democracies, abrasive judicial review is especially perilous, as this would only invite or provoke military dictators to abort the constitution by force. When a democracy is unstable or undermined by a dominant party/coalition, reform-oriented judges must always resist impinging on the core interests of the authoritarian regime.[29] Instead, wise judges must design constitutional rules that safeguard the institutional independence of the courts, keep the nation's democratic development on course, and bide their time in anticipation of the constitutional moment when the dominant party or military regime fades away. As law and politics interact in the construction of constitutional doctrines, Asian courts will continue to play this indispensable role in shaping the democratic order.

[29] Moustafa and Ginsburg (n 7), 15.

BIBLIOGRAPHY

Farid Ahmed, 'Bangladesh Ruling Party Wins Elections Marred by Boycott, Violence', (CNN, 7 January 2014) <http://edition.cnn.com/2014/01/06/world/asia/bangladesh-elections/>

Nizam Ahmed, 'The Parliament' in Ali Riaz and Mohammad Sajjadur Rahman (eds), *Routledge Handbook of Contemporary Bangladesh* (London, Routledge 2016) 82

C.C. Aikman, 'The Debate on the Amendment of the Indian Constitution' (1978) 9 *Victoria Wellington Law Review* 357

Richard Albert, 'Nonconstitutional Amendments' (2009) 22(5) *Canadian Journal of Law and Jurisprudence* 5

Rashaad Ali, 'Malaysian By-Elections: Najib's Winning Ways' (RSIS Commentary, 30 June 2016) <https://www.rsis.edu.sg/wp-content/uploads/2016/07/CO16165.pdf>

T.R.S. Allan, *Constitutional Justice: A Liberal Theory of the Rule of Law* (Oxford, Oxford University Press 2001)

Amnesty International, 'Malaysia Must End Unprecedented Crackdown on Hundreds of Critics through Sedition Act' (25 January 2016) <http://www.amnestyusa.org/news/press-releases/malaysia-must-end-unprecedented-crackdown-on-hundreds-of-critics-through-sedition-act>

T.R. Andhyarujina, 'The Unique Judicial Activism of the Supreme Court of India' (2014) 130 *Law Quarterly Review* 53

Associated Press in Dhaka, 'Bangladesh Election Violence Throws Country Deeper into Turmoil' (*Guardian*, 6 January 2014) <http://www.theguardian.com/world/2014/jan/06/bangladesh-election-violence-awami-league>

Association for Democratic Reforms, *Lok Sabha Election Watch 2014*, 327 <http://adrindia.org/sites/default/files/Lok_Sabha_Report_2014_compressed.pdf>

Granville Austin, *Working a Democratic Constitution: The Indian Experience* (New Delhi, Oxford University Press 1999)

N.W. Barber, '*Laws and Constitutional Conventions*' (2009) 125 *Law Quarterly Review* 294.

Francis Bennion and Oliver Jones (eds), *Bennion on Statutory Interpretation: A Code* (6th edn, London, Sweet & Maxwell 2013)

Carlos Bernal, 'Unconstitutional Constitutional Amendments in the Case Study of Colombia: An Analysis of the Justification and Meaning of the Constitutional Replacement Doctrine' (2013) 11 *International Journal of Constitutional Law* 339

Sarah Birch, *Electoral Malpractice* (Oxford, Oxford University Press 2011)

Harry Blair, 'Party Overinstitutionalisation, Contestation, and Democratic Degradation in Bangladesh' in Paul R. Brass (ed), *Routledge Handbook of South Asian Politics: India, Pakistan, Bangladesh, Sri Lanka and Nepal* (London, Routledge 2010) 98

Philip Bobbitt, *Constitutional Fate: Theory of the Constitution* (1st edn, New York, Oxford University Press 1984)

James W.J. Bowden and Nicholas A. MacDonald, 'Writing the Unwritten: The Officialisation of Constitutional Convention in Canada, the United Kingdom, New Zealand and Australia' (2012) 6 *Journal of Parliamentary and Political Law* 365

Louis D. Brandeis, *Letters of Louis D. Brandeis: Volume III, 1913–1915: Progressive and Zionist* (New York, State University of New York Press, 1973).

Johannes Chan, 'From Colony to Special Administrative Region' in Johannes Chan and CL Lim (eds), *Law of the Hong Kong Constitution* (2nd edn, Hong Kong, Sweet & Maxwell, 2015), 1

Heng Chee Chan, 'The Strategic Voter in the "New Normal"' (*Straits Times*, 19 September 2015) <http://www.straitstimes.com/opinion/the-strategic-voter-in-the-new-normal>

Sek Keong Chan, 'Judicial Review – From Angst to Empathy' (2010) 22 *Singapore Academy of Law Journal* 469

Chintan Chandrachud, 'Debating the NJAC Judgment of the Supreme Court of India: Three Dimensions' (UK Constitutional Law Association Blog, 3 November 2015) < https://ukconstitutionallaw.org/2015/11/03/chintan-chandrachud-debating-the-njac-judgment-of-the-supreme-court-of-india-three-dimensions/>

'Measuring Constitutional Case Salience in the Indian Supreme Court' (2014) 6 *Journal of Indian Law and Society* 42

Wen-chen Chang, 'Strategic Judicial Responses in Politically Charged Cases: East Asian Experiences' (2010) 8 (4) *International Journal of Constitutional Law* 885

Wen-chen Chang and Yi-Li Lee, 'Judicial Strategies to Resolving Presidential Election Disputes: the Case of Taiwan' in Po Jen Yap (ed), *Judicial Review of Elections in Asia* (London, Routledge 2016) 147

Channel News Asia, 'Electoral Boundaries Drawn for Next General Election' (Channel News Asia, 24 July 2015) <http://www.channelnewsasia.com/news/singapore/electoral-boundaries/2005186.html>

Guy-Uriel E. Charles, 'Democracy and Distortion' (2007) 92 *Cornell Law Review* 601

Moeen H. Cheema, '"Election Disputes" or Disputed Elections? Judicial (Non-) Review of the Electoral Process in Pakistan' in Po Jen Yap (ed) *Judicial Review of Elections in Asia* (London, Routledge 2016) 69

Moeen H. Cheema and Ijaz S. Gilani (eds), *The Politics and Jurisprudence of the Chaudhry Court: 2005–2013* (Karachi, Oxford University Press 2015)

Lian Cheng, 'Minimum Campaign Period Now 11 Days' (*Borneo Post*, 21 March 2013) <http://www.theborneopost.com/2013/03/21/minimum-campaign-period-now-11-days/>

Albert Chen, 'Law and Politics of the Struggle for Universal Suffrage in Hong Kong, 2013–15' (2016) 3 *Asian Journal of Law and Society* 189

(ed), *Constitutionalism in Asia in the Early Twenty-First Century* (Cambridge, Cambridge University Press 2014)

Gary Cheung and Jeffie Lam, 'Rise of Localists in Hong Kong Polls Set To Bring Headaches for Beijing, Analysts Say' *South China Morning Post* (5 September 2016) <http://www.scmp.com/news/hong-kong/politics/article/2015349/rise-localists-hong-kong-polls-set-bring-headaches-beijing>

Sujit Choudhry, 'How to do Constitutional Law and Politics in South Asia' in Mark Tushnet and Madhav Khosla (eds) *Unstable Constitutionalism: Law and Politics in South Asia* (New York, Cambridge University Press 2015) 18

M. Jashim Ali Chowdhury, 'Elections in "Democratic" Bangladesh' in Mark Tushnet and Madhav Khosla (eds) *Unstable Constitutionalism: Law and Politics in South Asia* (New York, Cambridge University Press 2015) 192

J. Chuang, 'Judiciary "disappointed"' (*Taipei Times*, 22 January 2005) 3

Constitutional and Mainland Affairs Bureau, 'Consultation Paper on Disqualification of Candidates with Unserved Prison Sentences and other Related Matters' (21 July 2014)

'Results of the Public Consultation on Disqualification of Candidates with Unserved Prison Sentences and other Related Matters and Proposed Way Forward' (17 November 2014) LC Paper No. CB(2)267/14–15(03)

Aurel Croissant, 'Electoral Politics in South Korea' in Aurel Croissant, Gabriele Bruns and Marei John (eds) *Electoral Politics in Southeast and East Asia* (Singapore, Friedrich Ebert Stiftung 2002) 233

Yasmin Dawood, 'Electoral Fairness and the Law of Democracy: A Structural Rights Approach to Judicial Review' (2012) 62 *University of Toronto Law Journal* 499

Surya Deva, 'Public Interest Litigation in India: A Quest to Achieve the Impossible?' in Po Jen Yap and Holning Lau (eds) *Public Interest Litigation in Asia* (London, Routledge 2011) 57

'Democracy and Elections in India: Reviewing the role of the Election Commission and the Courts' in Po Jen Yap (ed) *Judicial Review of Elections in Asia* (London, Routledge 2016) 38

Larry Diamond, 'The Democratic Rollback: The Resurgence of the Predatory State' (2008) 87(2) *Foreign Affairs* 36

A.V. Dicey and J.W.F. Allison (eds) *The Law of the Constitution* (Oxford, Oxford University Press 2013)

Rosalind Dixon and David Landau, 'Transnational Constitutionalism and a Limited Doctrine of Unconstitutional Constitutional Amendment' (2015) 13 *International Journal of Constitutional Law* 606

Rosalind Dixon and Samuel Issacharoff, 'Living to Fight Another Day: Judicial Deferral in Defence of Democracy' (2016) *Wisconsin Law Review* 683

Björn Dressel, 'Thailand's Elusive Quest for a Workable Constitution, 1997–2007' (2009) 31(2) *Contemporary Southeast Asia* 296

'Judicialisation of Politics or Politicisation of the Judiciary? Considerations from Recent Events in Thailand' (2010) 23(5) *Pacific Review* 671

(ed), *The Judicialisation of Politics in Asia* (Abingdon, Oxon, Routledge 2012)

Ronald Dworkin, *Taking Rights Seriously* (Cambridge, Massachusetts, Harvard University Press 1977)

Law's Empire (Cambridge, Massachusetts, Harvard University Press 1986)

John Hart Ely, *Democracy and Distrust: A Theory of Judicial Review* (Cambridge, Massachusetts, Harvard University Press 1980)

Lee Epstein, Olga Shvetsova and Jack Knight, 'The Role of Constitutional Courts in the Establishment and Maintenance of Democratic Systems of Government' (2001) 35 *Law and Society Review* 117

Audrey Eu, 'The Road of No Return Part 2: How the Courts could have Handled the Oaths Row' (*Hong Kong Free Press*, 7 December 2016) <https://www.hongkongfp.com/2016/12/07/road-no-return-part-2-courts-handled-oaths-row/>

Richard Fallon, 'Judicially Manageable Standards and Constitutional Meaning' (2006) 119 *Harvard Law Review* 1274

Shelley Feldman, 'Bangladesh in 2014: Illusive Democracy' (2015) 55(1) *Asian Survey* 67

John Ferejohn, 'Judicialising Politics, Politicising Law' (2002) 65 *Law and Contemporary Problems* 41

Federico Ferrara, *The Political Development of Modern Thailand* (Cambridge, Cambridge University Press 2015)

'Democracy in Thailand: Theory and Practice' in William Case (ed) *Routledge Handbook of Southeast Asian Democratisation* (London, Routledge 2015) 351

Brian Fong, 'Executive-Legislative Disconnection in Post-colonial Hong Kong' (2014) 1 *China Perspectives* 5

Freedom House, 'Bangladesh: Countries at the Crossroads 2007' (Freedom House), 25 September 2007 <https://freedomhouse.org/report/countries-crossroads/2007/bangladesh>

Lon Fuller, *The Morality of Law* (New Haven, Yale University Press 1964)

Brian Galligan and Scott Brenton (eds) *Constitutional Conventions in Westminster Systems: Controversies, Changes and Challenges* (Cambridge, Cambridge University Press 2015)

Stephen Gardbaum, 'Are Strong Constitutional Courts Always a Good Thing for New Democracies?' (2015) 53 *Columbia Journal of Transnational Law* 285

'Political Parties, Voting Systems, and the Separation of Powers' (2017) 65 *American Journal of Comparative Law* (forthcoming)

Yash Ghai, 'Sentinels of Liberty or Sheep in Woolf's Clothing? Judicial Politics and the Hong Kong Bill of Rights' (1997) 60 *Modern Law Review* 459

Tom Ginsburg, *Judicial Review in New Democracies: Constitutional Courts in Asian Cases* (Cambridge, Cambridge University Press 2003)

'Constitutional Courts in East Asia: Understanding Variation' (2008) 3 *Journal of Comparative Law* 80

'Constitutional Afterlife: The Continuing Impact of Thailand's Postpolitical Constitution' (2009) 7(1) *International Journal of Constitutional Law* 83

'Courts and New Democracies: Recent Works' (2012) 37 *Law and Social Inquiry* 720

Tom Ginsburg and Robert A. Kagan, 'Institutionalist Approaches to Courts as Political Actors' in Tom Ginsburg and Robert A. Kagan (eds) *Institutions and Public Law: Comparative Approaches* (New York: Peter Lang 2005) 1

Tom Ginsburg and Alberto Simpser (eds) *Constitutions in Authoritarian Regimes* (New York, Cambridge University Press 2014)

Jeffrey Goldsworthy, 'Homogenising Constitutions' (2003) 23 *Oxford Journal of Legal Studies* 505

Edmund Terence Gomez, 'Resisting the Fall: The Single Dominant Party, Policies and Elections in Malaysia' (2016) 46 *Journal of Contemporary Asia* 570

James Goodwin, 'The Last Defence of Wednesbury' (2012) *Public Law* 445

Jamal Greene, 'Selling Originalism' (2009) 97 *Georgetown Law Journal* 657

J.A.G. Griffith, 'The Brave New World of Sir John Laws' (2000) 63 *Modern Law Review* 159

Devin T. Hagerty, 'Bangladesh in 2007: Democracy Interrupted, Political and Environmental Challenges Ahead' (2008) 48 *Asian Survey* 177

Chaihark Hahm, 'Beyond "Law vs. Politics" in Constitutional Adjudication: Lessons from South Korea' (2012) 10 *International Journal of Constitutional Law* 6

Andrew Harding, 'The Death of a Doctrine? *Phang Chin Hock* v *Public Prosecutor*' (1979) 21 *Malaya Law Review* 365

'The 1988 Constitutional Crisis in Malaysia' (1990) 39 *International and Comparative Law Quarterly* 57

Andrew Harding and Penelope Nicholson (eds), *New Courts in Asia* (London, Routledge 2010)

Andrew Harding and Peter Leyland, *The Constitutional System of Thailand: A Contextual Analysis* (Oxford, Hart Publishing 2011)

Farooq Hasan, 'A Juridical Critique of Successful Treason: A Jurisprudential Analysis of the Constitutionality of a Coup d'état in Common Law' (1984) 20 *Stanford Journal of International Law* 191

Al Masud Hasanuzzaman, 'Civil-military Relations' in Ali Riaz and Mohammad Sajjadur Rahman (eds) *Routledge Handbook of Contemporary Bangladesh* (London, Routledge 2016) 115

Ran Hirschl, *Towards Juristocracy* (Cambridge, Massachusetts, Harvard University Press 2004)

'The Judicialisation of Politics' in Keith Whittington, R. Daniel Kelemen and Gregory A. Caldeira (eds) *The Oxford Handbook of Law and Politics* (Oxford, Oxford University Press 2010) 119

Hong Kong Electoral Affairs Commission, *Report on the 2012 Legislative Council Election Held on 9 September 2012* (22 November 2012) <http://www.legco.gov.hk/yr12-13/english/panels/ca/papers/ca1217cb2-306-e.pdf>

Hong Kong Special Administrative Region Government, *Consultation Report and Proposals on the Method for Selecting the Chief Executive by Universal Suffrage* (April 2015) <http://www.2017.gov.hk/filemanager/template/en/doc/report_2nd/consultation_report_2nd.pdf>

Ridwanul Hoque, 'The Recent Emergency and the Politics of the Judiciary in Bangladesh' (2009) 2(2) *National University of Juridical Science Law Review* 183

'Constitutionalism and the Judiciary in Bangladesh' in Sunil Khilnani, Vikram Raghavan and Arun K. Thiruvengadam (eds) *Comparative Constitutionalism in South Asia* (New Delhi, Oxford University Press 2013)

'The Judicialisation of Politics in Bangladesh' in Mark Tushnet and Madhav Khosla (eds) *Unstable Constitutionalism: Law and Politics in South Asia* (New York, Cambridge University Press 2015) 261

Tessa Houghton and Zaharom Nain, 'Watchdogs or Lapdogs? Monitoring Malaysia's Media Coverage of GE2013' in Johan Saravanamuttu, Lee Hock Guan and Mohamed Nawab Mohamed Osman (eds) *Coalitions in Collision: Malaysia's 13th General Elections* (Singapore, Institute of Southeast Asian Studies 2015) 159

Sara Hossain, 'Confronting Constitutional Curtailments: Attempts to Rebuild Independence of the Judiciary in Bangladesh' in Paul R. Brass (ed) *Routledge Handbook of South Asian Politics: India, Pakistan, Bangladesh, Sri Lanka and Nepal* (London, Routledge 2010) 191

Alison Hsiao, 'Legislature Approves Judicial Nominees' (*Taipei Times*, 26 October 2016) <http://www.taipeitimes.com/News/front/archives/2016/10/26/2003657934>

Human Rights Watch, 'Bangladesh: Abuses Grow in Crackdown on Protests' (Human Rights Watch, 25 August 2007) <https://www.hrw.org/news/2007/08/25/bangladesh-abuses-grow-crackdown-protests>

Jau-Yuan Hwang, 'Taiwan's Constitutional Court from 2003 to 2011: New Appointments and Different Performance' (2012) 53 *Seoul Law Journal* 41

Samuel Issacharoff, 'Judging Politics: The Elusive Quest for Judicial Review of Political Fairness' (1992) 71 *Texas Law Review* 1643

'Constitutional Courts and Democratic Hedging' (2011) 99(4) *Georgetown Law Journal* 961

'Constitutional Courts and Consolidated Power' (2014) 62 *American Journal of Comparative Law* 585

Fragile Democracies: Contested Power in the Era of Constitutional Courts (Cambridge, Cambridge University Press 2015)

Samuel Issacharoff and Richard Pildes, 'Politics as Markets: Partisan Lockups of the Democratic Process' (1998) 50 *Stanford Law Review* 643

International Crisis Group, 'Mapping Bangladesh's Political Crisis' (Asian Report N°264, 9 February 2015) <http://www.crisisgroup.org/~/media/Files/asia/south-asia/bangladesh/264-mapping-bangladesh-s-political-crisis.pdf>

'Thailand's Lengthening Roadmap to Elections' (Asian Report N°274, 10 December 2015) < https://www.crisisgroup.org/asia/south-east-asia/thailand/thailand-s-lengthening-roadmap-elections>

Gary Jacobsohn, 'An Unconstitutional Constitution? A Comparative Perspective' (2006) 4(3) *International Journal of Constitutional Law* 460

Swati Jhaveri and Anne Scully-Hill, 'Executive and Legislative Reactions to Judicial Declarations of Constitutional Invalidity in Hong Kong: Engagement, Acceptance or Avoidance?' (2015) 13 *International Journal of Constitutional Law* 507

Anil Kalhan, '"Gray Zone" Constitutionalism and the Dilemma of Judicial Independence in Pakistan' (2013) 46 *Vanderbilt Journal of Transnational Law* 1

Diana Kapiszewski, Gordon Silverstein and Robert A. Kagan (eds) *Consequential Courts: Judicial Roles in Global Perspective* (Cambridge, Cambridge University Press 2013)

Neal Kumar Katyal, 'Judges as Advicegivers' (1998) *50 Stanford Law Review* 1709

Aileen Kavanagh, 'Unconstitutional Constitutional Amendments from Irish Free State to Irish Republic' in Eoin Carolan (ed) *The Constitution of Ireland: Perspectives and Prospects* (Dublin, Bloomsbury Professional 2012)

Adeeba Aziz Khan, 'The Politics of Constitutional Amendments in Bangladesh: The Case of the Non-political Caretaker Government' (2015) 9 *International Review of Law* <http://www.qscience.com/doi/pdf/10.5339/irl.2015.9>

Hamid Khan, *Constitutional and Political History of Pakistan* (2nd edn, Karachi, Oxford University Press 2009)

Byung-Kook Kim, 'Party Politics in South Korea's Democracy: The Crisis of Success' in Larry Diamond and Byung-Kook Kim (eds) *Consolidating Democracy in South Korea* (Boulder, CO, Lynne Rienner Publishers 2000) 53

Jiyoon Kim, 'The Party System in Korea and Identity Politics' in Larry Diamond and Gi-Wook Shin (eds) *New Challenges for Maturing Democracies in Korea and Taiwan* (Stanford, Stanford University Press 2014) 71

Jongcheol Kim, 'Upgrading Constitutionalism: The Ups and Downs of Constitutional Developments in South Korea Since 2000' in Albert Chen (ed) *Constitutionalism in Asia in the Early Twenty-First Century* (Cambridge, Cambridge University Press 2014) 76

Marie Seong-Hak Kim, 'Travails of Judges: Courts and Constitutional Authoritarianism in South Korea' (2015) 63 *American Journal of Comparative Law* 601

Sanjay Kumar, 'A Shift towards Regionalisation of Indian Politics' in Sudha Pai (ed) *Handbook of Politics in Indian States: Regions, Parties and Economic Reforms* (New Delhi, Oxford University Press 2013) 148

Ming-Sung Kuo, 'Moving Towards a Nominal Constitutional Court: Critical Reflections on the Shift from Judicial Activism to Constitutional Irrelevance in Taiwan's Constitutional Politics' (2016) 25 (3) *Washington International Law Journal* 597

Jeffie Lam and Joyce Ng, 'Hong Kong Courts can Decide Fate of At Least 10 Lawmakers Despite Beijing Ruling' (*South China Morning Post*, 11 November 2016) <http://www.scmp.com/news/hong-kong/politics/article/2045224/hong-kong-courts-can-decide-fate-least-10-lawmakers-despite>

David Landau, 'Political Institutions and Judicial Role in Comparative Constitutional Law' (2010) 51 *Harvard International Law Journal* 319

'Abusive Constitutionalism' (2013) 47 *UC Davis Law Review* 189

'A Dynamic Theory of Judicial Role' (2014) 55 *Boston College Law Review* 1501

Chris Lau, 'Hong Kong Lawmakers Accused of Setting aside Solemnity in Taking Oaths' (*South China Morning Post*, 2 December, 2016) <http://www.scmp.com/news/hong-kong/politics/article/2051266/hong-kong-lawmakers-accused-setting-aside-solemnity-taking>

Chris Lau and Eddie Lee, 'Did CY Leung Mess Up his own Oath? Legal Challenge over Hong Kong Leader's 2012 Swearing In' (*South China Morning Post*, 11 November 2016) <http://www.scmp.com/news/hong-kong/law-crime/article/2045129/did-cy-leung-mess-his-own-oath-legal-challenge-over-hong>

'Pro-Beijing Group Member asks Hong Kong Court to Disqualify 11 Lawmakers over Legco Oaths' (*South China Morning Post*, 14 November 2016) <http://www.scmp.com/news/hong-kong/law-crime/article/2045801/pro-beijing-group-member-asks-hong-kong-court-disqualify-11>

Chris Lau, Eddie Lee and Tony Cheung (et al) 'Veteran Hong Kong Taxi Driver Group Member asks Court to Invalidate Eight Legco Oaths' (*South China Morning Post*, 10 November 2016) <http://www.scmp.com/news/hong-kong/law-crime/article/2044745/veteran-hong-kong-taxi-driver-group-member-asks-court>

Siu-kai Lau, 'Hong Kong's Partial Democracy under Stress' in Yue-man Yeung (ed) *New Challenges for Development and Modernisation* (Hong Kong, The Chinese University Press 2002) 181

David S. Law, 'The Anatomy of a Conservative Court: Judicial Review in Japan' (2009) 87 *Texas Law Review* 1545

Law Commission of India, *170th Report on Reform of the Election Law* (1999) <www.lawcommissionofindia.nic.in/lc170.htm>

Electoral Disqualifications (Report No. 244) (February 2014) <http://lawcommissionofindia.nic.in/reports/report244.pdf>

John Laws, 'Law and Democracy' (1995) *Public Law* 72.

Lawyers' Rights Watch Canada, 'J.B. Jeyaretnam' (Lawyers' Rights Watch Canada, 26 March 2012) <www.lrwc.org/j-b-jeyaretnam>

H.P. Lee, *Constitutional Conflicts in Contemporary Malaysia* (2nd edn, Oxford: Oxford University Press 2017)

Youngjae Lee, 'Law, Politics, and Impeachment: The Impeachment of Roh Moo-hyun from a Comparative Constitutional Perspective' (2005) 53 *American Journal of Comparative Law* 403

Yeonho Lee and Yoo-Jin Lim, 'The Rise of the Labour Party in South Korea: Causes and Limits' (2006) 19(3) *The Pacific Review* 305

Legislative Council Secretariat, *Paper for the Bills Committee on Village Representative Election Bill* (LC Paper No. LS 15/02-03) (18 November 2002)

Clive Lewis, *Judicial Remedies in Public Law* (4th edn, London, Sweet & Maxwell 2008)

Chien-Chih Lin, 'Majoritarian Judicial Review: The Case of Taiwan' (2014) *National Taiwan University Law Review* 103

Sonny Lo, *Competing Chinese Political Visions* (Santa Barbara, Praeger 2010)

Ngok Ma, 'Political Parties and Elections' in Wai-man Lam, Percy Luen-tim Lui, Wilson Wong and Ian Holliday (eds) *Contemporary Hong Kong Politics: Governance in the Post-1997 Era* (Hong Kong, Hong Kong University Press 2007) 117

Tayyab Mahmud, 'Praetorianism and Common Law in Post-Colonial Settings: Judicial Responses to Constitutional Breakdowns in Pakistan' (1993) *Utah Law Review* 1225

Malaymail, 'Election Commission changes names for 12 parliamentary, 34 state seats' (*Malay Mail*, 15 September 2016) <http://www.themalaymailonline.com/malaysia/article/election-commission-changes-names-for-12-parliamentary-34-state-seats>

Malaysian Electoral Roll Analysis Project (2003) <http://malaysianelectoralrollproject.blogspot.sg/>

Salman Masood, 'Pakistani Premier Warns of Plotting by Military' (*The New York Times*, 22 December 2011) <http://www.nytimes.com/2011/12/23/world/asia/pakistani-premier-yousaf-raza-gilani-lashes-out-at-his-military.html>

Manoj Mate, 'Public Interest Litigation and the Transformation of the Supreme Court of India' in Diana Kapiszewski, Gordon Silverstein and Robert Kagan (eds) *Consequential Courts: Judicial Roles in Global Perspective* (Cambridge, New York, Cambridge University Press 2013) 262

'High Courts and Election Law Reform in the United States and India' (2014) *Boston University International Law Journal* 267

'The Rise of Judicial Governance in the Supreme Court of India' (2015) 33 *Boston University International Law Journal* 169

'India's Participatory Model: The Right to Information in Election Law' (2016) 48 *Georgetown Washington International Law Journal* 377

Duncan McCargo, 'Network Monarchy and Legitimacy Crises in Thailand' (2005) 18(4) *Pacific Review* 499

'Competing Notions of Judicialisation in Thailand' (2014) 36 *Contemporary Southeast Asia* 417

F. Fraser Mendel, 'Judicial Power and Illusion: the Republic of China's Council of Grand Justices and Constitutional Interpretation' (1993) 2 *Pacific Rim Law & Policy Journal* 157

Gillian Metzger, 'Embracing Administrative Common Law' (2012) 80 *George Washington Law Review* 1293

David Gwynn Morgan, 'The Indian "Essential Features" Case' (1981) 30 *International and Comparative Law Quarterly* 307

Tamir Moustafa and Tom Ginsburg, 'Introduction: The Function of Courts in Authoritarian Politics' in Tamir Moustafa and Tom Ginsburg (eds) *Rule By Law: The Politics of Courts in Authoritarian Regimes* (New York, Cambridge University Press 2008) 1

Walter Murphy, 'Merlin's Memory: The Past and Future Imperfect of the Once and Future Polity' in Sanford Levinson (ed) *Responding to Imperfection: The Theory and Practice of Constitutional Amendment* (Princeton, Princeton University Press 1995) 163

Dhirenn Nair, 'Malaysia's Defiant Prime Minister: The 1MDB Purge' (*The Diplomat*, 9 August 2016) <http://thediplomat.com/2016/08/malaysias-defiant-prime-minister-the-1mdb-purge/>

Michael H. Nelson, 'Delaying Constitutionalism to Protect Establishment Hegemony in Thailand: Designing the Election System and the Senate in the Constitution of 2007' in Marco Bünte and Björn Dressel (eds) *Politics and Constitutions in Southeast Asia* (London, Routledge 2017) 49

Ng Kang Chung, 'Hong Kong Development Minister Slams Heung Yee Kuk Stance on Trading Small House Rights' (*South China Morning Post*, 25 January 2016) <http://www.scmp.com/news/hong-kong/politics/article/1905250/hong-kong-development-minister-slams-heung-yee-kuk-stance>

Pippa Norris, 'All Elections Are Not the Same: Why Power-sharing Elections Strengthen Democratisation' in Staffan I Lindberg (ed) *Democratisation by Elections: A New Mode of Transition* (Baltimore, John Hopkins University Press 2009) 148

James Ockey, 'Thailand in 2006: Retreat to Military Rule' (2007) 47(1) *Asian Survey* 133

Michael Pal, 'Breakdowns in the Democratic Process and the Law of Canadian Democracy' (2011) 57 *McGill Law Journal* 299

William Parlett, 'Courts and Constitution Making' (2015) 50 *Wake Forest Law Review* 921

Pemantau Pilihan Raya Rakyat, *Clean & Fair? An Election Observation Report of the 13th Malaysian General Election* (March 2014) <http://www.bersih.org/wp-content/uploads/2013/09/Pemantau-Report-English-Final.pdf>

Pasuk Phongpaichit and Chris Baker, 'Populist Challenge to the Establishment: Thaksin Shinawatra and the Transformation of Thai Politics' in Richard Robison (ed) *Routledge Handbook of Southeast Asian Politics* (London, Routledge 2011) 88

Daniel D. Polsby and Robert D. Popper, 'The Third Criterion: Compactness as a Procedural Safeguard against Partisan Gerrymandering' (1991) 9(2) *Yale Law and Policy Review* 301

Thitinan Pongsudhirak, 'Thailand's Uneasy Passage' (2012) 23(2) *Journal of Democracy* 47

'Thailand's Democracy in Military Custody' (*Straits Times*, 14 May 2016) <http://www.straitstimes.com/politics/thailands-democracy-in-military-custody>

Kitti Prasirtsuk, 'Thailand in 2014: Another Coup, a Different Coup?' (2015) 55 *Asian Survey* 200

Jon S.T. Quah, 'Taiwan's Anti-corruption Strategy: Suggestions for Reform' (2010) 2 *Maryland Series in Contemporary Asian Studies* 1

Taiyyaba Ahmed Qureshi, 'State of Emergency: General Pervez Musharraf's Executive Assault on Judicial Independence in Pakistan' (2010) 35 *North Carolina Journal of International Law and Commercial Regulation* 485

Judith Resnik, 'Managerial Judges' (1982) 96 *Harvard Law Review* 374

O. Chinnappa Reddy, *The Court and the Constitution of India: Summits and Shallows* (New Delhi, Oxford University Press 2008)

Reuters, 'Choi-gate: South Korean President's Approval Rating Tanks at 4%' (*Guardian*, 25 November 2016) <https://www.theguardian.com/world/2016/nov/25/choi-gate-south-korean-presidents-approval-rating-tanks-at-4>

'Indian Court Bans Politicians from Using Religion, Caste to Win Votes' (Reuters, 4 January 2017) <http://in.reuters.com/article/uk-india-law-religion-idINKBN14O1CO>

Woo-Young Rhee, 'The Electoral Process and the Judicial Review of Elections in the Republic of Korea' in Po Jen Yap (ed) *Judicial Review of Elections in Asia* (London, Routledge 2016) 136

Ali Riaz, 'Political Parties, Elections, and the Party System' in Ali Riaz and Mohammad Sajjadur Rahman (eds) *Routledge Handbook of Contemporary Bangladesh* (London, Routledge 2016) 65

Julian Rivers, 'Proportionality and Variable Intensity of Review' (2006) 65 *Cambridge Law Journal* 174

Kent Roach, 'Remedial Consensus and Dialogue under the Charter: General Declarations and Delayed Declarations of Invalidity' (2002) 35 *University of British Columbia Law Review* 211

Kent Roach and Geoff Budlender, 'Mandatory Relief and Supervisory Jurisdiction: When is it Appropriate, Just and Equitable?' (2005) 122 *South African Law Journal* 325

Kermit Roosevelt III, 'Aspiration and Underenforcement' (2006) 119 *Harvard Law Review* 193

Royal Thai Embassy of Singapore, 'Thailand's Constitutional Court Dismisses Democrat Party Dissolution Case' (29 November 2010) <http://www.thaiembassy.sg/press_media/news-highlights/thailands-constitution-court-dismisses-democrat-party-dissolution-case>

Yaniv Roznai, 'Unconstitutional Constitutional Amendments – The Migration and Success of a Constitutional Idea' (2013) 61 *American Journal of Comparative Law* 657

Jed Rubenfeld, *Freedom and Time: A Theory of Constitutional Self Government* (New Haven, Yale University Press 2001)

Bruce Ryder, 'Suspending the Charter' (2003) 21 *Supreme Court Law Review* (2d) 267

Lawrence G. Sager, *Justice in Plain Clothes: A Theory of American Constitutional Practice* (New Haven, Yale University Press 2004)

Niranjan Sahoo, 'Spectrum, Election and Corruption Conundrum' unpublished paper (2011) <http://www.orfonline.org/research/spectrum-election-and-corruption-conundrum>

Baqir Sajjad, 'Defence Budget Hiked by Usual 11pc' (DAWN, 4 June 2016) <http://www.dawn.com/news/1262657>

Aqil Shah, *The Army and Democracy: Military Politics in Pakistan* (Cambridge, Massachusetts, Harvard University Press 2014)

Saeed Shah, 'Pakistan Army Steps Up Confrontation with Government' (*Guardian*, 11 January 2012) <http://www.theguardian.com/world/2012/jan/11/pakistan-army-confrontation-government>

Martin Shapiro, 'Political Jurisprudence' (1963–4) 52 *Kentucky Law Journal* 294

'Gerrymandering, Fairness, and the Supreme Court' (1985) 33 *UCLA Law Review* 227

Martin Shapiro and Alec Stone Sweet, *On Law, Politics, and Judicialisation* (New York, Oxford University Press 2002)

Osama Siddique, 'The Jurisprudence of Dissolutions: Presidential Power to Dissolve Assemblies under the Pakistani Constitution and its Discontents' (2006) 23 *Arizona Journal of International and Comparative Law* 615

Singapore Government, *Report of the Constitutional Commission* 1966 (Singapore: Government Printer, 1966)

Catherine Soanes and Angus Stevenson (ed) *Concise Oxford English Dictionary* (11th edn, Oxford, Oxford University Press 2006)

Aditya Sondhi, 'Elections' in Sujit Choudhry, Madhav Khosla and Pratap Bhanu Mehta (eds) *The Oxford Handbook of the Indian Constitution* (Oxford, Oxford University Press 2016) 196

Richard Stacey, 'Constituent Power and Carl Schmitt's Theory of Constitution in Kenya's Constitution-making Process' (2011) 9 *International Journal of Constitutional Law* 587

Kevin M. Stack, 'An Administrative Jurisprudence: The Rule of Law in the Administrative State' (2015) 115 *Columbia Law Review* 1985

Matthew C. Stephenson, '"When the Devil Turns…": The Political Foundations of Independent Judicial Review' (2003) 32 *Journal of Legal Studies* 59

Straits Times, 'High Court strikes out PKR's civil suit against Malaysia's PM Najib' (*Straits Times*, 21 January 2016) <http://www.straitstimes.com/asia/se-asia/high-court-strikes-out-pkrs-civil-suit-against-malaysias-pm-najib>

David Strauss, 'The Ubiquity of Prophylactic Rules' (1988) 55 *University of Chicago Law Review* 190

Cass Sunstein, 'Trimming' (2009) 122 *Harvard Law Review* 1049

Alec Stone Sweet, *Governing with Judges: Constitutional Politics in Europe* (Oxford, Oxford University Press, 2000)

'Path Dependence, Precedent, and Judicial Power' in Martin Shapiro and Alec Stone Sweet (eds), *On Law, Politics, and Judicialisation* (New York, Oxford University Press 2002) 112

'Constitutions and Judicial Power' in Daniele Caramani (ed) *Comparative Politics* (Oxford, Oxford University Press 2014) 150

Alec Stone Sweet and Jud Mathews, 'Proportionality Balancing and Global Constitutionalism' (2008) 47 *Columbia Journal of Transnational Law* 72

Kevin Tan and Li-Ann Thio, *Singapore: 50 Constitutional Moments that Defined a Nation* (Singapore, Marshall Cavendish 2015)

Kenneth Paul Tan, 'Singapore in 2014: Adapting to the "New Normal"' (2015) 55(1) *Asian Survey* 157

Netina Tan, 'Manipulating Electoral Laws in Singapore' (2013) 32(4) *Electoral Studies* 632

'Pre-electoral Malpractice, Gerrymandering and its Effects on Singapore's 2015 GE' in Terence Lee and Kevin YL Tan (eds) *Change in Voting: Singapore's 2015 General Election* (Singapore, Ethos Books 2016) 169

Khemthong Tonsakulrungruang, 'Thailand: an Abuse of Judicial Review' in Po Jen Yap (ed) *Judicial Review of Elections in Asia* (London, Routledge 2016) 173

'The Anti-Majoritarian Constitutional Court of Thailand' (2017) 26 *Washington International Law Journal* 247

James Bradley Thayer, 'The Origin and Scope of the American Doctrine of Constitutional Law' (1893) 7 *Harvard Law Review* 129

The BBC, '"Santa protest" against South Korea President Park Geun-hye' (BBC) <http://www.bbc.com/news/world-asia-38427931>

The Electoral Boundaries Review Committee, *Report of the Electoral Boundaries Review Committee 2015* (24 July 2015) <http://www.eld.gov.sg/pdf/White%20Paper%20on%20the%20Report%20of%20the%20Electoral%20Boundaries%20Review%20Committee%202015.pdf>

The Government of the Hong Kong Special Administrative Region, 'Voter Registration Statistics: Functional Constituency' <http://www.voterregistration.gov.hk/eng/statistic20163.html>

Lawrence Tribe, 'A Constitution We Are Amending: In Defence of a Restrained Judicial Role' (1983) 97 *Harvard Law Review* 433

Mark Tushnet, 'Authoritarian Constitutionalism' (2015) 100 *Cornell Law Review* 391

Mark Tushnet and Madhav Khosla (eds) *Unstable Constitutionalism: Law and Politics in South Asia* (New York, Cambridge University Press, 2015)

Andreas Ufen, 'The 2013 Malaysian Elections: Business as Usual or Part of a Protracted Transition?' (2013) 32 *Journal of Current Southeast Asian Affairs* 3

'Laissez-faire versus Strict Control of Political Finance: Hegemonic Parties and Developmental States in Malaysia and Singapore' (2015) 47 *Critical Asian Studies* 564

Milan Vaishnav, 'The Market for Criminality: Money, Muscle and Elections in India' unpublished paper (2011) <https://casi.sas.upenn.edu/sites/casi.sas.upenn.edu/files/iit/Market%20for%20Criminality%20-%20Aug%202011.pdf>

Giancarlo Elia Valori, 'Legislative Elections in South Korea' (*Modern Diplomacy*, 21 April 2016) <http://moderndiplomacy.eu/index.php?option=com_k2&view=item&id=1363:legislative-elections-in-south-korea&Itemid=645>

Georg Vanberg, 'Constitutional Courts in Comparative Perspective: A Theoretical Assessment' (2015) 18 *Annual Review of Political Science* 167

Ozan Varol, 'Stealth Authoritarianism' (2015) 100 *Iowa Law Review* 1673

Adrian Vermeule, *Law and the Limits of Reason* (Oxford, Oxford University Press 2008)

John Vile, 'The Case against Implicit Limits on the Constitutional Amending Process' in Sanford Levison (ed) *Responding to Imperfection: The Theory and Practice of Constitutional Amendment* (Princeton, Princeton University Press 1995) 191

Vohra Committee of the Government of India Ministry of Home Affairs, *Vohra Committee Report.*

Bridget Welsh, 'Malaysia's Elections: A Step Backward' (2013) 24 *Journal of Democracy* 136

'Elections in Malaysia: Voting Behaviour and Electoral Integrity' in Meredith L. Weiss (ed) *Routledge Handbook of Contemporary Malaysia* (London, Routledge 2015) 11

James M. West and Dae-Kyu Yoon, 'The Constitutional Court of the Republic of Korea: Transforming the Jurisprudence of the Vortex?' (1992) 40 *American Journal of Comparative Law* 73

R. George Wright, 'Could a Constitutional Amendment be Unconstitutional?' (1991) 22 *Loyola University Law Journal* 741

Po Jen Yap, '10 Years of the Basic Law: The Rise, Retreat and Resurgence of Judicial Power' (2007) 36 *Common Law World Review* 166

'Defending Dialogue' (2012) *Public Law* 527

'A Typography of Constitutional Arguments in Hong Kong' (2014) 44 *Hong Kong Law Journal* 459

Constitutional Dialogue in Common Law Asia (Oxford, Oxford University Press 2015)

'The Conundrum of Unconstitutional Constitutional Amendments' (2015) 4 *Global Constitutionalism* 114

(ed) *Judicial Review of Elections of Asia* (London, Routledge 2016)

'New Democracies and Novel Remedies' (2017) *Public Law* 30

Po Jen Yap and Holning Lau (eds) *Public Interest Litigation in Asia* (London, Routledge 2011)

Jiunn-rong Yeh, 'Presidential Politics and the Judicial Facilitation of Dialogue between Political Actors in New Asian Democracies: Comparing the South Korean and Taiwanese Experiences' (2010) 8 (4) *International Journal of Constitutional Law* 911

The Constitution of Taiwan: A Contextual Analysis (Oxford, Hart Publishing 2016)

Alison Young, 'In Defence of Due Deference' (2009) 72 *Modern Law Review* 554

Katherine Young, *Constituting Economic and Social Rights* (Oxford, Oxford University Press 2012)

Simon N.M. Young, 'Judicial Review of Elections in Hong Kong: Resolving a Contradiction' in Po Jen Yap (ed) *Judicial Review of Elections of Asia* (London, Routledge 2016) 11

Simon Young and Richard Cullen, *Electing Hong Kong's Chief Executive* (Hong Kong, Hong Kong University Press 2010)

Simon Young and Anthony Law, 'Privileged to Vote: Inequalities and Anomalies of the FC System' in Christine Loh (ed) *Functional Constituencies: A Unique Feature of the Hong Kong Legislative Council* (Hong Kong, Hong Kong University Press 2006) 59

Chantal Yuen, 'Retired Photojournalist seeks Legal Challenge over Oaths of 14 Lawmakers and Chief Exec. CY Leung' (*Hong Kong Free Press*, 17 November 2016) <https://www.hongkongfp.com/2016/11/17/retired-reporter-seeks-legal-challenge-over-oaths-of-14-lawmakers-and-chief-exec-cy-leung/>

Suisheng Zhao, 'Reunification Strategy: Beijing Versus Lee Teng-hui' in Bruce J. Dickson and Chien-min Chao (eds) *Assessing the Lee Teng-hui Legacy in Taiwan's Politics: Democratic Consolidation and External Relations* (Armonk, New York, M.E. Sharpe 2002) 218

INDEX